# U2 and Philosophy

# Popular Culture and Philosophy®
## Series Editor: George A. Reisch
### (Series Editor for this volume was William Irwin)

**Popular Culture and Philosophy®**

# U2 and Philosophy

*How to Decipher an
Atomic Band*

Edited by

MARK A. WRATHALL

OPEN COURT
Chicago and La Salle, Illinois

*Volume 21 in the series, Popular Culture and Philosophy*™

**To order books from Open Court, call 1-800-815-2280, or visit our website at www.opencourtbooks.com**.

Open Court Publishing Company is a division of Carus Publishing Company.

**Library of Congress Cataloging-in-Publication Data**

U2 and philosophy / edited by Mark A. Wrathall..
     p. cm. — (Popular culture and philosophy ; v. 21)
    Summary: "A collection of essays about the rock band U2 and lead singer Bono focusing on philosophical and ethical aspects of their music and political activities" — Provided by publisher
    Includes bibliographical references and index.
    ISBN-13: 978-0-8126-9599-1 (trade pbk. : alk. paper)
    ISBN-10: 0-8126-9599-2 (trade pbk. : alk. paper)
    1. U2 (Musical group) 2. Music — Philosophy and aesthetics.
3. Rock music — Social aspects — Ireland. 4. Popular culture — Ireland. I. Wrathall, Mark A. II. Series.
ML421.U2U13 2006
782.42166092'2 — dc22

                  2006011454

# Contents

# Acknowledgments

This book is not authorized or endorsed by U2. All quotations from the songs of U2 are employed strictly for purposes of scholarly argument.

I gratefully acknowledge permission to quote from the following:

"Dear God." Words and Music by Andy Partridge. © 1986 EMI Virgin Music Ltd. All Rights in the U.S. and Canada Controlled and Administered by EMI Virgin Songs, Inc. All Rights Reserved. International Copyright Secured. Used by permission.

"Engel." Music and Lyrics: Till Lindemann / Richard Z. Kruspe / Doktor Christian Lorenz / Oliver Riedel / Christoph Doom Schneider / Paul Landers. © by TamTam Fialik Musikverlag / Musik—Edition Discoton GmbH (BMG Music Publishing Germany), München. Used by permission.

"Sehnsucht." Music and Lyrics: Till Lindemann / Richard Z. Kruspe / Doktor Christian Lorenz / Oliver Riedel / Christoph Doom Schneider / Paul Landers. © by TamTam Fialik Musikverlag / Musik—Edition Discoton GmbH (BMG Music Publishing Germany), München. Used by permission.

# Thinking about U2

MARK A. WRATHALL

For over two decades, U2 has been one of the biggest acts in rock music. During that time, the group has produced over a dozen platinum and multi-platinum records and won numerous Grammy Awards, while garnering critical acclaim for the thoughtfulness of their lyrics and the artistry of their music.

But U2 is known almost as much for their religiosity and political activism as for their music. U2's music has always been suffused with Christian themes and thick with scriptural references. When the audience at a U2 concert sings along to songs like "40" or "Yahweh," they are literally joining the group in prayer. At the same time, U2's Christianity is not just something to profess, but something to live. It thus manifests itself in the form of the group's commitment to political and social change. The members of U2 have used their stature as pop-cultural icons to raise public awareness of a variety of political, social, and cultural issues. Bono has recently taken the lead in mobilizing assistance for the AIDS crisis in Africa, debt relief for third world nations, and fighting extreme poverty around the world. In 2005 he was named one of *Time* magazine's persons of the year for his efforts. U2 concerts mix political appeals into the set, smoothly segueing between hit songs and calls to social action. U2 is, in short, anything but a typical rock band.

Fine—so U2 is unusual. But why should we think that U2 is *philosophically* interesting?

Many philosophers would turn up their noses at the thought of treating contemporary popular music as a serious topic for philosophical reflection. But pop music is a multi-billion dollar industry that has shaped the way we think, dress, and speak. It has been faulted (or credited, depending on your perspective) with undermining morals and encouraging rebellion against traditional values. Some have even argued that Rock music has changed the world politically—by, for example, channeling and encouraging the dissatisfaction with the communist regime of East Germany, thereby contributing to the fall of the Berlin Wall. Pop music has become so pervasive that today one can find even, say, anti-Western dissatisfaction expressed in the idiom of rap music by Islamic youth around the world. In light of such facts, the interesting question is not why we're writing about popular music, but why popular music has attracted so *little* philosophical attention.

There's a long tradition in philosophy of studying popular culture as a source of insight into ourselves. Nietzsche taught that the first rule for understanding a philosophy or a society is to see how it stands with respect to life. The things we say, the music we listen to, the way we organize our cities, the things we eat and drink, and the philosophical theories we espouse—all these things betray a certain stand on life. They show what we think is important and what kind of things we think make life worthwhile. If Nietzsche is right about this, then popular culture and popular forms of music are promising, fertile topics for philosophical study. The fact that U2 is so enormously popular thus says something important about *us*. U2's popular success is, in other words, a philosophically interesting phenomenon in its own right because it holds up a mirror in which we can see what we care about and what we are moved by.

I would suggest that one important source of their popularity, and, subsequently, of philosophical lessons to be learned from the study of U2's music, is the way that the members of the group struggle to deal with widely-shared modern contradictions arising from the technological-global world economy. Our age has witnessed dramatic changes in the style of life brought about by the extension of technology into every corner of our existence. Modern industrialized economies are the most productive in the history of humankind. This has given us citizens of industrialized nations an unprecedented wealth and freedom to choose how to live our lives—none of us is restricted anymore to life options we inherit from our families or local cultures about such things as what to eat and wear, how to recreate and work, and so on. But the global-technological nature of modern life has produced ethical tensions with which we all struggle to greater or lesser degrees. While technology frees us on the one hand from inherited constraints, we lose on the other hand a sense of identity with a deep connection to our homes and local cultures, connections that once gave life a sense of purpose and meaning.

The chapters in the first section of this book consider U2's effort to come to terms with our contemporary world-historical situation. As Marina McCoy's chapter (Chapter 1) reminds us, the longing for profound meaning and purpose in life is not a new one. In Plato's ethics, we deal with this longing by ascending from bodily desires to the intellectual pursuit of the ultimate object of love in the form of the beautiful itself. McCoy introduces us to the central role that various notions of love play in U2's music by showing how U2's early songs illustrate the Platonic approach to love.

Hubert Dreyfus and Mark Wrathall (Chapter 2), by contrast, review the work of existentialist philosophers on the problem of finding meaning in the contemporary world. The existential tradition of philosophy has rejected Plato's effort to overcome bodily desires and attachments. Instead, as Dreyfus and Wrathall explain, existentialist philosophy argues that we must learn to embrace the contradiction between body and mind. Much of U2's work in and following *Achtung Baby* can be profitably understood in the light of this existential tradition and, in particular, Danish philosopher Søren Kierkegaard's work. Wrathall (Chapter 3) continues the exploration of this theme in U2, spelling out the approach U2 has adopted for dealing with the contradiction. U2, Wrathall argues, can be seen as carrying on the existentialist Christian tradition of Kierkegaard, Pascal, and Dostoevsky—a tradition which insists that religious ideas have a worldly significance, and that a meaningful existence is one which learns how to discover satisfaction of our spiritual longings in this life. Jeff Malpas (Chapter 4) also draws on existential philosophy in tracing the search for a home or a sense of place through U2's music and lyrics.

It's no accident that Malpas's essay focuses primarily on *The Joshua Tree*. Starting with *Achtung Baby*, critics and the band-members themselves have described U2's music as abandoning the earnestness that characterized their earlier albums in favor of a postmodernist playfulness. Kerry Soper (Chapter 5) illuminates this by showing how Bono can be seen as working out on a very public stage the search for an authentic sense of identity in a world where traditional sources of identity have been undermined. Iain Thomson (Chapter 6) deepens our understanding of postmodernism by simultaneously showing how U2's music embodies certain postmodern traits and, in the process, using that music to help get clear about what postmodernism as a philosophical movement really is.

Together, these chapters help us appreciate the members of U2 as prominent examples of how to balance the modern western condition of historically unprecedented prosperity with moral and ethical responsibilities. Much of U2's success, in other words, is attributable to the way they confront publicly the same tensions of modern life which discomfort all of us to a greater or lesser degree. We need not share their approach to navigating the shoals of modern life in order to appreciate and learn from their efforts to own up to the dilemmas we all face.

There is another contradiction produced by the technological world order. As economies and societies become intertwined through the technologization and globalization of world culture, a sense of political disempowerment grows at the very same time that our responsibility for the poverty and suffering of far distant people increases. We feel disempowered because the organization of social life (the allocation of resources, states of war and peace, the availability of medicine, job opportunities, and so on) is increasingly driven by forces beyond any individual's control. Nobody can be morally comfortable, for example, with the fact that AIDS victims are dying "three to a bed" in a hospice in Uganda for the want of drugs that are readily available in western industrialized countries (see "Crumbs from your Table"). But most of us feel completely helpless to affect the basic economic and political forces that lead to this situation. Each individual is, as a result of the global-technological world order, impotent to change fundamentally the way things work.

But there is a sense in which our responsibility grows along with the globalization of the economy. Our standard of living is maintained by harnessing the labor of others around the world, consuming the resources that others also need, and polluting the environment that we all share. Our practices of consumption encourage corporate and governmental policies on trade, the environment, and so on, that directly impact the lives of millions of others. But the ties that bind us to our fellow citizens around the world are so personally attenuated that they appear merely as anonymous others, thus making it easier to shirk the responsibility we bear for the impact we have on them.

Of course, no band has more persistently engaged with the question of political and ethical responsibility than U2—to both the annoyance and the delight of critics and fans. The chapters in the second section of the book examine the philosophical issues raised by U2's efforts to come to terms with the problem of political and ethical responsibility. The call to responsibility, for U2, forces us to own up to the existence of evil and suffering in the world. Because U2 experiences the existence of suffering as a call to action, they can reasonably see, as Trenton Merricks explains (Chapter 7), the existence of suffering in the world as actually reinforcing religious faith rather than undermining it. In Chapter 8, Jennifer McClinton-Temple and Abigail Myers explore in more detail the nature of U2's ethical response to the world. U2's music, they argue, exhibits an ethics of care— "a method for making moral decisions which places particular emphasis upon the principle that people should look out for and protect one another, given the particulars of relationships between persons involved in a given situation." Craig Delancey (Chapter 9) explores a philosophical basis for U2's self-appointed role as a public conscience, goading us to resist the tendency toward political complacency in the face of the banalization of modern life. Stanley Benfell (Chapter 10) shows how U2's music deals with apocalyptic themes of death and world destruction by encouraging us to take responsibility for our lives. In this respect, Benfell argues, U2's music bears interesting parallels to German philosopher Martin Heidegger's (1889–1976) account of authentic existence as being towards death.

Another source of U2's success is the way that it, more than most bands, has been very interested in and concerned with the medium of rock music itself as a means of communication. Right from the beginning of their career, U2's members have seen the performance of their music, rather than its recording, as its true realization. It is in the moment of performing before an audience that the act of communication can be authentically fulfilled. In authentic communication, the participants in the conversation do not rely on clichés or fall into conventional modes of speech. Instead, they come to share a way of being disposed to and oriented to the particular situation they face together. Bono describes this experience in the following way: "when it's really going off, you have the sense that you're really in the song, and the song is really in the room: all of you, crowd and performers, disappear into it. It's an extraordinary thing."[1] Aiming for this experience demands of the band that they abandon clichés and explode conventional means of expression, searching for an expression into which everyone can meld.

U2's constant experimentation with musical styles and its refusal to continue comfortably sounding the same are manifestations of an effort to keep the communication with the audience alive and authentic. Great communicators, whether poets or politicians, artists, philosophers or musicians, have always shown an ability to take up and transform established styles of expression. Edge realized this at a very early stage of the band's evolution. Being in the band, he explains, "challenges everything that you believed about what the electric guitar was for. Suddenly the question is, 'What are you *saying* with it?' Not 'Can you play this lick?' or 'What's your speed like?' It's 'What are you saying with your instrument? What is being communicated in this song?' Suddenly guitars were not things to be waved in front of the audience but now were something you used to *reach out* to the crowd. . . . I had to totally re-examine the way I played."[2] The focus on communication forged Edge's distinctive style as he learned to recognize that "notes actually *do* mean something. They have power. I think of notes as being expensive. You don't just throw them around" (*U2 at the End of the World*, p. 44).

Notes *mean* something for U2, Béatrice Han-Pile (Chapter 11) shows, because they communicate a mood, a feeling, a way of being disposed to the world. One common mood or disposition that U2 songs communicate is the despair of existence in the modern world. Edge notes that "the spirit of what we've been trying to express since the beginning" is "the feeling of alienation and loss, the feeling of not being at one with your circumstances"[3] But Bono's lyrics also sometimes go beyond merely putting words to the mood of the music; the words and the music frequently come into dialogue. Bono noted of the

---

[1] Michka Assayas, *Bono in Conversation* (New York: Riverhead, 2005), p. 120.
[2] Quoted by Bill Flanagan in *U2 at the End of the World* (New York: Delta, 1995) p. 44.
[3] Hank Bordowitz, ed., *The U2 Reader* (Milwaukee: Hal Leonard Corporation, 2003), p. 70.

songs on *Achtung Baby*—songs whose lyrics do express the "feeling of alienation and loss" that Edge refers to—that the music itself points toward an answer to the thoughts expressed in the lyrics: "Even if some of the subjects were dark, the music had within it the antidote for the subject matter." (*Bono in Conversation*, p. 137) This dialogue between music and lyrics is beautifully illustrated in "Miracle Drug" from *How to Dismantle an Atomic Bomb*. The song, as a whole, can be seen as a kind of theodicy—a philosophical justification of God's goodness in the face of the existence of suffering and evil in the world. In the central section of the song, Bono sings despairingly: "God, I need your help tonight." Edge's guitar answers the call for help, uplifting and re-energizing the listener. And to make sure that the musical answer isn't missed, Edge sings the following refrain, putting the musical theodicy to words: "Beneath the noise / Below the din / I hear a voice / It's whispering / In science and in medicine / 'I was a stranger / You took me in.'" In this passage, Edge quotes Jesus's explanation of why, at the final judgment, the righteous will be accepted into God's presence (see Matthew 25:35). By equating science and medicine with works of Christian charity, Edge offers U2's answer to the problem of the existence of evil. The answer is found in the insight that God has already given us the means to relieve each others' suffering. Logic, reason, science—all of which are sometimes thought of as enemies of religious faith—are seen and experienced by U2 as manifestations of God's love for us. This is an interesting philosophical position in its own right (for more on U2 and the problem of evil, see Merricks, Chapter 7). But here my interest in this passage stems from the glimpse it gives us of the way communication works in U2's music. Bono's lyrics often express the underlying mood of the music. But at other times, Edge, Adam and Larry respond to Bono's lyrics by setting the listeners mood, showing in the process what kind of disposition for the world is needed to overcome anxiety and intellectual doubts about the meaningfulness of modern existence.

U2's understanding of the significance of music, and the relationship between feelings and the intellect, points to a number of issues with which philosophers have perennially struggled. Han-Pile (Chapter 11) reviews a variety of philosophical accounts of the nature of music itself, and argues that U2's emphasis on mood supports a phenomenological interpretation of music in terms of its role in altering our dispositions for the world. Timothy Cleveland (Chapter 12) also explores the way U2 gives priority to feelings over thoughts. U2's view has important implications for the way we think about the nature of knowledge itself. Theodore Gracyk (Chapter 13) takes up the nature of meaning and communication in musical lyrics. Chris Tollefsen (Chapter 14) and David Werther (Chapter 15) are each interested in the way that U2 exploits the relationship between music and feelings. Tollefsen, following Plato, argues that music's appeal to emotions rather than the intellect makes it a dangerous and deceptive medium. U2, Tollefsen argues, are masters of illusion rather than truth—a fact we should be critically aware of when listening to them. Werther, by contrast, mounts a defense of U2's exploitation of the emotional power of music along the lines suggested by Aristotle. Because of U2's commitment to moral ideals, Werther argues, their music can play a worthwhile role in the moral education of their listeners.

Philosophers believe that you miss too much if you *don't* stop to think. This book, I believe, shows that this is certainly true of U2's music. I hope these essays will make U2's fans more appreciative of the group's music by showing the coherence and depth of thought behind it. But more than that, because truer to the spirit of the U2 itself, I hope this book will be taken as an invitation to further critical thought and reflection about the serious issues that concern the group. After all if you don't think, you don't try and make sense, you don't theorize, you will, to paraphrase Edge, end up numb.

# PART I

# See the World in Green and Blue

## U2 and the Philosophy of Existence

1

# "We Can Be One": Love and Platonic Transcendence in U2

MARINA BERZINS McCOY

Many of the early songs of U2 share a common theme of long-ing for an object of love.[1] To a person in love, the idea of love seems intuitive and clear: we think that we know what it means to love without having to analyze it. But upon further reflection, just what the term "love" means becomes more difficult to sort out. If I say that I love my mother, or I love a boyfriend, or I love to play basketball, I seemingly have very different things in mind. What is love about primarily? Because love is never just about the object of our love, but always also about the person who is doing the loving, a second kind of question naturally arises: what does it say about human beings to say that love is central to our lives? That is, what does it mean to *be* a lover?

More often than not, pop songs have dealt with these ques-tions in terms of romantic love. At first blush, this seems true of U2's music as well. In "New Year's Day," for example, the singer speaks of his desire to be reunified with someone from whom he has been separated—he is not only separated but is "torn" asunder from his beloved.[2] Without her, he is somehow incom-plete. This is not just a man who misses his sweetheart and is telling her so. Instead, we hear the suffering of a man who is not entirely himself without his other half. The lyrics imply that

---

[1] I have focused primarily on the early music of U2 since the themes of Platonic desire are most apparent here. U2's later music shifts towards an emphasis on the relationship between transcendence and particular things rather than the longing for the transcendent.
[2] The term "singer" here refers to the song's narrator, rather than Bono.

3

the original unity here is not the singer but rather a prior unity between himself and the object of love. The song is not altogether hopeful that the reunification with take place any time soon: "though I want to be with you, be with you, night and day / Nothing changes on New Year's Day." While New Year's is traditionally a time for fresh starts, whatever is keeping his beloved from him seems to be a perpetual obstacle. Still, his need for her is no less pressing.

Plato's dialogue the *Symposium* deals with the theme of love and longing. In the *Symposium*, a number of friends give speeches in praise of love. Each in turn offers an account of the nature of love or *eros* (a Greek term that has connotations of sexual and romantic love, rather than the sort of love that we have for our friends, parents, or children). Many of U2's songs exhibit this Platonic approach to love.

## Longing for the Other Half

One of the most amusing accounts of *eros* offered in the dialogue describes love in terms of longing for our "other half," through the voice of the character Aristophanes, a Greek comedic playwright. Aristophanes tells a story about the origin of humanity that is supposed to reveal the nature of love. He humorously suggests that once there were not two sexes but instead three: males, females, and androgynous beings who had sexual organs of both genders. Human beings used to have four arms, four legs, and two faces; they were round creatures who moved about by somersaulting across the ground. Since the gods saw human beings as a threat, they decided that one way of limiting human beings would be to cut them in half; so each human being was divided into two. Each part that constitutes the present state of humanity is only half of an original creature, always searching for its other half. Love is all about finding the rest of ourselves; we in our present condition are not whole. When someone meets his or her "other half," Aristophanes says:

> they are then marvelously struck by friendship and kinship and Eros, and scarcely willing to be separated from each other even for a little time. These are the people who pass their whole lives with each other, but who can't even say what they wish for themselves by being with each other. No one can think it is for the sake of sex-

ual intercourse that the one so eagerly delights in being with the other. Instead the soul of each clearly wishes for something else it can't put into words; it divines what it wishes, and obscurely hints at it.[3]

Aristophanes goes on to say that the real nature of love is a longing for wholeness (*Symposium*, 93a). As in the song "New Year's Day," Aristophanes suggests that each of us is incomplete by ourselves, and needs his or her beloved in order to be whole again. No human being is sufficient on his own; instead, we are all in need of someone else who completes us.

Aristophanes points out that we generally don't understand this truth about ourselves. Even after they find each other, the lovers in the passage above don't know exactly what it is that makes them each long for time with the other so much. It's not the shared activity, the conversation, or the sex that makes being with the other half so desirable, although we might make the mistake of thinking that one of these things is all we are after. We each have just a "hint," a vague intuition of what it is that we are missing. Even finding our other half does not allow us to fully understand ourselves; ordinary humans never really understand the origin of their incompleteness. (They don't know the story that Aristophanes tells, after all.) Romantic love and sexual desire turn out to be about more than what they first appear to be; they are about a deeper need for wholeness. However, in Aristophanes's account, we are never fully united with our lovers and so never really completed.

While it might seem as though U2's "New Year's Day" could be understood as Aristophanes proposes, it would be a misunderstanding to view it as a song merely about romantic love. While it resonates with us on the level of romantic love, the song is also about the imprisonment of Poland's Solidarity movement leader Lech Walesa and the Soviet domination of Poland.[4] Some of the lyrics of "New Year's Day" allude to the

---

[3] *Symposium*, 192c–d. All quotations from the *Symposium* are taken from the translation by R.E. Allen: Plato *The Symposium* (New Haven: Yale University Press, 1991).

[4] Christopher Connelly, "Keeping the Faith," *Rolling Stone* 444 (14th March, 1985), p. 25. Apparently the song began as a love song from Bono to his newlywed wife Ali but was later transformed into a song about the Solidarity movement in Poland; its original meaning was probably about separation due to war or political unrest more generally.

problems of war: "Under a blood red sky / A crowd has gathered in black and white / Arms entwined, the chosen few / The newspapers says, says / Say it's true it's true . . . / And we can break through / Though torn in two / We can be one." The lovers' separation in this case is caused by war and domination; one can't understand their personal difficulty apart from its political causes. The object of longing in the song is not only for reunion with the beloved, but also for a different kind of unity: peace, political unity, concord. U2 uses the imagery of romantic love and the desire for reunification with a lover to describe a more fundamental political problem. Love, then, has a scope much wider than we might usually think: we can love not just an individual person, but a country, a people, humanity, peace, or justice. Regarding romantic love as the only form of love turns out to be inadequate.[5]

## Still Haven't Found What I'm Looking For

Plato shares this understanding of love as having a much wider scope than the romantic or sexual, even the somewhat psychologically complex version offered by Aristophanes. The *Symposium* goes on to provide other accounts of love after Aristophanes's account.[6] The poet Agathon describes love as being young, delicate, and happy. For Agathon, there is no violence in love, and love possesses the classical Greek virtues of justice, temperance, moderation, and wisdom. While Agathon's description gives love high praise, it lacks entirely Aristophanes's sense of longing, neediness, and even suffering as important components of *eros*. When next Socrates gives his own account of love, as told to him by the prophetess Diotima, he implicitly criticizes this "cleaned up" vision of love.[7] Love, according to Diotima, is neither perfectly good nor perfectly beautiful, though it is also not bad or ugly. Instead, Love is something in between beauty and ugliness, and in between the

---

[5] Or consider "Surrender"'s mention of love in relation to politics: "Oh, the city's afire / A passionate flame / It knows me by name / Oh, the city's desire / To take me for more and more / It's in the street, getting under my feet / It's in the air, it's everywhere."
[6] Other accounts of love also precede Aristophanes's story in the *Symposium*, but are not dealt with here.
[7] For our purposes here, we take Socrates to represent Plato's ideas, not necessarily those of the historical Socrates.

good and the bad (*Symposium*, 202b). If we think of Love as the Greek god Eros, then he must have been the child of Penia (want or need) and Poros (resourcefulness). Eros has qualities of both of his parents. He is ever in want, but also always seeking what he needs, courageously and intently going after good and beautiful things (*Symposium*, 203b–e). In this sense, Socrates affirms that both Agathon and Aristophanes were partially right: real love strives for good things, but the lover also by definition longs for something that he still does not possess. He is always in between a state of total lack and total possession of the good.

U2's music clearly emphasizes this in between element of Eros as well. "Walk away, walk away, walk away, walk away, I will follow" is suggestive of someone who is willing to persist in going after what he loves, even if the beloved is somewhat elusive.[8] "Drowning Man" lyrically promises a love that will somehow survive the temporal: "Take my hand / You know I'll be there / If you can / I'll cross the sky for your love / And I understand / These winds and tides / This change of times / Won't drag you away." But the aching tones in Bono's voice suggest the suffering along with promise. U2's use of the image of not yet being home is also a common theme in many of their songs.[9] This sense of restlessness is perhaps nowhere more evident lyrically than in "I Still Haven't Found What I'm Looking For," in which the singer describes a variety of objects of desire, none of which truly satisfy him: "I have climbed highest mountain / I have run through the fields . . . / I have run / I have crawled / I have scaled these city walls . . . / I have kissed honey lips . . . / But I still haven't found what I'm looking for."

The singer describes a variety of challenges he has overcome—some of them clichéd metaphors for success—in order to be reunited with his beloved. But none of these achievements is ultimately satisfying, not even the reunion with the

---

[8] Bono describes this song as being about the unconditional love of a mother for her child. See David Breskin, "U2's Passionate Voice," *Rolling Stone* 510 (8th October, 1987), p. 44.

[9] For example, "Three Sunrises"'s claim that "love won't find / Find its own way home" is also evocative of the perpetual movement of love. See also references to home in "Fire," "A Sort of Homecoming," "Shadows and Tall Trees," "The Unforgettable Fire," and "Twilight."

beloved. It's clear that the dissatisfaction of the lover doesn't come from any shortcoming on her part: her kisses taste sweet and her touch really does heal him in some way. Still, he longs for something more. Later in the song, the speaker turns to other things that might satisfy him, as he moves to religious images; but even these don't seem to satisfy him. He remains restless and needy. As Bono said in an interview, "'Still Haven't Found What I'm Looking For' is an anthem of doubt more than faith."[10] But such "doubt" is a kind of an exhibition of faith, in one's recognition of needfulness. Socrates says in the *Symposium* that "ignorance is difficult just in this, that though not beautiful and good, nor wise, it yet seems to itself to be sufficient. He who does not think himself in need does not desire what he does not think he lacks" (204a). Conversely, having a sense of one's own lack of self-sufficiency means recognizing the possibility of a transcendent good that can satisfy us.

## The Ladder of Love

Socrates reports the teachings of a prophetess, Diotima, who taught him all about love. Diotima also claims that human beings are in a state of restlessness, but then we can progress and move ever closer towards the ultimate object of our desire. In what is probably the most famous passage in the *Symposium*, the "ascent" (*Symposium* 209e–212a), Socrates recalls how Diotima described to him a "ladder of love" which a lover can ascend. Diotima says that we begin with the love of single body—the lover is attracted to and longs for another person because of his or her physical attractiveness (210a). However, as time goes on, if the lover progresses, he will realize that this love of just one single body is not enough. He will see that what is attractive to him is beauty in all bodies; beauty is beauty wherever it is found (210b). Eventually, the lover will see that loving what is beautiful in the soul of another person is even better than his earlier love of bodies. Here Diotima's appeal to the beauty of the soul continues Aristophanes's ear-

[10] See the interview by David Fricke, "U2 Finds What It's Looking For," *Rolling Stone* 640 (1st October, 1992), pp. 40–46.

lier thought that simple sexual union is not, after all, what we really desire: there is something more fundamental about another person that we can't quite touch but want to be closer to. U2's "City of Blinding Lights" also addresses this idea of the beauty of the soul. Its contrasts between inner and outer beauty suggest that the beauty of a soul is more important than outward appearances: "Don't look before you laugh. Look ugly in a photograph . . . Oh you look so beautiful tonight." Diotima says that when one loves the soul of another person, the lover wants to nourish what is good in the other and wants to help the other person to become better (210c). Eventually the lover's object of love will be whatever is beautiful in the laws and traditions of the city. We move beyond love of particular people to love of city and community. Similarly, "Like a Song" addresses the need for love in a time of civil war: "Angry words won't stop the fight. Two wrongs won't make it right. A new heart is what I need. Oh, God, make it bleed." Just as U2's songs often link images of romantic love to love of the city, Diotima likewise links the two.

This link between love of another human being and politics might seem a little strange to us. What could one have to do with the other? The key according to Diotima lies in education. When the lover cares for his beloved, he wants the beloved's character to grow and to improve, she says. If we care for someone else's soul, we want them to possess good personal qualities. For example, we want to foster the growth of their understanding or encourage their courageousness. Friends want this for one another, as do parents for their children. But the natural place in which we usually learn these qualities is not just from our parents or our friends, but also from the larger society and its institutions. Caring for one soul might naturally enough lead to caring about social institutions that contribute to our well being. We are not just isolated individuals, but part of a larger society, which is itself worthy of love. (Consider Bono's involvement in addressing the AIDS crisis and Third World debt relief.) One might even start to find knowledge in all of its different branches to be a beautiful thing (210c–d), since finding good political solutions requires knowledge in order to make good decisions. If this happens, Diotima says, the lover has gone even further up the ladder of love.

## Love and the Divine

The ladder goes on, but according to Diotima, love *can* find its ultimate object. Unlike Aristophanes, who suggested that the lovers really could never get what they wanted, or even understand the true nature of their own desires, Diotima holds out the possibility that our restless search for what we want can come to an end. That object of desire, the true thing that we have wanted all along even if we did not know it, is difficult to describe; it transcends all particular things.

> He who has been educated in the things of love up to this point, beholding beautiful things rightly and in due order, will then, suddenly, in an instant, proceeding at that point to the end of the things of love, see something marvelous, beautiful in nature; it is *that*, Socrates, for the sake of which in fact all his previous labors existed. (*Symposium*, 210e)

This "marvelous" thing has several important qualities: first, it never comes into being nor perishes; neither does it grow or diminish (211a). Unlike Eros itself, it is not in between beauty and ugliness, or relatively beautiful, but is the Beautiful itself (211b–d). It is the source of all the beauty that we find in particular things, such as bodies, speeches, knowledge, institutions, art, and so on, but is not reducible to any one of those things. This "Beauty itself" is so beautiful that all one would want to do if she or he could see it would be to contemplate it; everything else would fall away. Just as U2's "A Man and a Woman" claims, "The soul needs beauty for a soul mate," Diotima suggests that we all long for transcendence. We yearn for something that is above and beyond all the particulars of this world, even as it gives meaning to those things.

In U2's music, the concept of the ultimate good is described through Christian religious language—for good reason, as Christian philosophers such as Augustine and Aquinas were strongly influenced by Platonism. For example, Augustine in his autobiography, the *Confessions*, reflects on what this restlessness that seems to be endemic to us might indicate about love. There, he describes his pursuit of a variety of things in his youth and early adulthood in a quest to satisfy his desires, things such as fame, sex, entertainment, and even theft and vandalism. None of these things ultimately made him happy. Only in God did he find the sort of fulfillment for which he had been searching. In the introduction to the *Confessions*, he writes, "Our hearts are restless until they rest in thee [God]."[11] U2's album *October* in particular is full of Christian imagery. "Gloria" speaks of the need for God for self-fulfillment: "I . . . I try to stand up / But I can't find my feet / I try, I try to speak up / But only in you I'm complete / Gloria . . . in te domine / Gloria . . . exultate." Or consider the lyrics of "With a Shout": "I wanna go / To the foot of the messiah / To the foot of he who made me see / To the side of a hill / Where we were still / We were filled / With our love / We're gonna be there again / Jerusalem Jerusalem."[12] In these songs, Love's object is presumed to be possible to find, even if the full reunion is not yet here.

Even the Edge's description of what he aims for in his playing suggests that he uses the guitar to get at something beyond both himself and the instrument: "Basically, I don't play proper guitar . . . For a start, I avoid the major third like the plague. I like the ambiguity between the major and minor chords, so I tread a very fine line sometimes between the two. I tend to isolate chords down to two or three notes and then octaves of the notes. Like for an E chord, I play just Bs and Es, including my big-E string . . . I haven't formed ruts down the fingerboard by playing the same things. It's still very much unexplored territory. Maybe that's why I don't feel attached to my instruments. It's almost like I'm going to dominate them in some way. I don't feel like they're part of me; they stand between me and something new."[13] In other ways, U2's music seems always to be reaching for something beyond the ordinary. Unlike many pop songs that tend to be highly repetitive and to go with a common pattern of verse, refrain, verse, refrain, and so on, U2's earlier songs more often than not follow a different structure. For example, "Like Song" from the *War* album has no clear refrain at all. "Seconds" has a refrain but one that changes lyrically from verse to verse, as the song builds to a climactic finish. Bono's propensity to "break" his voice, for example, in "Sunday, Bloody Sunday,"

---

[11] Augustine, *Confessions* (Indianapolis: Hackett, 1970), p. 3.

[12] While many of U2's members clearly have Christian affiliations, they also go out of their way in interviews to avoid specific questions about their religious beliefs and practices.

[13] See interview by Jas Obrecht, "Close to the Edge: U2's Guiding Light Finds True Creative Spirit" at http://www.guitar.com.

expresses an aching sense of longing found in many U2 songs. Bono even describes *Gloria* as being in part about the difficulty of describing something beyond words, emotions difficult to express.[14]

## Love's Satisfaction

While the character of Diotima makes the claim that love can, finally, be satisfied, it is clear that Socrates has only heard of this as a divine teaching, something revealed to him, but not yet personally experienced. The story Diotima tells is highly mediated: it is a story told to Socrates, which Socrates tells to the group at the symposium, which is itself a tale recounted by Apollodorus—and of course, even that tale is itself a fiction told to us by Plato! Plato suggests, by the very construction of the dialogue, that no human being has ever come to the very end of the ascent.[15] If Socrates, the hero of the story, has not himself reached the ultimate end, then what hope is there for the rest of us? Perhaps for Plato the situation is tragic. If we all long for the good but cannot find it, then we may be akin to Aristophanes's lovers who never even find our other halves, yet cannot escape wanting to find them. "I can't live with or without you," a lover might then say of his object of love.

However, a closer reading of Diotima's speech suggests that there is room for optimism, even if we never in this lifetime reach the end of our quest. For while the simple love of one body, or even many bodies, is disparaged as inadequate and shallow, Diotima's language to describe the life of the person who is further up the ladder is positively fecund and creative. The person who loves knowledge must, "looking now to the beautiful in its multitude, no longer delight like a slave, a worthless, petty-minded servant, in the beauty of one single thing . . . but rather, having been turned toward the multitudinous ocean of the beautiful and contemplating it, he begets many beautiful and imposing discourses and thoughts in ungrudging love of

---

[14] *U2 Magazine*, No. 11 (1st June, 1984).
[15] This might even include Diotima; like other Greek prophetesses (the oracle at Delphi, or fictional prophetesses such as Cassandra), she is not a god herself but only speaks on behalf of the gods. She therefore need not have seen the vision of the good itself in order to talk about it.

wisdom . . ." (210d). It is the person who loves knowledge, but is not yet complete in his knowledge that wants to talk, to discover, to create art, to give birth to children and to ideas—and perhaps would also be the one who wants to sing. Plato suggests that it is here on the ascent, and not in the contemplation of an eternal and unending Beauty (as desirable as that really is) that human living and loving takes place.

But the end of the ascent does relate that love and creativity and care for the "multitudinous" to a single Beauty itself. That is, for Socrates, the philosopher sees that to love the multiple things of this world is *already* to love and to depend on (if not to possess and know) Beauty. "With or Without You" is *not* a tragic song; it is a song about longing but not despair. Bono describes the line, "and you give yourself away . . ." as being about surrender, being open to something outside of ourselves. Bono said, "In 'With Or Without You' when it says "and you give yourself away and you give yourself away"—everybody else in the group knows what that means. It's about how I feel in U2 at times— exposed. I know the group thinks I'm exposed and the group feels that I give myself away." In response to the further question, "But there is a spiritual value about giving yourself, your ego, away?" Bono replied, "That goes back to the song 'Surrender'. I always believed in the Biblical idea that unless the seed dies, is almost crushed into the ground, it won't bear fruit."[16]

Plato's *Symposium* does not end with Diotima's speech, however. Alcibiades, the beloved of Socrates, bursts into the conversation, drunk and agitated. He complains that while Socrates is moderate and even unexpectedly beautiful in his soul, he has always refused to play the part of the lover to Alcibiades. Alcibiades implies that Socrates never really loved *him*, the particular, individual person. (Socrates has been similarly accused of neglect of his wife, Xanthippe.) But Plato implicitly raises a question here, never fully answered: is love ever love of a person, rather than an abstract notion such as Beauty itself? What about that love of the "other half" that Aristophanes had described as fundamental to our experience? Is the profundity of love to be found in something beyond all particulars, or precisely in those things?

---

[16] Niall Stokes, "The World About Us" *Hot Press* (26th March, 1987).

The later music of U2 takes a turn towards expressing the problem of transcendence and particulars, as Mark Wrathall shows in Chapter 3 of this volume. But for the moment, U2's lines about love sometimes leave us looking more like Alcibiades than like Socrates: "Say I'm a fool / They say I'm nothing. / But if I'm a fool for you / Oh, that's something."[17]

---

[17] Thanks to Kerry Cronin, Dan Dwyer, Greg Fried, John McCoy, John Siracusa, and Mary Troxell for helpful comments on previous drafts. I am also grateful to Mark Wrathall and Bill Irwin for their suggestions.

# 2

# Staring at the Sun:
# U2 and the Experience of
# Kierkegaardian Despair

HUBERT L. DREYFUS and
MARK A. WRATHALL

Thinkers in the West since Plato (429–347 B.C.) have tried to understand the nature of the human self. Like many others since, Plato understood the self as a combination of two components: body and soul. The members of U2 also understand human nature in this dualistic way, and have searched through their music for a way of resolving the tension between the different components of the self. When Bono, speaking of their music, noted in 1987: "I'd like to achieve a balance between the head and the heart,"[1] he expressed one version of this dualism about the self, and pointed toward "balance" as one possible way of resolving the tension. When Edge observed a decade later that "the challenge for us is to factor our spirituality into the mix along with our sexuality,"[2] he simultaneously articulated a different version of the dualism, but also attested to the enduring importance of the problem for the group.

## "Are You Still Holding On?" Philosophical Dualism and Christian Pessimism

According to the ancients, the self begins with these aspects in conflict, which leads to a confused and unstable life, but, once one realizes that *only one aspect is essential*—that one is either

---

[1] "Luminous Times: U2 Wrestle with Their Moment of Glory," *Musician* (1st October, 1987), p. 72.
[2] Ann Powers, "The Future Sound of U2," *Spin* 12 (March 1997), p. 50.

essentially a soul, and not a body, or vice versa—the conflict and instability are overcome. To arrive at peace and fulfillment, then, all one has to do is realize one's true nature and satisfy the self's deep needs while renouncing one's superficial and inessential desires.

So, for Plato for instance, life is all about learning to free ourselves from bodily attachments, and living the life of the mind. According to Lucretius (first century B.C.), who was a materialist, by contrast, one had to get over religious superstitions about the soul and live a life of bodily pleasures.

On the Greek account, any attempt to "balance" the factors or to "factor them both into the mix" would lead to a self in hopeless self-contradiction. It could not fully do justice to all its bodily, finite, temporal needs and capacities while at the same time fully expressing all its intellectual, infinite, eternal needs and capacities. It seemed to the Greeks, in fact, that the more you express one set of factors, the less you are able to express the other set. In Plato's famous "allegory of the cave," the philosopher who returns from the world of ideas to the world of earthly concerns is as blind as someone who has been staring at the sun would be if he or she were to crawl into a cave:

> Coming suddenly out of the sunlight, his eyes would be filled with darkness. He might be required once more to deliver his opinion on those shadows, in competition with the prisoners who had never been released, while his eyesight was still dim and unsteady; and it might take some time to become used to the darkness. They would laugh at him and say that he had gone up only to come back with his sight ruined; it was worth no one's while even to attempt the ascent.[3]

So it seemed to the ancient Greeks that if human beings were to be happy, only one set of factors could be essential. Early Christian theologians like St. Augustine (354–430) introduced the Platonic version of this view to Christian thought, and it is probably fair to say that it is the mainstream view in Christian theology. Our ability to dwell in this world (the "earthly city") impairs our ability to receive the higher things of God ("the

---

[3] Plato, *The Republic of Plato* (London: Oxford University Press, 1941), pp. 230–31.

heavenly city").[4] Indeed, it seems that this kind of Christian Platonism very nearly led to the premature end of the group U2 when, following the release of *Boy*, the Christian fellowship with which Bono, Edge, and Larry were involved claimed that God wanted the group to quit, since the life of a rock star seemed incompatible with the life of devotion to God.[5]

But this same sort of view is reflected in many of U2's own songs. The group adopts imagery drawn from the Christian interpretation of Plato's cave allegory, where the sun represents God. U2's songs return again and again to the idea that religious faith makes us unable to live in this world, in which there's no longer even room for love and saintliness. "Jesus's sister's eyes are a blister" ("If God Will Send His Angels")—the faithful are blinded, presumably from "staring at the sun." In "Staring at the Sun," the singer declares that he's "not the only one / Who's happy to go blind." Indeed, from the traditional Christian or Platonic perspective, it's a good thing to have one's focus on God blind one to a world where "love took a train heading south," "the cops collect for the cons," "the cartoon network turns into the news" ("If God Will Send His Angels") where "intransigence is all around" ("Staring at the Sun").

Of course, the rejection of the world doesn't lead U2 to give up on the longing for God and for the divine. It's just that it seems a fulfillment of this longing is only possible by renouncing the world. That's precisely the theme of "Gone," where the singer declares: "I'll be up with the Sun / I'm not coming down."

As we'll see, however, U2's traditional Christian pessimism turns into a kind of despair once they recognize that metaphysical or Platonic Christianity is a kind of escapism, a deliberate rejection of an essential part of us as earthly beings. This despair—the need for the eternal here in the temporal—gets its fullest expression on the aptly-entitled *All That You Can't Leave Behind* album. "Heaven on Earth / We need it now / I'm sick of all of this / hanging around / I'm sick of sorrow / I'm sick of the

---

[4] See Augustine, *City of God* (London: Penguin, 1984): "because there is in man a rational soul, he subordinates to the peace of the rational soul all that part of his nature which he shares with the beasts. . . . But he needs divine direction. . . . And so long as he is in this mortal body, he is a pilgrim in a foreign land, away from God" (XIX, 14).
[5] See "Bono: *The Rolling Stone Interview*, " *Rolling Stone* 986 (3rd November, 2005), p. 56.

pain / I'm sick of hearing / again and again / that there's gonna be Peace on Earth." This sickness—Kierkegaard called it "despair" or "the sickness unto death"—points to a fundamental problem with the Platonic or traditional Christian picture of the self, because it suggests that no side of the self is unessential.

## U2 and "Sickness unto Death"

Christian thinkers such as Blaise Pascal (1623–1662), Søren Kierkegaard (1813–1855) and Fyodor Dostoevsky (1821–1881) claimed that both sides of the self are essential, thus leading to a view of the self as in essential contradiction. As Pascal put it:

> What a chimera then is man! What a novelty! What a monster, what a chaos, what a contradiction! Judge of all things, imbecile worm of the earth; depositary of truth, a sink of uncertainty and error; the pride and refuse of the universe![6]

This view of our dual nature is a theme U2 repeatedly returns to—singing, for example, of the "I and I" in "Elevation"—the I that's "high, higher than the sun," and the I that's "a mole, digging in a hole." This view is summed up elegantly in "So Cruel": "head of heaven, / fingers in the mire." If we are essentially dual in this way, then any attempt to overcome one side in favor of the other inevitably ends in despair. According to Pascal, a person's highest achievement was not to deny or overcome this contradiction—by getting rid of half the self—but to live in such a way as to fully express the tension of the contradiction. "We do not display greatness by going to one extreme," he said, "but in touching both [extremes] at once, and filling all the intervening space" (*Pensées*, § 353).

Kierkegaard likewise thinks that the classical approach fails to explain the possibility of despair, an essential aspect of human life. He holds that the self's defining property is that it is a relation that relates itself to itself, and that such a relation has a complex structure which he calls a "synthesis" of two sets of factors: on the body side, temporal, finite, and fixed, and, on the soul side, eternal, infinite and free. In a synthesis, unlike a combination, both aspects are essential.

---

[6] Blaise Pascal, *Pensées* (New York: Dutton, 1958), p. 121.

Kierkegaard agrees that, according to the Judeo-Christian tradition, the self is a contradictory *synthesis* between two sets of factors and that *each set is essential* and requires the other. He calls this a dialectical relation. That means that both sets of factors are aspects of one whole. You can't satisfy one set of factors without satisfying the other. Bono makes the same point when he observes: "People are made to choose between flesh and the spirit, when people are both."[7]

But how are we to respond to this essential contradiction and the despair that grows out of it? One response is to attempt to hide from oneself the fact that one is in a contradiction. Kierkegaard called this state "spiritlessness." In spiritlessness one senses that the self is a contradiction that has to be faced, but one lives in distraction so that one never has to take a stand in thought or action as to how to get the factors together. Pascal gives as examples of distraction playing tennis, or sitting alone in one's room solving hard philosophical problems. (No doubt he had Descartes in mind.)

In his essay, *The Present Age*,[8] written in 1846, Kierkegaard warns that his age is characterized by a disinterested reflection and curiosity that levels all differences of status and value. In his terms, this detached reflection levels all qualitative distinctions. Everything is equal in that nothing matters enough that one would be willing to die for it. Friedrich Nietzsche gave this leveling a name; he called it 'nihilism'. U2 calls it 'pop'. In pop culture, we throw ourselves into lightweight, meaningless activities to distract ourselves from the contradiction at the root of our existence.

Kierkegaard thought the most important distraction in his time was the Public Sphere, especially the newspaper, which has since degenerated into the talk show, where one could discuss events and people anonymously without ever having to take responsibility for one's views. One could also debate, on the basis of principles, how the world should be run, without running the risk of testing these principles in action. This form of distraction is now consummated in chat rooms and news groups on the Internet, but, of course, there are many other

---

[7] In Bill Flanagan, *U2 at the End of the World* (New York: Delacorte, 1995), p. 82.

[8] Søren Kiekegaard, *The Present Age* (New York: Harper and Row, 1962).

ways to avoid facing the contradictory nature of the self besides surfing the Net.

"Playboy Mansion," in particular, has an excellent discussion of Kierkegaardian leveling, which obliterates all the meaningful differences that make it possible to make the kind of commitment that could overcome spiritlessness. Our age, U2 notes sardonically, has reduced all that was once holy, sacred, or important to items for consumption: "Coke is a mystery / Michael Jackson . . . History"; "perfume is an obsession / and talk shows . . . confession." As a result, our highest longings are reduced to a passing desire for satisfaction, for the Playboy Mansion rather than heavenly mansions. The dream of Christian redemption is replaced with the dream of hitting the jackpot in a Casino: "Don't know if I can hold on / Til the colours come flashing / And the lights go on / Then will there be no time for sorrow / Then will there be no time for shame."

"Discotheque" likewise addresses the spiritlessness we feel when leveling has destroyed all meaningful distinctions, but nevertheless left us addicted to what few, banal pleasures we have left: "You know you're chewing bubblegum / You know what that is but you still want some / You just can't get enough of that lovie dovie stuff."

But the spiritlessness made seductive by the banality of our age fails, according to Kierkegaard, because if a human being acts only as a combination of factors, he or she is not yet a self. To be a self, the relation must relate itself to itself, by taking a stand on both sets of factors through its actions. It must manifest that something about the self is essential by making something in its life absolute. It is not enough merely to try to "balance" or "mix" the factors together.

As we've already seen, the Platonic Christian tradition sought for what is essential by denying that the other set of factors is essential. Kierkegaard calls the result of this approach a "negative unity." One gets a unified self by denying one of the sets of factors and acting as if only the other aspects of the self are essential. For example, if one makes possibility absolute and lives for constant change, constantly open to new possibilities, one is in the aesthetic sphere—Kierkegaard's anticipation of Nietzsche and the post-moderns—but the end result is despair at having no self at all, no existence worth having. Kierkegaard explains that, for such a person, "possibility seems greater and greater to the self; more and more becomes possible because nothing becomes actual. In the end it seems as though everything were possible, but that is the very moment that the self is swallowed up in the abyss."[9] U2 sings of such a person in "Last Night on Earth.": "She feels the ground is giving way," U2 explains, and "she thinks we're better off that way." She learns "to give it away," to do without any hope that anything will give her "lasting satisfaction"[10]—"she's not waiting on a saviour to come." But for all its coherence, this sort of life can't escape the nagging sense of despair: the "world turns" and she "gets dizzy," there's "something she might be missing." To avoid the despair, Kierkegaard thinks, we need to have a synthesis of both possibility and necessity.

Another example comes with those who deny their finite and temporal sides, and instead try to make the infinite and the eternal absolute. As Kierkegaard puts it, such mystical types can't bring their God-relationship together with a decision whether or not to take a walk in the park. This is the approach represented by the singer in "Staring at the Sun," who is "happy to go blind" to this worldly existence by looking to an infinite source of meaning. But at the same time, he recognizes this as a kind of fleeing. The ones who are staring at the sun are "afraid of what you'll find if you took a look inside." What you find is "an insect in your ear"—earthly desires and attachments—and "if you scratch it won't disappear / it's gonna itch and burn and sting." Scratching—trying to get rid of these attachments—"brings / waves [of passion] that leave me out of reach / breaking on your back like a beach."

Moreover, the song recognizes that loving relations and passions are not just accidental to our nature—"creeps a crawling over me / over me and over you stuck together with God's glue." Our insect-passion side is God-given, in that it ties us in love to the people around us. If we choose the 'staring at the sun' option, we have to give up on these passionate relationships and, in the process, miss out on true human greatness: "I'm nearly great / but there's something missing / I left in the duty free" that is, it had to be left behind in the transition to eternity.

---

[9] Søren Kierkegaard, *Sickness unto Death*, p. 66.
[10] Friedrich Nietzsche, *The Gay Science* (New York: Vintage, 1974), §295.

Like Kierkegaard, then, U2 recognizes that both forms of search for a positive unity will inevitably end in despair because a true unity can only come about by relating to oneself through another—a relation that is impossible for someone trying to establish a unity on their own. The "something missing" in "Staring at the Sun" is the woman the singer loves, who was left behind in his longing for the infinite and eternal. Mark Wrathall shows in the next chapter how U2 has dealt with this option. Here we want to conclude by exploring in the next section the way that Kierkegaard uses the inescapable fact of despair as an argument for the Christian view of the world.

## "You Know There's Something More": The Argument for Christianity

In *Sickness unto Death*, Kierkegaard tries to show that every possible attempt to combine the factors by essentialising one or the other side of each pair of factors leads to despair, as does every way of trying to do justice to both on your own. And, according to Kierkegaard, everyone who has not managed to perform the impossible task of getting his or her self together in a stable, meaningful life is in despair.

You might well think that this is all ridiculous, since you, at least, are not in despair. You may feel that you are having a great time enjoying all your possibilities, or living a fulfilling life taking care of your family, or that your life is worth living because you are working to eliminate suffering, and so forth. You may think, in general, that you are fulfilling your capacities and everything is working out fine.

One response that U2 and Kierkegaard share is to reflect on and describe these kinds of unresolved lives—to do phenomenology. Kierkegaard and Bono both share a penchant for writing pseudonymously. Whether it is Johannes Climacus or the Fly, Vigilium Haufniensis or Macphisto, these pseudonyms allow them to explore a form of life from the inside out: "rather than write about the character, *become* the character."[11]

When Bono steps out of character to describe the different ways of living a life, however, his descriptions suggest that those

---

[11] Bill Flanagan, *U2 at the End of the World* (New York: Delta, 1995), p. 57

who have failed to do justice to both sets of factors inevitably have a sense that something is missing. Sadie, an acquaintance of Bono's that he writes about in "Surrender," "tried to be a good girl and a good wife / raise a good family / lead a good life." But she left it all because she couldn't shake the sense that "it's not good enough." Those seeking love in the "Discotheque" have the same experience: they "take what you can get / 'cause it's all that you can find / but you know there's something more . . ."

In addition to offering this kind of phenomenological description, Kierkegaard also offers a kind of argument to show that even those who might think they are living a worthwhile life, in fact are in despair. What right does he have to say this? His answer is in *Sickness unto Death*:

> Despair differs dialectically from what one usually calls sickness, because it is a sickness of the spirit. And this dialectical aspect, properly understood, brings further thousands under the category of despair. If at any time a physician is convinced that so and so is in good health, and then later that person becomes ill, then the physician may well be right about his having been well at the time but now being sick. Not so with despair. Once despair appears, what is apparent is that the person was in despair. In fact, it's never possible at any time to decide anything about a person who is not saved through having been in despair. For when whatever causes a person to despair occurs, it is immediately evident that he has been in despair his whole life. (*Sickness*, p. 54)

Kierkegaard is pointing out that despair is not like sadness, regret, disappointment, depression, and so on. Rather, unlike these downers, despair exhibits what Kierkegaard calls "the dialectic of eternity." If you are sad, you know that it is temporary. Even if something so terrible happens to you that you feel that you were happy once but that whatever has happened makes it impossible for you ever to be happy again, that is certainly misery, but it is not despair. Despair is the feeling that life isn't working for you and, given the kind of person you are, it is impossible for things to work for you; that a life worth living is, in your case, literally impossible.

That means that once a person experiences despair—"it will be evidence that his [previous] success was an illusion" (*Sickness*, p. 51)—all that person's past joys *must have been* self deceptions. That in turn means that, if you ever experience despair, you realize that you have always been in despair and you always will be. So Kierkegaard concludes that, since the self is a contradiction, even though you now feel that things are going well for you, you must right now be in despair and not know it. Only if you have faced your despair—the sickness unto death—and been cured can you be sure you are not now in despair. So, given the contradictory nature of the self, all of us, with the exception of those who have faced despair and been healed, must right now be in despair.

The ultimate despair, Kierkegaard contends, is denying that one is in despair by denying the demand that we express the two sets of factors in our lives in a way that enables them to reinforce each other. This is not the distraction of the present age where one represses the call to be a self. Rather, someone in this ultimate form of despair sees that in our religious tradition the self has, indeed, been constituted as having a set of essential but incompatible factors, but claims that this is merely a traditional, essentialist view that we should opt out of. Since the traditional Judeo-Christian understanding of the self leads people to despair, we should simply give it up and adopt a vocabulary and practices that are healthier and more useful to us now.

How can we decide who's right here, Kierkegaard or the pragmatist? We think this is a question we can only approach experimentally. In *Sickness Unto Death*, Kierkegaard tries to show that the Christian claim that the self is a contradiction is confirmed by a purportedly exhaustive categorization of all the ways of being a self available to us and how each fails.

At this point, we once again return to the phenomenological approach—we see to what extent the existentialist description of the emptiness and banality of present culture, together with the longing for something deeper resonates with our common experience of the world. U2's music offers just such a description. Its general appeal suggests that, if Kierkegaard's critique is not correct, it is at least not easily dismissed.

# 3

# "If You Want to Kiss the Sky, Better Learn How to Kneel": Existential Christianity in U2

MARK A. WRATHALL

> Whoever has never yet been seized with vertigo through a philo-sophical question has also never yet questioned philosophically.
> —MARTIN HEIDEGGER, *The Basic Concepts of Metaphysics*

> . . . your head can't rule your heart
> and fear has taken over every thought . . . .
> I'm at a place called Vertigo
>   —U2, "VERTIGO" (Jacknife Lee 10" version)

The feeling of vertigo that Heidegger (1889–1976) and Bono allude to is the dizziness or disorientation that comes from being in a place that we can't understand. We find our head spinning, our minds overwhelmed by the undeniable reality of the situation we find ourselves in. For Heidegger, this kind of experience is the starting point for philosophical reflection, because this is an experience of being brought up short, confronted with the limits of our understanding.

According to Kierkegaard (1813–1855), one of the most important sources of philosophy-inspiring vertigo is the dual nature of human existence. Our efforts to produce a synthesis between our bodily desires and spiritual longings produces a despair that is a kind of vertigo: "The possibility of vertigo lies in the combination of the psychical and the physical . . . What vertigo is with respect to the combination of the psychical and the physical, despair is for the spirit, with respect to the combi-nation of the finite and the infinite, freedom and necessity, the divine and the human . . . . In a healthy state or when there is balance between the psychical and the physical, there is no vertigo in human beings. And the same with despair."[1] This kind of vertigo, it turns out, is in fact what Bono has in mind. The struggle between head and heart, the driving beat of existence that he can't make sense of, takes him to a place called vertigo.

How to make a whole out of our divided nature—to unite mind *and* body; reason *and* passion; spirit *and* body, to "take this soul / stranded in some skin and bones / and make it sing" ("Jahweh")—how to do this is a problem that has motivated existentialist thinkers like Blaise Pascal (1623–1662), Fyodor Dostoevsky (1821–1881), Søren Kierkegaard, and Friedrich Nietzsche (1844–1900). Most thinkers in the West since Plato (429–347 B.C.) have understood the nature of the human self in divided terms. On this conception, one cannot fully do justice to all one's bodily, finite, temporal needs and capacities while at the same time fully expressing all one's intellectual, infinite, eternal needs and capacities. It seems to many, in fact, that the more you try to satisfy bodily desires, the less you are able to express your spiritual or intellectual longings, and *vice versa*. So it seems to them that if human beings are to be happy, only one side of their being can be essential. One must either become numb to the bodily desires in order to live the life of the mind or spirit; or one must abandon oneself to the pursuit of transitory worldly pleasures, at the cost of giving up on one's highest yearnings (for more on this, see Chapter 2 in this volume).

There's a long tradition of trying to resolve the conflict between the body and the intellect, this world and eternity, by taking only one side of human existence as essential, thus holding that one is either essentially a soul, and not a body, or *vice versa*. To arrive at peace and fulfillment, then, all one has to do is realize one's *true* nature and satisfy the self's deep needs while renouncing one's superficial and inessential desires. This is a dominant approach in Christianity, where believers aim to, in Luther's words, "mortify the flesh." In this respect, traditional Christianity agrees with Plato in insisting that the eternal spirit of man is essential, and that the body, with all its desires and appetites should be denied. This leads to a kind of pessimism,

---

[1] Søren Kierkegaard, *Søren Kierkegaards Papirer*, Volume VIII: 2 (Copenhagen: Gyldendal, 1968), pp. 261–62. I am indebted to Nate Kramer for helping me with the translation of this passage.

in which the faithful look in vain to find anything in this world that lives up to the truths their faith leads them to expect. This pessimism is expressed in vintage U2 songs like "I Still Haven't Found What I'm Looking For": one can 'climb the highest mountains', 'scale city walls', 'kiss honey lips,' 'speak with the tongue of angels,' and still one doesn't find what one needs. The pessimistic Christian can only look forward to "the Kingdom Come / then all the colours will bleed into one" for final satisfaction of her longings.

But how does the pessimist deal with the undeniable reality of the world around her? Like the singer of "MoFo," she spends her life "lookin' for a sound that's gonna drown out the world," that is, looking for some way to sever all her bodily attachments to the fallen world around her.

### "I'll Be Up with the Sun": Pessimism and Existential Despair

For existentialist thinkers like Pascal, Kierkegaard, Nietzsche, and Dostoevsky, however, pessimism is not a feasible stance. The existentialists argue that both sides are essential to human nature, and that any attempt to get rid of one side will inevitably fail. The key to living a worthwhile life, for the existentialists, is not to deny the contradiction built into human existence, but to somehow learn to affirm it. Bono, by the way, shares this view of human nature: "As a person, as a performer, you're looking for wholeness. On a spiritual level, I think that's God's design for us. Wholeness. And that often amounts to embracing contradictions."[2]

If the existentialists are right about this claim, then we should find evidence in even the most resolutely sensual or most resolutely intellectual life that there is something missing. The existential name for the feeling or mood that results is anxiety (*Angst*), the experience (as Heidegger defines it) in which we find that "the world has the character of completely lacking significance,"[3] and thus is incapable of providing anything that can give ultimate meaning to our lives. Here's where rock 'n' roll becomes an interesting phenomenon for philosophical study. To

---

[2] Richard Blow, "Bono Turns up the Political Heat," *George* 5 (April 2000), p. 94.
[3] Martin Heidegger, *Being and Time* (New York: Harper and Row, 1962), p. 231.

the extent that Rock is an expression of the sensuous life, then the discovery in Rock music of existential anxiety will attest to the existential thesis about the essential wholeness of human existence.

And, in fact, a careful listener finds over and over again in the corpus of Rock music just such expressions of anxiety. It's evident in the mood of "MoFo" as much as the lyrics—the music is drenched with the anger, turmoil, and despair that come from a need to fill the "Godshaped hole" in our soul, combined with an inability to fill it with anything we find in the world around us. U2 here is giving voice to the view of human nature expressed by Blaise Pascal (1623–1662), French philosopher and grandfather of existentialism. Human experience "proclaims," he wrote:

> that there was once within us true happiness of which all that now remains is the outline and empty trace. Man tries unsuccessfully to fill this void with everything that surrounds him, seeking in absent things the help he cannot find in those that are present, but all are incapable of it. This infinite abyss can be filled only with an infinite, immutable object, that is to say, God himself.[4]

Pascal's void that can only be filled by God, the God-shaped hole that Bono sings about, shows that human nature longs for something that can't be satisfied by ordinary carnal pleasures. Such expressions of despair over our inability to find "the baby Jesus under the trash" might not surprise us coming from committed Christians like the members of U2. But interestingly enough, we find the same expressions of anxiety and despair from some of the most resolutely anti-religious and sensual groups I can think of. If they experience anxiety in the face of the world, an inability of the world to fulfill their most profound longings, then surely everyone will.

Take, for example, the songs of Rammstein, many of which address the kinds of longing that arise from both the religious anxiety produced by denial of our earthly side, and the sensuous anxiety produced by denial of our spiritual side. Rammstein's expression of the latter contains an important insight. The traditional Christian ascetic ideal, because it sees the good life as involving a complete denial of bodily pleasures

---

[4] Pascal, *Pensées* (Oxford: Oxford University Press, 1995), p. 52.

(including companionship with other embodied beings), will only produce anxiety in embodied beings like us.

> Who on earth is good in life
> becomes an angel after death.
> You ask while glancing toward the heavens
> Why it is we cannot see them
>
> [Angels singing:] Only when the clouds go to sleep
> can one see us in the heavens
> we are anxious and alone.
>
> [Till's response:] As God knows, I don't want to be an angel.[5]

If union with God requires us to abandon all sociality and bodily pleasures, Rammstein suggests, the result will only be anxiety and, among many, a refusal of the life of faith. Many of U2's songs suggest the same, if not as bluntly as Rammstein. In the melancholic "The First Time," for example, the story of the prodigal son is presented with a twist: after the father gives the son "the keys to his kingdom (coming)," the singer notes: "I left by the back door / And I threw away the key. / For the first time, I feel love."

It's no surprise, of course, to find rock 'n' roll groups rejecting the ascetic life. What is interesting, however, is finding that groups like Rammstein also recognize that the life devoted to sensuality is equally destined to failure. In "Sehnsucht," "Longing," they sing of the dissatisfaction one finds in a life devoted to sensuous pleasure: "Longing hides / like an insect. / In sleep you don't notice / that it stings you. / I will not be happy anywhere."[6]

In the face of the anxiety that results from our inability to satisfy both sides of our nature at the same time, perhaps the most common reaction is to seek distraction—to keep oneself so busy with meaningless and trivial things that one doesn't notice that one cannot be happy anywhere. Sex, drugs, and rock 'n' roll, of course, are the typical sources of distraction in our age (for more on the idea of distraction, see Chapter 2 in this volume).

---

[5] "Wer zu Lebzeit gut auf Erden / wird nach dem Tod ein Engel werden / den Blick gen Himmel fragst du dann / warum man sie nicht sehen kann. / Erst wenn die Wolken schlafengehen / Kann man uns am Himmel sehen / wir haben Angst und sind allein / Gott weiss ich will kein Engel sein" ("Engel")

[6] "Sehnsucht versteckt / sich wie ein Insekt / im Schlafe merkst du nicht / dass es dich sticht / glücklich werd ich nirgendwo . . ." ("Sehnsucht")

But existential Christians like Pascal, Kierkegaard, and Dostoevsky argue that such distractions can't ultimately change the fact that, because of the essential contradiction in our nature, we inevitably find ourselves in despair. Despair is the state of being incapable of satisfying our most profound longings, of wanting something that can't be had (this despair is expressed in songs like Nine Inch Nails's "Something I Can Never Have").

U2 sings in "Gonc" of abandoning all worldly concerns for union with the Sun, that is, with God: "Goodbye, you can keep this suit of lights / I'll be up with the sun / I'm not coming down." But this is a strategy that works only if we can do without our worldly attachments and passionate bodily relations to others.

That we cannot do without these worldly attachments is attested to by musicians like Trent Reznor, who sings despairingly of the worldly gravity that drags us back "Down in it." The protagonist of "Down in it" describes the experience of being pulled inexorably back into worldly relationships—relationships, however, which produce only anxiety and despair—despite his best efforts to transcend the world. His attempt at denying his worldly side, in other words, ends up driving him into despair.

In rock music we find anecdotal confirmation of the existentialist theses that: 1. the human being is a contradiction, who desires on the one hand a relationship to the infinite, eternal, and world-transcendent, and on the other hand passionate, sensuous relationships to particular, finite, and temporal beings; and 2. this contradiction produces anxiety and despair over our inability to simultaneously satisfy our spiritual longings and our passionate desires. This confirmation is impressive, given that signs of a longing for the eternal, and anxiety and despair over a failure to satisfy these longings are found in groups as diverse as Rammstein, Nine Inch Nails, and U2.

## "Heaven on Earth, We Need It Now": U2 and the Existential-Christian Solution

It seems like we're stuck in an impossible dilemma. We can't give up on our longing for the divine, and we can't deny our passionate attachment to the world. For the Christian existentialist, this condition points us toward the need for a Savior: the only possible solution is to find some way to discover God in the world. Christian existentialists reject the pessimistic idea that satisfaction of our highest longings can be deferred until the next life. As Bono succinctly expresses the point, pessimists are "zealots" who

> have no love for the world. They're just getting through it to the next one. It's a favorite topic. It's the old cliché: 'Eat shit now, pie in the sky when you die.' But I take Christ at his word: 'On Earth as it is in Heaven.'"[7]

Yet the existentialists equally reject the idea that we can do without satisfaction of our highest longings. The slogan for such Christian existentialists could easily be the introductory line of "Peace on Earth": "Heaven on earth / We need it now / I'm sick of all of this / hanging around."

Despair, as we've seen, grows precisely out of "needing it now" but being unable to have it. The problem is that we long for something that, it seems, can't possibly be realized "in the flesh." For the Christian existentialist, the key is to discover a way to understand our longings so that they can be realized on earth. This will require a changed conception of both our spiritual side and our sensual nature. Faith in God, the Christian existentialist believes, shows us how to do this. In a faithful existence, the world is disclosed in such a way that we can achieve this resolution of the contradiction at the heart of our existence. What will the resolution be like? It will somehow show us both (a) how to pursue something eternal, infinite—worthy of neverending longing; and (b) allow us to live on earth, in the kind of passionate relationships to others that don't end up driving us to despair by undermining our higher longings.

U2 gives us a picture of what the solution looks like in "Beautiful Day." The song begins with the Christian's dilemma. "You have to care" about the world because you're stuck here:

> You're out of luck and the reason that you had to care,
> The traffic is stuck and you're not moving anywhere.
> You thought you'd found a friend to take you out of this place,
> Someone you could lend a hand in return for grace.

---

[7] *Bono in Conversation with Michka Assayas* (New York: Riverhead, 2005), p. 203.

A pessimistic Christian hopes that Christ's grace will remove the believer from the world. But it doesn't do that—and we're left to fall in love with this world, even with all its imperfections: "you love this town even if it doesn't ring true." So now the solution can't be to escape from the world—out of all time and place, to be up with the Sun. Instead, the solution is to be taught to disclose the world differently—that is, be taken to "that other place." This other place is the world seen in the Christian way, the world itself "in green and blue." Where "Acrobat" demands the full realization of our eternal hopes now, the existential Christian discloser of the world doesn't, because he has learned to feel God in the world: "What you don't have you don't need it now. What you don't know you can feel it somehow." The resolution comes when one realizes that there is a way to get the contradictory sides of our nature together. We do this by realizing, as Bono puts it, that "what look like opposites . . . may not be."[8]

That's the solution. But how can faith lead to this resolution of the dilemma? To answer this question, we need to say something about the existentialist understanding of faith.

## "A Place that Has to Be Believed to Be Seen": Faith as World Disclosure

Take a look at Heidegger's description of faith:

> the essence of faith can formally be sketched as a way of existence of human being [*Dasein*] that, according to its own testimony . . . arises *not from* human being [*Dasein*] or spontaneously *through* human being [*Dasein*], but rather from that which is revealed in and with this way of existence, from what is believed. For the "Christian" faith, that being which is primarily revealed to faith, and only to it, and which, as revelation, first gives rise to faith, is Christ, the crucified God. . . . The crucifixion, however, and all that belongs to it is a historical event, and indeed this event gives testimony to itself as such in its specifically historical character only for faith in the scriptures. One "knows" about this fact only *in believing.*[9]

[8] Bill Flanagan, *U2 at the End of the World* (New York: Delta, 1995), p. 82.
[9] Martin Heidegger, "Phenomenology and Theology," in W. McNeill, ed., *Pathmarks* (Cambridge: Cambridge University Press, 1998), pp. 43–44 (translation modified).

For Heidegger, in other words, faith is a mode of existence—a way of acting and living—that reveals the world, and Christian faith arises out of the world as it is revealed through faith in Christ. Note the circular character of this description—faith is a way of living in the world that arises from the world being disclosed or revealed through faith. To have faith, then, the world must be able to support a certain mode of existence—certain practices and dispositions—but the world only shows up in a such a way that it can support that mode of existence to one who already has the mode of existence. The Christian world is, in other words, "a place that has to be believed to be seen" ("Walk On"). Pascal, in a similar way, noted that "it is clear that those with a keen faith in their hearts can see straightaway that everything which exists is the work of the God they worship." On the other hand, "those in whom this light [of faith] has been extinguished, . . . scrutinizing with all their intelligence everything they see in nature which can lead them to this knowledge . . . find[] only obscurity and darkness" (*Pensées*, §644, p. 139).

U2 expresses precisely this same Pascalian-Heideggerian view in songs like "When I Look at the World." On such a view, we are no longer worried about our failure to find cognitive verification of our faith in the world. Instead, we are satisfied if a Christian experience of the world shows us how to see this world without "blinking" or "looking away." Addressing a saint-like figure—a person who's learned to feel the world in the right way—the singer longs to "see what you see" "when you look at the world." Cognitively, the saint's Christian faith remains deferred ("your thoughts are too expensive / to ever want to keep"). But through her faith, she can inhabit the world without despair—she has "an expression / So clear and so true / That it changes the atmosphere / When you walk into the room." U2's longing has become not the longing to escape the world—to be up with the Sun—but the longing "to be like you / to feel it like you do".

This is quite a different way of understanding faith than, as is commonplace, thinking of it as a mental attitude. In particular, one typically thinks of faith in terms of a certain degree of confidence in the truth of a proposition—a state in which one accepts a sentence as true, even when one lacks absolute certitude of its truth. For thinkers like Pascal and Kierkegaard, however, such a degree of confidence is based on faith understood

in existential terms. Confidence in the truth of certain propositions grows out of the way that faith in Christ produces a
changed experience of the world. "The Christian thesis,"
Kierkegaard wrote, "is not: *intelligere ut credam* (I understand
in order that I might believe), nor is it *credere, ut intelligam* (I
believe in order that I might understand). No, it is: Act according to the command and orders of Christ; do the will of the
Father—and you will become a believing person."[10] Thus faith
is to be understood, in the first instance, as the existential state
of those who are able to act and live in a Christian way.

    Without an ability to live a Christian life and inhabit a
Christian world, mere belief in God or the truth of religious
claims is not faith, it is superstition. Superstition is belief in the
existence of entities and events which do not manifest themselves in the ordinary course of experience. If someone does
believe "that rock 'n' roll can really change the world,"[11] it need
not be a superstitious belief. This is because, while there might
be an objectively low degree of probability that just listening to
a song will really change all the greed and hatred and evil
actions in the world, people might nevertheless, in the normal
course of affairs in the world, change their behavior as a result
of listening to a particularly inspiring song. By contrast if I
believe that there is a God in spite of the fact that there's no
place for God in my way of making sense of the world, then the
belief is a superstition. It's not just that there is a low probability that God does exist, it's rather that, given my experience of
the world, it is utterly incomprehensible how there could be a
God. I am left merely "speaking of signs and wonders," while a
true experience of God demands "something other"—namely,
loving action to relieve the suffering of others (consider
"Crumbs From Your Table").

    We don't always use the word 'faith' to denote a mere men-
tal state of belief. Faith also involves actually relying on or having confidence in the object of one's faith—we say we "believe
in something" to express this. We would not ordinarily say of
someone that she has faith in something if she is incapable of

---

[10] *Søren Kierkegaard's Journals and Papers*, Volume 3, (Bloomington: Indiana University
Press, 1975), p. 363. I am grateful to James Faulconer for bringing this passage to my
attention.
[11] Bono claims that he does not in "God Part II."

acting in reliance on that thing. Pascal captures this by noting that faith is a "disposition within [the] heart" (*Pensées*, §412). The idea of a disposition of the heart goes beyond simply being disposed to act in a certain way. It also includes being primed to feel or experience things in a certain way. If we say that someone has a "sunny disposition," we are saying that she responds to all situations cheerfully, and generally focuses on the bright side of even bad events. So what kind of disposition is Christian faith? It involves both a kind of feeling or readiness to experience things in such and such a way, and a kind of practical orientation or readiness to act in a certain way. Pascal gets at this in a backhanded way in the following passage:

> There are few true Christians. Even as far as faith goes. There are many who believe, but through superstition. There are many who do not believe, but through licentiousness. There are few in between. I do not include those who lead a truly devout life, nor all those who believe through a feeling of the heart (*Pensées*, §210; see also *Pensées*, §142).

We would not say, in other words, that someone has Christian faith who is unable to live a Christian life. This is true, even if that person had a rationally grounded knowledge of God.[12] So faith is located in the existential register, meaning the presence or absence of faith is a matter of the kind of stance one takes on life, the practices one engages in, the ways one feels about things. True faith is found in one's disposition (feelings of the heart) and the actions that arise from those dispositions (living a devout life). Bono echoes this view in his description of his own approach to religion: "God is love, and as much as I respond in allowing myself to be transformed by that love and acting in that love, that's my religion" (*Bono in Conversation*, p. 200). True *dis*belief, by the same token, is found in a corrupt and licentious life (taking pleasure in what is not pleasing to God, doing actions that God condemns).

Philosophers have long recognized that, in developing habits and practicing actions for dealing with a particular domain, we

---

[12] *Pensées*, §690: "Such knowledge," Pascal argues, "is useless and sterile. Even if someone could be persuaded that the proportions between numbers are intangible, eternal truths, dependent on an earlier truth in which they exist, called God, I would not consider that he had made much progress towards his salvation."

acquire skillful dispositions so attuned to that domain that we can perceive things of which we were oblivious before. Take, for example, Adam Clayton's description of his early experience with the band: "punk rock had just happened, so it wasn't really important that you knew how to play . . . . I certainly didn't know anything about playing." As a result, "the ambition" of the band, he explains, "was just to end the song together!" Things changed as they all became more skillful: "as our songwriting became more developed and there were better chord progressions, I found I would fall into more interesting things. I wouldn't literally know where I was headed when I started out, but Larry's drums have always told me what to play, and then the chords tell me where to go."[13] As his skills developed, in other words, he was able to experience the musical situation in a way that he could not before he possessed those skills. Adam offers here a very sound and rich description of what skill acquisition is like. As one becomes more skillful, one simply allows the situation that one's skills reveal to dictate how to respond.

For Pascal, religious faith works the same way. He explains:

> You want to find faith and you do not know the way? You want to cure yourself of unbelief and you ask for the remedies? Learn from those who have been bound like you, and who now wager all they have. They are people who know the road you want to follow and have been cured of the affliction of which you want to be cured. Follow the way by which they began: by behaving just as if they believed, taking holy water, having masses said, etc. That will make you believe quite naturally, and according to your animal reactions. (*Pensées*, §680)

Faith is, then, the condition of one who has acquired the skills of religious living, and thus has the dispositions to feel and act appropriately in the world that appears when one has those skills. Notice that this description replicates the circularity in Heidegger's earlier descriptions of faith—faith is "a way of existence that arises from the world revealed by this way of existence."

---

[13] Gregory Isola, "Reluctant Rock Star: How U2's Adam Clayton Learned to Play–and Conquer the World Onstage," in Hank Bordowitz, ed., *The U2 Reader* (Milwaukee: Hal Leonard Corporation, 2003), pp. 197–98.

Faith will then not be amenable to proof in the way one verifies a cognitive state or proposition (demonstrating that it is true). But it will have the kind of confirmation or success conditions that all other skills have. Music skills are confirmed or successful when they allow the musician to cope with the concert hall or the recording studio. Religious faith will be confirmed or successful when it gives me the practices and dispositions I need to cope with the world as a whole. As Father Zosima notes in *The Brothers Karamazov*, Dostoevsky's classic depiction of existential Christianity, "one cannot prove anything here, but it is possible to be convinced." He goes on to explain that one is convinced "by the experience of active love. . . . The more you succeed in loving, the more you'll be convinced of the existence of God and the immortality of your soul. And if you reach complete selflessness in the love of your neighbor, then undoubtedly you will believe, and no doubt will even be able to enter your soul."[14] The confirmation and conviction come, in other words, through one's success in living in the world in the way indicated by faith. Bono hints at the same view when he describes songs like "40" as prayers "pulling at the hem of an invisible deity whose presence we glimpse only when we act in love."[15]

## "Your Love Is Teaching Me How to Kneel": Love and Existential Faith

The existential Christian thus argues that faith is confirmed if it turns out that it is only the Christian who, through the saving grace of Christ, is able to resolve her despair. U2's music shows a similar understanding of the validity of faith—the true possessor of faith is the saint of "When I look at the World," rather than the superstitious preacher of signs and wonders in "Crumbs From Your Table." "When there's all kinds of chaos / and everyone is walking lame," the saint doesn't even "blink . . . or look away"—that is, she's not tempted at all to make the pessimistic move of renouncing the world.

---

[14] Dostoevsky, *The Brothers Karamazov* (New York: Vintage, 1990), p. 56.
[15] *Selections from the Book of Psalms, with an Introduction by Bono* (New York: Grove Press, 1999), p. xi.

For the existential thinker, then, Christian doctrines need to be understood in terms of the human practices which instantiate those doctrines. Their 'truth' is demonstrated when the practices they generate allow us to resolve the contradiction of human existence. Take, for example, the Christian doctrine of grace— the doctrine that God and God alone forgives and redeems sinners. For an existential Christian faith in grace would be mere superstition if it amounted to the vague hope that somehow, inexplicably, God would purify our souls. For the doctrine to actually work to change our lives and allow us to disclose the world differently, we need some experience of grace embodied. This is precisely what U2 describes in "Grace": "Grace, it's the name for a girl. It's also a thought that changed the world." That is, we get an understanding of the thought by meeting someone like the girl alluded to in the song—a person who has a certain set of loving practices. "She's got the time to talk," she "finds beauty in everything," "she takes the blame," "she covers the shame." If we ever have dealings with such a person, we discovery the worldly manifestation of Christian grace. Through her acts of love, "what once was hurt, / what once was friction, / what left a mark, / no longer stings / because Grace makes beauty / out of ugly things."

In general, then, the crucial Christian idea that God is love becomes existentialized in U2's music, meaning it is given a concrete manifestation in the world. This is, for Bono, the profound, existential meaning of God's incarnation in Christ:

> The idea that God, if there is a force of Love and Logic in the universe, that it would seek to explain itself is amazing enough. That it would seek to explain itself and describe itself by becoming a child born in straw poverty, in shit and straw . . . a child . . . I just thought: 'Wow!' Just the poetry . . . Unknowable love, unknowable power, describes itself as the most vulnerable. . . . Love needs to find form, intimacy needs to be whispered. To me, it makes sense. It's actually logical. It's pure logic. Essence has to manifest itself. It's inevitable. Love has to become an action or something concrete. It would have to happen. There must be an incarnation. Love must be made flesh. (*Bono in Conversation*, p. 125)

Christians as diverse as Dante, Kierkegaard, and Dostoevsky have understood that we live faithfully to this doctrine when we give ourselves fully in love to some particular person or people. Christian love isn't an abstract love of humanity, a love that "tries to throw its arms around the world," it is a love of a husband or wife, a brother or sister, a child or father, a neighbor—a concrete love that ends up changing the way we are disposed to the actual people and things and situations that we encounter. For the existential Christian, we discover God in the world through that kind of love. Bono has shown an intuitive grasp of this idea in interviews. "I'm always attracted to subjects you can't really get a grip on, like sex or God. I think I sometimes confuse them both!" (*Bono in Conversation*, p. 128). There's a humorous side to this comment, of course, but it contains a crucial insight. Just as Grace is a person who allows the Christian ideal of grace to be disclosed in the world through her actions, so our loving relationships to other people allow God's divine love to be disclosed in the world. "Erotic love can turn into something much higher, and bigger notions of love, and God, and family," Bono notes. "It seems to segue very easily [for] me between all those" (*Bono in Conversation*, p. 120).

In U2's lyrics, this idea is expressed over and over again by tying concrete instances of human love to images of the Sun, which is the metaphor for God's presence in the world. Take, for example, the troubled relationship Bono sings about in "A Man and a Woman." "Everything is not okay," but his lover doesn't need to "worry about a thing today" if they can "take the heat from the sun." The existentializing of God in love of a woman is made explicit as Bono discovers that his effort "to be complete"—to resolve the contradiction of human existence—cannot succeed without his lover: "Little sister, I've been trying to feel complete again. / But you're gone and so is God. / The soul needs beauty for a soul mate. / When the soul wants, the soul waits."

These last lines allude to the way the soul is tied to earthly desires and passions. It is "love and faith and sex and fear and all the things that keep us here" that prevent us from making the pessimistic move.

But for all the trouble in his relationship to his lover, the singer of "A Man and a Woman" is ultimately free of the despair that overcame the protagonist of "Staring at the Sun," who discovered that he was "nearly great but there's something missing" because his lover "never really belonged to me." In "A Man and a Woman," by contrast, he discovers that his lover "was already mine."

U2 gives us more insight into their existentialized account of divine love in "Mysterious Ways." The title, of course, alludes to a line from William Cowper's hymn "Light Shining Out of Darkness": "God moves in mysterious ways, His wonders to perform." In U2's version, however, "God" is replaced by a woman in the chorus: "It's alright, it's alright, it's alright. / She moves in mysterious ways." "Mysterious Ways" is addressed to a man who's "been living underground," that is, the kind of person Dostoevsky described in his classic "Notes From Underground."[16] Those who live underground, according to Dostoevsky (and U2 seems to intend to invoke this idea), are those who live in despair at the paradoxical condition we've described above. The underground man explains that "at all times I was aware of a great many elements in me. . . . I felt how they swarmed inside me, these contradictory elements. I knew that they had been swarming inside me my whole life and were begging to be let out; but I wouldn't let them out."[17] The reason the underground man never resolves these contradictions, Dostoevsky makes clear, is that he despises his earthly side—he calls it his insect side—and longs to live in the perfect, divine sphere of "beautiful forms of being." As a result, his love is "never directed at anything human" (*Notes from Underground*, p. 40).

U2's existentialist advice spells out what Dostoevsky leaves implicit. The resolution for the underground man will only come when he stops "running away from what you don't understand" and "takes a dive with your sister in the rain." An actual, concrete love can teach us what Grace already understands—the healing power of human contact.[18]

---

[16] Beth Maynard has pointed out to me that the man called "Johnny" in "Mysterious Ways" is the John the Baptist character of Oscar Wilde's play "Salome." But U2 go on to criticize the character on Dostoevskian grounds: just like Dostoevsky's underground man, he's been running away from concrete, personal love.

[17] Fyodor Dostoevsky, *Notes From Underground* (New York: Norton, 2001), p. 4, distinguishes between love and romance. "Only true love can keep beauty innocent," that is, only the right kind of love can keep our earthly passions from obscuring our higher longings." Bono sings of such counterfeits of divine love in songs like "Do You Feel Loved" ("it looks like the sun, but it feels like the rain").

[18] Of course, not any thing that passes for love will resolve the contradiction. "A Man and a Woman" distinguishes beween love and romance. "Only true love can keep

When we find true love, our whole world is given meaning by our relationship to the object of our love. In this way, love gives us something transcendent. At the same time, love is an experience of exhilarating, passionate, sensual, and bodily desire. Thus, the love of a man and a woman can solve the paradox by uniting our passionate, exhilarating sensual desires with our longing for something transcendent and meaning-giving: "Let her talk about the things / you can't explain. / To touch is to heal, / to hurt is to steal. / If you want to kiss the sky, / better learn how to kneel . . . On your knees boy!" Kneeling is precisely the right image for contact with the earth and the heavens at the same time.

And so we can now return full circle to the experience of vertigo with which we began. In "Vertigo," the dizziness and disorientation that has the protagonist on the verge of giving up on the world and checking out is stopped when he encounters the "the girl with crimson nails [who] has Jesus round her neck": " I can feel your love teaching me how to kneel."[19]

---

beauty innocent," that is, only the right kind of love can keep our earthly passions from obscuring our higher longings. Bono sings of such counterfeits of divine love in songs like "Do You Feel Loved" (it looks like the sun, but it feels like the rain").

[19] I would like to thank Beth Maynard for her many helpful comments on this paper. I'm particularly grateful to the students and fellow U2 fans at Brigham Young University who have, over many years, helped me recognize the philosophical profundity of Bono, Edge, Adam, and Larry.

# 4

# Philosophizing Place in
# *The Joshua Tree*

JEFF MALPAS

What's the relation between a human life and the place or places in which that life is lived? What does it mean to be at home, to have a sense of place? How should we understand the alienation, homelessness, and loss that is so often reported as a characteristic feature of modern life?

Although such questions may be viewed by some philosophers as best left to cultural theorists or empirical psychologists, they are nevertheless questions that have appeared, in one form or another, in the work of a number of existentially-oriented thinkers—particularly the German philosopher Martin Heidegger.[1] Themes of place, home, and belonging, as well as of displacement, alienation, and loss, also have a special importance in the music of U2, and especially in what is usually acknowledged to be their critically most significant album, *The Joshua Tree*. The Edge described the music of *The Joshua Tree* as music that "actually brought you somewhere physical as opposed to an emotional place—a real location,"[2] and bassist Adam Clayton described the progression of the tracks on *The Joshua Tree* as "like a journey"—it's a journey that takes us from Ireland to Central America, from Wales to New Zealand, from Reagan's America to Pinochet's Chile.

---

[1] For more on these themes as they figure in Heidegger's work, see my *Heidegger's Topology: Being, Place, World* (Cambridge, Massachusetts: MIT Press, 2006); also Julian Young, *Heidegger's Later Philosophy* (Cambridge: Cambridge University Press, 2002).

[2] In *Classic Albums: U2's The Joshua Tree*, directed by Philip King and Nuala O'Connor (London: Independent Television, 1999).

## A Desert Landscape

In the words and music of U2's *The Joshua Tree*, however, almost all of the places to which we are taken appear as places of loss and desolation—places in which we find ourselves, not at home, but often, as Clayton says of the opening track of the album, "running for our lives." The very title of the album, *The Joshua Tree*, refers us to a place "on the margins"—the desert landscape of the Joshua Tree National Park and the small desert township of Joshua Tree (near Palm Springs), both in Southern California[3]—it also refers us to the Joshua tree whose strange awkward shape figures prominently on the album's cover. The tree has a special significance since it can be seen not only as symbolic of the desert as such, but also of journeying and the end of journeying, of the loss of home and its rediscovery. It's said that the Joshua tree (which is actually a giant member of the Lily family known botanically as *Yucca brevifolia*) was named after the Old Testament prophet Joshua by Mormon settlers as they crossed into the region west of the Colorado River in the nineteenth century. The tree presented an image of supplication, its limbs stretched out to the sky and to God—an image that's said to evoke the Old Testament prophet Joshua pointing the way towards the land of Israel. As an image of supplication, the Joshua tree embodies ideas of hope—of a new home, of salvation, of divine blessing. Yet as hope comes out of need, so the Joshua tree also invokes notions of struggle, toil, and potential loss; as the tree points towards the promised new home that may be attained, so it draws attention to current homelessness and alienation.

Wherever else *The Joshua Tree* may take us, it's the desert landscape that dominates the album as a whole—one of the working titles U2 used for the album was simply "Desert Songs" (the other being "The Two Americas"). The image of the desert—and of its empty, open spaces—may be thought

---

[3] Neither place appears explicitly in the album—although the album cover includes photos of the band against a desert landscape and decaying buildings, most of the shots were taken in Death Valley, some one hundred miles northwest of Joshua Tree, during a three-day road trip in December 1986. One reason for nevertheless taking the association with the settlement of Joshua Tree to be significant is that it was there that Gram Parsons, once of the Byrds and Flying Burrito Brothers, died of an overdose in 1973; it thus already had a place in rock history before U2.

particularly resonant with the character of U2's own sound.[4] As many critics have commented, that sound, achieved through a distinctive guitar technique as well as vocal style, is one that seems particularly attuned to open space. The soaring, 'anthemic' quality of much of U2's music might also be taken to be evocative of the grand 'epic' experience often associated, at least in the popular imagination, with the vast openness of the desert landscape. Yet there's also a feel of constant movement that characterizes the tracks on *The Joshua Tree*—especially evident in the restless energy of "Where the Streets Have No Name." If the sound of the album invokes the open space of the desert, it does so through invoking our *movement* through that space. Such movement, and the restlessness that goes with it, also points to the spirit of search that pervades the album—and of the dislocation and uncertainty out of which such searching comes. The lyrics of *The Joshua Tree* themselves constantly refer to such uncertain and restless movement—"searching," "stumbling," "tripping," "climbing," "touching," "holding-on," "shaking." Since we come to places, as well as lose them, through movement—the movement towards and within, and the movement away from—so the restless character of U2's music and lyrics serves to reinforce the more explicit concern with place, home, belonging and loss.

## An Irish Band

The way in which these latter concerns do indeed appear as central themes in *The Joshua Tree*, and throughout much of U2's work, has been recognized by a number of critics,[5] and is a feature of their music often taken to be associated with the

---

[4] Somewhat paradoxically so, since, as Gerry Smyth points out, in *Space and the Irish Cultural Imagination* (New York: Palgrave Macmillan, 2001), p.177, sound tends to dissipate in the emptiness of the desert landscape—the desert is mostly silent.

[5] Including John Waters, but also Kieran Keohane, "Traditionalism and Homelessness in Contemporary Irish Music," in Jim MacLaughlin, ed., *Location and Dislocation in Contemporary Irish Society:Perspectives on Irish Emigration and Irish Identities in a Global Context* (Cork: Cork University Press, 1997), pp. 274–303; Allan F. Moore, *Rock, The Primary Text: Developing a Musicology of Rock* (Buckingham: Open University Press, 1993), and Gerry Smyth, "'Show Me the Way to Go Home': Space and Place in the Music of U2," in *Space and the Irish Cultural Imagination*, pp. 159–187.

character of U2 as an essentially Irish band.[6] Not only does
Ireland itself have a "marginal" status as it stands between both
America and Europe, but issues of home and place also loom
large in Irish consciousness—Bono himself talks of the Irish as
outsiders, "misfits, travellers, never really at home, but always
talking about it."[7] These themes seem to have been reinforced in
Bono's case by the Protestant-Catholic split within his own family, and the tragic loss of his mother in 1974. It certainly seems
to be true that "home" was already an ambiguous notion for the
young Bono,[8] and in Lypton Village, the group of like-minded
friends who met regularly at Bono's house (and who provided
the names 'Bonovox', hence 'Bono', and 'The Edge'), Bono
seems to have found something of an alternative mode of
belonging—perhaps an alternative version of 'home' and 'place'.

Yet although issues of place and alienation, of home and
homelessness, of identity and belonging, may well be taken to
have a special resonance for Irish culture and experience, they
are not peculiarly Irish themes. In a famous passage from the
1848 *Communist Manifesto*, Karl Marx and Friedrich Engels
speak of the enormous changes that modernity had already
brought with it by the middle of the nineteenth century:

> . . . uninterrupted disturbance of all social conditions, everlasting
> uncertainty and agitation distinguish the bourgeois epoch from all
> earlier ones. All fixed, fast-frozen relations, with their train of
> ancient and venerable prejudices and opinions, are swept away, all
> new-formed ones become antiquated before they can ossify. All
> that is solid melts into air, all that is holy is profaned, and man is
> at last compelled to face with sober senses, his real conditions of
> life, and his relations with his kind. The need of a constantly
> expanding market . . . chases the bourgeoisie over the whole sur-

---

[6] "Show Me the Way," p. 172—Smyth quotes directly from John Waters, *Race of Angels*
(London: Fourth Estate, 1994), p. 121.

[7] In Richard Kearney, ed., *Across the Frontiers: Ireland in the 1990s* (Dublin: Wolfhound
Press, 1988), p.191.

[8] Bono addresses this in "Sometimes You Can't Make it On Your Own": "Where are we
now? I've got to let you know / A house still doesn't make a home / Don't leave me
here alone," and in the following quote: "The death of my mother really affected my
confidence. I would go back to my house after school, but it wasn't a home. She was
gone. Our mother was gone, the beautiful Iris. . . . I felt abandoned, afraid"—see
Assayas, *Bono in Conversation with Michka Assayas* (New York: Riverhead, 2005), p. 12.
Thanks to Mark Wrathall for bringing this quotation to my attention.

face of the globe. It must nestle everywhere, settle everywhere, establish connections everywhere.[9]

## An Album of Doubt

Not only in the nineteenth century, but also—and perhaps even more so—in the twenty-first, the common experience of modernity would seem to be one of change and uncertainty, and with it a loss of any clear sense of place or home. While Heidegger uses different terms from Marx and Engels and doesn't give any special role to economic factors, he also talks about the dislocation and disturbance that is characteristic of modernity. Yet Heidegger presents such dislocation and displacement specifically in terms of a homelessness that does not consist in any lack of housing, but in an inability properly to dwell,[10] and he regards such homelessness as deeply problematic—as a form of destitution.[11] More generally, it seems that while notions of "place," "home," and "belonging" may appear to be out of kilter with the modern experience of the world, still those notions continue to play an important part in human life and thought— we still need, in some sense, to belong, to have a sense of place, to have a sense of home. Bono has commented that "I didn't know I was Irish until I went to America" (*Across the Frontier*, p. 187), but in similar fashion, one might say that one never knows what it is to belong until the fact of such belonging comes into question.

In an interview with *Rolling Stone* in 1992, Bono commented that the opening track of *The Joshua Tree* itself was "an anthem of doubt more than faith"—a comment that is surely true not only of the opening track, but of the album as a whole. Such a comment connects directly with the restless, often driving feel that characterizes much of the album's sound, but it also reflects an uncertainty about the relation to home and to place that the

---

[9] Karl Marx, "The Communist Manifesto," in Jon Elster, ed., *Karl Marx: A Reader* (Cambridge: Cambridge University Press, 1986), p. 227. The general tone of Marx and Engels's comments is echoed in many other places and by many other writers across the political and social spectrum.

[10] Matin Heidegger, "Building Dwelling Thinking," in *Poetry, Language, Thought* (New York: Harper and Row, 1971), p. 161; see also "The Thing," *Poetry, Language, Thought*, pp. 165–66.

[11] Heidegger, "What Are Poets For?" in *Poetry, Language, Thought*, p. 91.

album evokes. In none of the places to which *The Joshua Tree* takes its listeners is there any surety, any safety, any final dwelling place—from some of those places, in fact, the only option is flight, and all of those places are characterized by loss. One response to this might be to conclude that *The Joshua Tree* simply represents the true state of the contemporary world, or, as Marx and Engels put it, our "real conditions of life," namely, that there are no places in which one can belong, and 'home' is indeed a mistaken, or even outmoded, ideal. If that were so, however, then one might expect *The Joshua Tree* to project something other than the sense of search and journey that pervades the album—one does not search for what one already knows cannot be found. "I Still Haven't Found What I'm Looking For," the album's second track, projects just this sense of continuing search in the face of uncertainty, yet an uncertainty also coupled with a strong sense of commitment: "You know I believe it / But I still haven't found what I'm looking for." One might argue that the continuing commitment to that search is mistaken, but the fact of such commitment seems incontrovertible.

## In Search of Identity and Belonging

The sense of search and of journey that belongs to *The Joshua Tree* does, of course, have strong spiritual, and more specifically Christian, connotations. But it would be a mistake to take the images of search and journey, of place, home, and belonging that emerge here as merely the medium for a straightforwardly religious message. Quite apart from the way in which U2 have attempted to distinguish the spiritual from the religious, what's at issue in talk of the "spiritual," and to some extent even in talk of the religious, is a matter of who and what we are, and where and to whom we properly belong. It's no accident, then, that images of search and journey, of place and home, loom so large even in spiritual and religious discourse. The search for faith, and for God, is also a search for identity and belonging. This is particularly important, it seems to me, in the case of a band such as U2, who come out of a cultural and social background that is so much imbued with a sense of the religious and the spiritual as important frames within which questions of identity and belonging are to be pursued.

Whether we talk in terms of identity and place or of God and spirit, however, it's still our own existence and the meaning of that existence that is primarily at issue. Inasmuch as our human existence is always an existence worked out in and through specific places, and the very content of our lives is drawn from those places, then it becomes apparent that questions of God and spirit, if we chose to frame matters in those terms, must also be directly tied to questions of the proper spaces and places of our lives and our relation to those places. To stand in a relation to God, is also to find oneself in a certain relation to the places in which one dwells—a relation that may be expressed in terms of belonging, or perhaps also, in terms of a certain form of being 'at home'. In this respect, the character of contemporary life as 'homeless', and even 'alienated', is itself tied to the character of that life as without meaning, without any sense of spirituality, without God.

This returns us, however, to the question as to whether the sense of search that pervades *The Joshua Tree* is simply misguided or mistaken. Is there really any point to such searching in the contemporary world—can it arise out of anything other than blindness or self-deception? Just as Marx and Engels declared the loss of any sense of solidity or certainty in the modern world, so a little later in the nineteenth century, Friedrich Nietzsche proclaimed the "death" of God. The two claims are not unrelated—not only do Marx and Engels themselves refer to the way in which "all that is holy is profaned," but the advent of modernity seems to constitute the loss of *any* fixed point, whether understood in terms of God, place, home, or almost any other concept, around which human lives can be oriented and secured. For this reason, Heidegger can talk both about the homelessness of modernity and the flight of the gods as equally characteristic of the modern age (pp. 91–95). Yet although, in the twentieth-first century, it may be thought almost commonplace to view the world as a thoroughly secularized, globalized space of constantly shifting economic, social, and cultural "formations," it may also be presumptuous to conclude that therefore the ideas of place, home, and belonging—and perhaps also of God and spirit—have lost all relevance and significance. It may well be that for all the changes that have occurred in the world, those changes have not altered the basic character and needs of human beings as such.

The sense of search, and of uncertainty, that remains in the songs of *The Joshua Tree*, and that continues to underpin U2's music even now, can be seen to reflect the real character of human life as always articulated in and through its concrete locatedness. We do not make our lives out of abstract ideals, universal declarations, or globalized "connectivity." What gives content and direction to our lives, and so gives content and direction to who and what we are, are the people, places, land-scapes, and things with whom we are actively engaged, and that call forth our attention, our care, our concern. In this latter respect, it is especially significant that the articulation of partic-ular political and social concerns that may be seen to be present in *The Joshua Tree*—whether it be famine in Ethiopia, American foreign policy in El Salvador, drug-taking and urban decay in Dublin, or human rights in Chile—is always expressed through the evocation of a certain "physical," and not merely "emo-tional" place. Here, indeed, is the "cinematic music" to which the Edge referred—music that takes the listener *to a place*, and in doing so connects the listener with the concreteness of that place, enabling the listener to feel and respond through a con-nectedness that is, in a certain sense, "physical"—a sense of "being there."

## Heaven Knows This Is a Heartland

It is precisely our being "in place" that connects us with the peo-ple and the things that we find around us—it also connects us with ourselves, since it is in our relation to who and what sur-rounds us that we encounter and articulate who and what we are. The way we find ourselves "in place" is also how we find ourselves "in" our own lives—in our concrete movements and actions in respect of other persons and things, as well as our-selves, and the relations that are constituted through such move-ments and actions. Moreover, in being "in place" in this way, we also find ourselves enmeshed in a set of relationships and inter-actions that are themselves changing and fragile, and that there-fore demand our attentiveness, our concern and our care. This is just what it is to be "in place": it is to be oriented in relation to our surroundings such that aspects of those surroundings motivate and direct our own actions and movements as well as being affected by them; it is to be bound by our care and concern for what lies around us; and this is also what it is to "belong." In this latter respect, belonging, and so too the ideas of place and home, always carry with them a sense of inevitable loss. Nostalgia, in the literal sense of "homesickness," can be seen, for this reason, as a necessary accompaniment of such belonging.

Physical dislocation, and so a literal "homelessness," whether of the refugee, the emigrant or the wanderer, is a widespread feature of contemporary life. Yet there's an even more widespread form of dislocation and homelessness that arises out of our inability to recognize the way in which, no matter where we are, we are always already "at home"—the way in which our lives are already given over to the places in which we find ourselves and can only be worked out in relation to those places. Both these forms of alienation are, of course, connected, and both appear in the words and music of *The Joshua Tree*. The physical alienation, dislocation, and devastation that is to be found in the Ethiopian refugee camp, in the Central American village, or in the Dublin high-rise are themselves products of the alienation and dislocation of much of contemporary life and culture, and of its economic, social, and political structures. Yet although this world is one in which we may wonder what sense is any longer to be attached to ideas of home or homeland, of a place of the heart or a heartland, still the idea or its image remains: "In this heartland / In this heartland soil / In this heartland / Heaven knows this is a heartland."[12]

The sense of uncertainty that is present in *The Joshua Tree* partly derives from the uncertainty that is present here—in the fact that, on the one hand, it seems that ideas of place, home, and belonging no longer have any meaning or applicability in the modern world, and, on the other, that those very ideas nevertheless continue to pull on us in a powerful way. The problem, however, is not that the contemporary world has erased the human relatedness to place, or made notions of home and belonging obsolete, but that it has instead covered over such belonging, such place-relatedness—hiding it and rendering it obscure to us. This is largely a consequence of the

------

[12] "Heartland," from U2's 1987 album *Rattle and Hum*, but originally recorded as part of the sessions for *The Joshua Tree* in 1986.

way the contemporary world appears itself to have become increasingly uncertain and insecure, increasingly prone to change and disruption in new and unexpected ways, while at the same time what it is to belong, to be at home, or to be in place, is taken to entail a contrasting certainty, security or stability. Yet in reality, at the very core of our being "in place" is our being taken up in care and concern for what is around us— things arc brought close to us, and we close to them, through such care and concern—and if that is so, then our being "in place," our belonging, cannot be a matter of our being somewhere certain, secure and unchanging in the way that seems so commonly assumed. That which is demanding of our care and concern is indeed that which is vulnerable, subject to change and loss, and it is only in the care and concern that is thus demanded of us that we are brought into any closeness with things, with others, or with ourselves.[13]

While it's certainly true that the places to which *The Joshua Tree* takes us are indeed places of uncertainty, desolation, and loss, they are nevertheless also places in which these things can be felt and experienced only because of what is not lost, because of what is not desolated, because of what remains certain—namely our continued relatedness to those places, and to others, our continued belonging to the places in which our lives are articulated and in which the meaning and significance of those lives takes concrete form. This form of certainty, however, brings no final safety or security with it—it grounds, but does not bring an end to, the character of our lives as always in question, as always also uncertain, as always given over to journey and to search. Perhaps this conclusion could not have been explicitly formulated by the members of U2 during the creative process that gave rise to *The Joshua Tree* itself, but they did not need to do so—it is the work, the album itself, and the music it contains, that speaks, that traces out the lines at issue here, that takes us on its own journey—a journey that brings us back to the one place we can never leave, the place that we ourselves are, that is our own world, our own place.

The lines of sound and song that U2 travel in *The Joshua Tree* are like tortured wires—they mark out a pathway of sorts, but

---

[13] For more on this, see my *Place and Experience*, Chapter 8.

it's a path that trips, and sometimes cuts, a path that is in no way comfortable or comforting—a path that takes us past sites of cruelty, hypocrisy and pain. It's the path one walks when one is no longer sure which way to go—when the streets along which one walks no longer have names—and yet still one must somehow find one's way. For many people, this describes the central feature of our contemporary situation. In a world in which one can no longer rely on old ways, in which there is no longer a place that one can unequivocally call "home," in which home itself appears under threat, the only paths available will be uncertain and shifting, and where those paths point is likely to be equally uncertain, if not illusory. The paths of song and sound that make up *The Joshua Tree* take us to many places, but no one of these places seems to provide anything more than another site of uncertainty and loss. The paths that are followed by *The Joshua Tree* are thus not those of the nomad who is at home in the desert landscape, but the stranger lost in a land that may have once been familiar, and is now alienated and alienating. The places to which *The Joshua Tree* takes us are thus the places in which we now find ourselves—they trace out paths across a contemporary world.

## Finding Home

The tortured image of the Joshua tree may itself seem to mimic the uncertain pathways the album follows, but the Joshua tree is also named after a prophet—one who shows the way out of desolation and into the promised land. If it seems that there is no such land to which *The Joshua Tree* directs us, that may mean only that we have mistaken the direction in which to look. Whether or not it was part of U2's own conception in making the album, *The Joshua Tree* nevertheless directs our attention, not to a land beyond or outside of our own, but to the places that are already here—before our eyes and at our feet. These places are not certain nor are they secure—quite the opposite: as human life is uncertain, so too are the sites in which human life is lived similarly uncertain, similarly prone to harm and to loss.

If a central problem in the contemporary world is finding a way of dwelling in that world, of finding a sense of place and of home, a sense of belonging, then this is only to be achieved by coming to an understanding of the way in which all such dwelling is constituted only through the commitment that is itself expressed in uncertainty and doubt, in search and journey, in care and concern. We do not come to belong or properly to dwell by remaining only in one place, but rather by recognizing the way in which our lives are only to be given in and through the particular places in which we already find ourselves, and which are shaped by us as even as we are shaped by them.

We come to belong by tracing out the paths that connect us to one another, as they also connect us to the places in which our lives are lived, and that connect those places into the world as a whole. The paths of song and sound that U2 trace out thus delineate the spaces and places of belonging, of place and of home, as they connect sites of alienation, loss and desolation— as they also take us from Ireland to America, from Lypton Village to the Joshua Tree.

# 5

# The Importance of Being Bono: The Philosophy and Politics of Identity in the Lyrics and Personae of U2's Frontman

KERRY SOPER

Paul Hewson, the lead singer of U2, like other internationally famous pop stars such as Prince, Sting, and Madonna, is known only by an iconic stage name, "Bono." Larger than life, his image and identity are part of a constructed persona: a swaggering, sunglass-wearing, microphone-wielding rock star. But whereas most constructed pop stars seem to be just that—superficial constructions of physical beauty or stylized rebellion—Bono, along with a handful of other exceptions such as Bob Dylan, Bruce Springsteen, and Michael Stipe (of R.E.M.), is unique in being something more. Behind, or intertwined with, this constructed persona, is an artist who is exceptionally sensitive about issues of integrity and authenticity. In interviews and lyrics he thoughtfully explores—even occasionally agonizes over—the nature of his identity, the substance of his art, and the social responsibilities of a politically engaged rock star.

This intense self-reflection might seem narcissistic coming from a less serious, or less accomplished, artist. But Bono has unique qualities—such as the ability to be self-reflexive, self-deprecating, and sincere—that not only make it tolerable, but often fascinating and inspiring. Moreover, from the perspective of a fan, he seems justified in indulging in this public self-analysis because it feels like an extension of his confessional and intellectually-engaged lyrics. Because his lyrics are such a direct and raw expression of his passions, doubts, and epiphanies, we want and expect interviews that elaborate upon, or act as an extension of, his art. In fact, a great part of his appeal is based in the poetic and entertaining ways he articulates—in both lyrics and interviews—the moral dilemmas, insecurities, and occasional epiphanies that most people face on a less dramatic scale. In effect, as an amplified everyman, he models for fans of U2 the complexities, pitfalls, and potential triumphs of constructing an "authentic self" in a world fraught with tricky "post"-paradigms: postnationalism, poststructuralism, postcolonialism, postmodernism paradigms that complicate the effort of constructing a solid identity and committing one's self to earnest causes, stable religious beliefs, and meaningful moral action.

Let's look at some interviews, lyrics, and stage shows to chart Bono's efforts to construct this authentic, purposeful self at the intersection of three competing conceptions of social identity construction generally recognized among contemporary philosophers: pre-modern, modern, and postmodern.[1] I'll also try to describe Bono's successful navigation through, and borrowings from, these paradigms as he succeeds in constructing a model of ethical and artistic engagement—a resolution that I label "Postmodern Christian Pragmatism."

## Bono and Pre-modern Conceptions of Identity

Before the mid-nineteenth century (or so it has been speculated) people developed stable, static identities based on the religious, ethnic, and social contexts in which they were born and raised. Because pre-modern European societies had fairly rigid caste systems and the average person rarely ventured far from where he or she were born and raised, a person's identity was inherited, rather than "found" or constructed. In these times traditional institutions such as religion, and hierarchies of race and gender, exercised great power in assigning, and often limiting, one's life choices or conception of self. Looking back from our present cultural vantage point where fluid self-construction is taken for granted, it is tempting to pity people from these earlier, more restrictive times; but fewer choices and more stable

---

[1] Douglas Kellner, "Popular Culture and the Construction of Postmodern Identities," in Scott Lash and Jonathan Friedman, eds., *Modernity and Identity* (Oxford: Blackwell, 1992), pp. 141–177. Kellner summarizes nicely the characteristics of each paradigm while also reflecting in critical ways on the theoretical limitations of reducing entire eras to broad constructs.

identity markers may have also made for less angst—a malady often associated with the social flux of the twentieth century.

Bono comes from an Irish cultural tradition that has held tightly to pre-modern identity markers. As a colonized, largely agrarian people who retained their allegiance to Rome during the Protestant reformation, the Irish were often passed over, or removed themselves, as new social choices were introduced. In addition, some of their colonizers used racist ideologies in the nineteenth century to mark the Irish as an inferior, swarthy, "Africanoid" race that had no hope of bettering their individual or collective life situations because they were clannish, hopelessly Catholic, and supposedly provincial, lazy, and drunken.[2] Because the Irish were caricatured and maligned for so many decades, it is often suggested that they developed a case of "double consciousness"—an inferiority complex of self-defeating behavior or chronic self-loathing that sprang from seeing themselves through the eyes of their oppressors.[3]

As an internationalized pop star, Bono has often constructed his identity in rebellion against restrictive notions of Irishness, or outside of the pre-modern constructs provided by his heritage, and as a result, has occasionally been criticized for selling out on Irish heritage. Sinead O'Connor's manager, Fachtna O'Ceallaigh, a long time critic of U2, for example, said in 1993 that Bono appears to be "ashamed to be Irish" and charged that he mouthed the "words of the oppressor against the oppressed," when speaking about the conflicts in Ireland.[4] O'Ceallaigh's view is incorrect, in part, because it is limited by a romantic, pre-modern conception of essentialized Irishness—that there is some pure, foundational Irish identity that is tied to genetics and a nationalistic heritage. The view is also marked by the dogmatic notion that a true Irish consciousness is only activated through an enlightened, radical faith in, and engagement with, the Nationalist rebel cause. Finally, it is a flawed judgment because what he perceives as Bono's failings—his caution, complexity, and ambivalence—can also be seen as virtues in a political and cultural mix so fraught with competing worldviews and dangerous brands of violent

---

[2] Perry L. Curtis, Jr., *Apes and Angels: The Irishman in Victorian Caricature* (Washington, D.C.: Smithsonian Institution Press, 1997), p. 123.

[3] W.E.B. Dubois, *The Souls of Black Folk* (New York: Vintage, 1990), p. 8.

[4] Dermott Hayes, "Do You Know This Man," *Select Magazine* (1st June, 1993), p. 3.

fundamentalism. In an interview after the release of *War*, Bono
effectively articulated both his ethnic pride and cautious ambivalence: "I am an Irishman and we are an Irish group . . . But I'm
frightened of borders, frightened of restrictions on those levels
and I get scared when people start saying they're prepared to
kill to back their belief . . ."[5]

Even if Bono does not continually wear his ethnicity like a
badge of pride, he is clearly both aware of, and takes pride in,
his culture's tumultuous heritage; for example, he still uses
Dublin as his home base; he refers knowingly to early Irish-
American history and sometimes uses Irish identity as a
metaphor in songs like *New York*; and he and the band contributed a thoughtful, Irish-themed song, "The Hands that Built
America," to Martin Scorsese's *Gangs of New York*.

As pre-modern identity frames began losing their power in
the late nineteenth century and early twentieth century,
American-Irish immigrants were uniquely stubborn in resisting
complete assimilation and holding onto traditional religious and
cultural identity markers. This legacy of resistance to external
pressures factors into Bono's construction of his own identity in
significant ways. For example, from the band's earliest albums
he has not shied away from using his Irish heritage—with all of
its complicated political conundrums—and his Christian faith, as
metaphors for universal struggles against tyranny, cycles of violence, and movement toward sexual, psychological, or spiritual
liberation ("Gloria," "With a Shout," "New Year's Day," "Sunday
Bloody Sunday," "Pride In the Name of Love," "Beautiful Day,"
"Yahweh"). Like a charismatic embodiment of this collective,
tumultuous heritage, Bono seems to draw inspiration both from
the sense that his people were robbed for many years of their
autonomy or were scapegoated by others and from this tradition
of stubborn resistance to paradigms of identity imposed by
other cultural powers.

## Bono and Modernist Conceptions of Identity

Because of the social disruptions and technological shifts of the
mid-to-late nineteenth century, many people's foundational con-

---

[5] Liam Mackey, "Articulate Speech of the Heart," *Hot Press* (22nd July, 1983), p. 1.

ceptions of their identities were disrupted. New philosophies also emerged at the turn of the twentieth century that challenged authoritative ideological systems such as institutional Christianity that had grounded peoples' traditional sense of self. Nietzsche posited that truth was a social construction exerted as a form of cultural power, and that Christians had killed their God by warping theology into a contradictory, life-denying philosophical system; Freud explained the human psyche in nonreligious terms, emphasizing the constructedness of social identity; and Marx charged that traditional institutions and ideologies were illusions or opiates that saddled people with false consciousnesses.

While the angst caused by societal tumult and philosophical shifts became a dominant theme in early to mid-century art, many modernist thinkers and artists also found ways of celebrating the new flux associated with identity. Freudian and Marxist theory promoted the idea that it was liberating to shed one's flawed psyche or traditional identity in order to find one's true self; and existentialism, in particular, which was first given rough shape by Kierkegaard and later elaborated upon by mid-twentieth century writers such as Albert Camus and Jean-Paul Sartre, emphasized the need to discover one's authentic self and engage in purposeful moral action within the void left after traditional belief systems had been abandoned. The modernist movement in art even celebrated as a virtue the shedding of one's provincial surroundings and all of its accompanying baggage of traditional religious, ethnic, or nationalist allegiances. The modernist artist was expected to be a liberated visionary, beholden to no paradigms except the search for truth or enlightenment through aesthetic experimentation.

As a budding artist in his teenage years, Bono embraced vaguely modernist notions of identity construction and the role of the artist in society. Although technically the era of Bono's youth—the 1970s—is considered to be "postmodern," modernist paradigms had (and still persist in having) a power over our cultural imagination. Indeed, the popular myth that one must leave behind a provincial past and break bonds with traditional folk or family traditions in order to find one's true self, to see the world clearly, and to create something truly *avant-garde*, held great appeal for the young Bono.

Bono traces the rough outlines of this modernist concept as an aspiring painter and actor in his teen years while attending a progressive, nondenominational school, Mount Temple, in Dublin: he reveled in being different from his schoolmates, took pride in not being interested in football (soccer), and enjoyed sitting around with like-minded friends, concocting plans to leave their town and make a mark on the world. He was also the first among his group to embrace punk music, identifying with its democratic proposition that anyone could adopt the pose of the angry, enlightened, societal visionary.[6] Like a discontented modernist artist who could see more clearly than those around him, Bono also wanted to escape Irish culture's myopic embroilment in religious and political strife—conflicts that were perhaps an outgrowth of people being too invested in essential, pre-modern conceptions of who they were.

The peculiarities of Bono's upbringing enabled him to embrace the modernist idea of a malleable identity with ease. As Dubliners, his family was more cosmopolitan than many rural Irish. Dubliners, in fact, had a history of more readily opening themselves to other worldviews and cultural practices (often from invading forces) than other parts of Ireland. His parents' courageous marriage across the Protestant-Catholic cultural divide (his father was Catholic, his mother a member of the Church of Ireland, representing the tradition of Anglican Protestantism) also enabled and complicated his identity construction. According to biographer Eamon Dunphy, Bono existed as a young man in a spiritual "twilight world" between the two religious traditions, a social and spiritual outsider who felt Catholic among Protestants, and out of place among Catholics (*Unforgettable Fire*, pp. 26–27.) But straddling this cultural divide also inspired his moral-artistic visions—in cries for bridging cultural divides like *Pride, In the Name of Love,* or eschewing zealous allegiance to dogmatic political or religious position as in "Sunday Bloody Sunday": "I won't heed the battle call. / It puts my back up, puts my back up against the wall."

As a teenager, Paul Hewson made the first step in becoming a modernist-style artist by renaming himself, at the suggestion of a friend, as "Bono Vox" (good voice, in Latin)—a heroic but

---

[6] Eamon Dunphy, *Unforgettable Fire: The Definitive Biography of U2* (New York: Warner, 1987), p. 65.

playful name that he eventually reduced to "Bono" (*Unforgettable Fire*, p. 75). In the same year (1977) he joined with Adam Clayton, "The Edge," and Larry Mullen Jr. to create the band U2. Initially they were much like most young, aspiring rock stars—eager to achieve fame and wealth at all costs. And on a local level they quickly began to realize this goal. Although they were not especially accomplished musicians at this point, and Bono did not have an impressive voice, their charisma, and energy in live performances attracted a devoted following. In 1980, their first album, *Boy* (1980), attracted a small but enthusiastic fan base.

Building upon this popularity, but remaining true to their grassroots vision and style, Bono and the band became "auteurs," a unique form of *popular,* modernist artist. They used their growing popular clout and unique methods to experiment and articulate a distinctive vision not typical of packaged rock stars, but they were also highly popular, tuned into the interests and needs of their audience in a way uncharacteristic of modernist experimentalists. As auteurs, they have consistently swum against prevailing currents in the music industry and resisted institutional or economic pressures that would have cheapened their art. For example, their first albums, *Boy* and *October*, were unfashionably earnest, religious, and rootsy at a time when the record industry was packaging and promoting ironically detached, synthesizer-laced New Wave music. The band also worked outside the traditional record industry mechanisms of marketing by developing a devoted fan base through arduous grassroots touring. After these strategies brought the band mass success in 1983 with the albums *War* and *Under a Blood Red Sky,* they had enough leverage to renegotiate their contracts, effectively achieving economic and artistic independence more completely.

The effort to articulate a coherent philosophy in their music did not proceed without some missteps and difficulties. After their first album, when they were on the brink of making it big, a complex intersection of pre-modern and postmodern pressures stalled them for a time, complicated their long-term aspirations, and then set them on a career arc marked by chronic soul searching and thoughtful reinvention. From both pre-modern and modernist directions came Bono's, Edge's, and Larry's conversion to a charismatic Christian movement called

Shalom—a movement that advocated the idea of the acceptance of Christ as a Savior as a commitment to social justice. On one level, this conversion was a regrounding in the foundational constructs of a Christian worldview. On another, its progressive theology was a liberating, enlightened replacement to the seemingly corrupt or regressive structures of traditional Catholicism and Protestantism. (Shalom meetings ended with people hugging and singing, breaking down barriers.)

Their second album, *October* (1981), highlighted the band's emerging religious beliefs in songs such as "Gloria" and "With a Shout": "I wanna go to the foot of the Messiah, / To the foot of he who made me see." Bono's embrace of the movement's tenets was so deep and sincere that for a time he toyed with abandoning the rock star career—a lifestyle seemingly incompatible with Christian principles. Modernist conceptions of self, and the social role of the constructed, elevated rock star, in particular, did not work with Shalom's theology which taught that one should relinquish his or her ego in order to be filled with the Spirit of God. Eventually the dilemma was resolved when Bono realized first that he had to leave the movement because its ideals were too narrow and idealistic, and second, that he could be a musician and still remain devoted to his core Christian beliefs. The music and his rock-star persona could be the vehicles for expressing this faith and promoting social change.

## Bono and Postmodern Conceptions of Identity Construction

When U2 gained international popularity with their next album, *War,* in 1983, they entered into a popular music scene in which some of the most critically acclaimed performers such as Prince and The Talking Heads were embracing a postmodern concept of what it meant to be an artist or rock star. Unlike the modernist visionary trying to transform society, the postmodern artist was simply a cool conduit of recycled cultural data. David Byrne, lead singer of The Talking Heads, embodied this concept nicely; he presented himself not as an anthem-shouting visionary, but rather as a detached interpreter who deconstructed his own pop-star persona and created collage-like music through the ironic quoting other forms and figures.

The postmodern concept of the artist emerged primarily with 1960s pop artists—Andy Warhol being the quintessential example—but postmodern conceptions of identity construction can also be traced, in part, to the psychoanalytic philosopher Jacques Lacan. In the 1960s and 1970s he took Freudian theory into post-structuralist territory by positing that the natural state of the psyche is one of fragmentation and discord; as a result, it is unfixable and a stable identity cannot be established. According to Lacan, because of complications built into childhood phases of development, we are destined to pursue throughout our lives three objectives that can never be satisfied: a search for solid identity, a re-creation of the sense of plenitude we experienced when we were one with our mothers, and an achievement of idealized sexual gratification. As we move beyond early childhood, these searches are transferred into the "symbolic realm" of language, literature, entertainment, and music. While engaging with these substitute gratifications, we construct temporary, shifting, shallow identities that are borrowed from the culture at large—often from iconic celebrities and stars who seem to embody more stable, heroic, and beautiful versions of what we aspire to be.

Because Bono and U2 still maintained deep ties to pre-modern identity markers—while also embracing modernist conceptions of artistic liberation and enlightenment—it's understandable that they initially resisted adopting postmodern forms and attitudes. For one thing, this detached and ironic pose did not match the band's personality and worldview. Still proud of their Irish identities, still devoted to generalized Christian ideals of integrity, faith, and social responsibility, and still invested in the belief that they could use their music to promote positive social change, they defined themselves in contrast to postmodern pop stars. As Bono stated in an interview linked to the release of the film, *Rattle and Hum*, "I don't have an ironic persona like David Byrne or David Bowie to stand behind. . . . Some artists perform with a wink. That's just not the way with U2."[7] Instead, they wanted to sing earnest anthems that communicated their real convictions.

---

[7] Adam Block, "Pure Bono," *Mother Jones* (May 1989), p. 34.

Despite this rejection of the ironic postmodern pose, some aspects of postmodern theory meshed well with the worldview of Bono and the band. Postmodern theorists such as Jean Francois Lyotard describe the need for a general skepticism towards reductive ideologies—and this includes the overly authoritative, supposedly progressive claims of modernist paradigms such as Freudianism, Marxism, and extreme forms of political rebellion based on nationalist identities. Although probably not familiar with Lyotard's ideas in an academic form, Bono had embraced this skepticism in an intuitive way in his worldview and lyrics in albums as early as *War*—especially in relation to nationalist and religious arrogance. As a young man he had developed a distrust of fanatical certitude, or extreme allegiance to dogmatic revolutionary causes, as a result of growing up in a politically and religiously divided culture. He saw first-hand the violence and ugliness that can emerge in a society when one mixes the following impulses: a clannish devotion to one's tribal identity; a fanatical confidence in the certitude of one's religious or political convictions; and a zealous commitment to radical political theory that promotes change through terroristic violence. The lyrics of "Two Hearts Beat as One," from *War,* articulate this postmodern skepticism "I don't know, / I don't know which side I'm on, / I don't know my right from my left, / Or my right from wrong."

So as U2 became hugely popular, they embraced a unique blend of pre-modern, modern, and postmodern poses: Christian, Irish rockers who were enlightened visionaries singing revolutionary anthems that warned against the dangers of dogmatism and fanaticism. Songs such as "Sunday Bloody Sunday" and "Pride, in the Name of Love" are good examples of these anthems that are paradoxically martial in their tone, but more about peace, tolerance, and humility, in their lyrics (a sort of militant pacifism). Along with Jesus Christ, the band embraced as their heroes figures such as Gandhi and Martin Luther King Jr.—visionaries who promoted social change through peaceful resistance and the leveling of cultural hierarchies or ethnic distinctions.

This earnest pose and thoughtful message helped to fuel their popularity, inspiring some fans to become devoted disciples. There were substantial ideas and solid convictions undergirding the pleasing art, and these convictions were universal

enough (or vague enough) to resonate with people from varying cultural and religious backgrounds—people who, like Bono,
were also struggling with the challenge of believing in something semi-solid as older ideologies gave way to the healthily
skeptical, but potentially empty, relativism of the postmodern
world.

But the same qualities that made Bono and the band so
heroic and appealing among fans, led to criticism and backlash
from the press. Some critics pointed out that most fans probably
missed the lyrics' nuanced message, and the fact that Bono felt
compelled to state explicitly on stage during the *War* tour that
"This is not a rebel song!" before singing "Sunday Bloody
Sunday" seemed to support this point. Perhaps the distinction
between a martial tone and more open-ended, peace and
understanding-promoting lyrics was blurred by the surface pleasures of music listening or the excitement of a concert environment.

U2 also ran into trouble when their earnest posture and
seemingly self-righteous message began to wear thin on critics
and some fans. As they became enormously wealthy and
famous, it became harder to maintain the image of the earnest
visionaries and some critics charged that there was an artificiality or hypocrisy to the band's persona. For example, their image
on the back of the *Joshua Tree* album was seen by some as pre-
tentious. They posed in earthy, subdued clothing, and had the
fixed, humorless expressions of working-class prophets or
desert-dwelling monks. Some observers also complained that
Bono seemed a bit patronizing and self-aggrandizing when he
would wrap himself in a white flag during concerts or pull a
young black girl out of the audience in a broad gesture of racial
tolerance during the Live Aid concert in 1985.

Looking back, many of these complaints seem to be unfair or
based largely on surface impressions. In interviews and lyrics
Bono and the band during *The Joshua Tree* period were expressing ideas that had none of the marks of arrogance or confidence
that one would normally associate with self-appointed visionaries. In the song "I Still Haven't Found What I'm Looking For,"
Bono seems to suggest that continual questioning and perpetual
journeying are the essence of our existence; there are no relationships or ideologies—not even one of Christian faith—that
can remedy this need to search. With what could be considered

a postmodern modesty of conviction, Bono commented about the implications of this song's lyrics: "We're very clear, and it's very clear in our music that we don't have any answers. But that the questions are at least worth asking ("Pure Bono," p. 54). Nevertheless, critics seemed determined to see the band as arrogant and overly serious. The backlash came to a climax after the release of their film *Rattle and Hum* in 1989. Bono appeared slightly self important in the film's interview clips and he was criticized for seeming to compare himself to American icons such as Johnny Cash, Elvis Presley, B.B. King, and old Chicago bluesmen such as Muddy Waters. In one scene, the band made a pilgrimage to Graceland and contemplated Elvis's legacy with a grave seriousness. What the band perceived as sincere homage was interpreted as self-aggrandizement. Moreover, Bono did, in fact, display some romantic naivete in the way that he fetishized the authenticity of old bluesmen. He enthused, "In Memphis recently Adam and I went out into the cotton fields and found this off-limits juke-joint on Sunday afternoon where they serve moonshine and play the blues. We found one of the old bluesmen there who didn't leave to go to Chicago like Muddy Waters, B.B. King and the others. He was playing in this shed, this kind of dwelling right on the edge of the cotton field. It was an extraordinary music."[8]

The most cynical interpretation of these tributes and comparisons was that here was another instance of white rockers trying to enhance their authenticity or hip quotient by tapping into rock's authentic African American roots or by appropriating black musical forms. A more generous and accurate reading could be that U2 was celebrating a musical heritage that insisted on roots traditions and heroic and stable (albeit constructed) personae—as opposed to either hiply superficial postmodern forms or overly homogenized pop. Moreover, with the knowledge that the Irish have significant historical connections to black culture—that they were equated with blacks, that they shared some of the psychological trouble with double consciousness, that they found similar ways to hold onto traditional folk forms in the tumult of the twentieth century—also makes Bono's tributes seem more benign and sincere.

-------

[8] "Bono off the Record," *Propaganda* 9 (1st January, 1989), p. 1.

Wounded by the critical backlash, Bono and U2 retreated from the public eye and promised to "reinvent" themselves, to engage in what Bono described as "four men chopping down the Joshua Tree." When they re-emerged several years later, they embraced, albeit with greater sophistication and more ongoing depth than most bands, the prevailing postmodern conceptions of art production and identity. In a *Rolling Stone* interview in the wake of the release of their next album, *Achtung Baby* (1991), Bono acknowledged the constructedness of their identities: "let's play with it, and let's distort it and manipulate it and lose our-selves in the process of it. But let's write about losing ourselves in the process of it, 'cause that's what's happening to everybody else on a smaller scale anyway" ("Pure Bono," p. 45).

Musically and lyrically the band also embraced more explic-itly postmodern modes and poses. For example, beginning with *Achtung Baby* (1991), and carrying through *Zooropa* (1993), and *Pop* (1997), the band engaged in practices considered distinctly postmodern: collaging, ironic quoting, and the channeling of media images in their music. Moreover, with the help of the pro-ducers Daniel Lanois and Brian Eno they developed a funkier, more eclectic, and more ambient sound; they incorporated world music influences; and they dabbled in the "playgiarism" of found noises, distorted feedback, and sampling. During this period of reinvention the band also opened itself to the influ-ence of figures from the world of highbrow postmodern music such as John Cage and Phillip Glass.

In terms of identity construction, Bono embraced postmod-ern notions with enthusiasm, reinventing himself several times over and wearing masks as if he were a male version of Madonna, the quintessential postmodern pop star. Most famously, he adopted the shifting identities of "The Fly," "Mirrorball Man," and "Mister MacPhisto" in stage performances. Offstage, The Fly became his principle identity—a strutting, leather clad hipster who wore wrap-around sunglasses and spoke with a persistently ironic, world-weary tone—a far cry, it seemed, from the righteous prophet of the early albums. Displaying self-reflexivity and an organic understanding of post-modern conceptions of identity, he explained his embrace of shifting identities: ". . . there were reports of egomania, and I just decided to become everything they said I was. Might as well. The truth is that you are many people at the same time, and you don't have to choose. It's like Edge describes me—as a nice bunch of guys."[9]

Although from a distance it seemed as if Bono was giving in to the type of cynical, winking postmodernism that he had resisted in the previous decade, there were facets to the band's music and his behavior that were still connected to long-term, core convictions—evidence that he was still influenced by the pre modern and modern constructs that gave his persona and art such gravity and appeal. Despite the interchangeable facades, he remained devoted to social and political causes. In 1999 he showed up dressed as The Fly at a Greenpeace demonstration protesting the Sellafield nuclear power plant in England. Since postmodern poses were most often associated with a hiply ironic political detachment and a blanket contempt for anything overly earnest or heroic, Bono's consistency of conviction and purposeful action even pointed to a new way of combining old and new cultural paradigms.

Other facets of Bono and U2 such as lyrics, music videos, and stage shows also articulated postmodern attitudes in atypically complex ways. Consider the lyrics of the song "Even Better than Real Thing": Although Bono seems to be singing praises to a lover, the video of the song emphasizes the postmodern theme of hyper-reality. Echoing Jean Baudrillard's theory of how postmodern culture is immersed in simulations—copies of ideas or images that improve upon reality and ultimately have no stable reference to an original—the video alternates between images of the band spinning, ungrounded, through space, and fleeting clips of hyper-real culture. These images include three-dimensional, wax replicas of the Beatles dressed in their Sergeant Pepper's costumes (a copy of an image—the album cover—that was already a jokey collage of borrowed identities in the Beatles' hands); the artist Jeff Koons getting fake-married to an Italian model; and grainy, pixilated images of the paraphernalia associated with virtual reality and cyber sex. But grounding these images are Bono's lyrics and vocal delivery that seem to suggest that one antidote to this rootless, detached culture is the sensual and spiritual connection of real lovers in real time and space. The song concludes that the lover, rather than

---

[9] Alan Light, "Behind The Fly," *Rolling Stone* (4th March, 1993), p. 45.

fleeting, hyper-real images, is the real thing—or even better than the real thing.

Nuanced, postmodern notions of identity were also articulated in a number of songs including "Mofo." This song, from the *Pop* album, gives organic expression to Lacanian notions of how one is driven continually (and perhaps futilely) to establish a solid identity, re-establish the plenitude one once felt with one's mother, and the achievement of sexual and romantic fulfillment: "lookin' for to save my soul / lookin' in the places where no flowers grow / lookin' for to fill that GOD shaped hole / mother mother sucking rock and roll . . . / mother am I still your son, you know I've waited for so long to hear you say so . . . / lookin' for a sound that's gonna drown out the world."

Most of the Lacanian themes are represented here, including the idea that these searches are transferred by artists into the symbolic realm—in Bono's case to the musical and lyrical realm of rock 'n' roll. But it's Bono's persistent hope in the promises of Christianity that help the song to transcend the pessimism that might dominate these postmodern musings. He holds out the possibility that God can fill the void or help him to establish a foundational identity.

In stage shows like the *Zoo TV* tour (1992) and the *Popmart* tour (1997), the group also addressed postmodern cultural ills, and embodied postmodern forms in sophisticated ways. The *Zoo TV* tour acted as a giant conduit of fragmented media images as Bono and the band played against the backdrop of random satellite feeds. But this fragmentation was filtered through songs that highlighted the opiating or manipulative effects of mass entertainment. The opening sequence to the show—a clip of young Hitler youth pounding drums in *Triumph of the Will*—could be interpreted as a satiric red flag, articulating a skepticism toward arrogantly confident ideologies (in this case, fascism), and indicating that fans should be alert to the power of imagery and music as seductive carriers of specious ideas. In other words, even as Bono and the band were giving voice to the hungry media machine, they were also trying to say something satiric about these forces. In sum, Bono and U2 were able to rise above the "pastiche" of much postmodern music and culture (the uncritical channeling of eclectic images and styles with a detached, hiply ironic attitude). Instead, they articulated postmodern ideas with depth and poignancy; embodied postmodern forms while still engaging in coherent cultural satire; and remained committed to core convictions and social causes.

Despite these successes, there were complications and missteps during these years. As with their early anthems, there was no way of knowing if fans really understood the satiric, layered quality of the stage shows and songs. The intense cheers erupting among fans when the Hitler youth began their drum sequences during the *Zoo TV* tour suggests that the martial tone once again might have trumped the nuanced message. And what percentage of the audience would even recognize the reference to *Triumph of the Will* and thus absorb the critical point? Moreover, several songs on the *Pop* album also seemed to be quoting or sampling other musical styles (electronica, in particular) in ways that at times felt opportunistic or shallow.

U2's most recent albums, *All That You Can't Leave Behind* (2000*)*, and *How to Dismantle an Atomic Bomb* (2004), have been interpreted by some critics and fans as a return to roots, as if Bono and the band had finished with their postmodern fun and were returning to the solid pre-modern groundings and modernist seriousness that shaped their early albums. Although Bono himself has admitted that he does indeed want to reconnect with the earnestness and innocence of his early self, this story of complete return is only partially accurate, because of two misreadings of the band's career arc.

First, it does not acknowledge the consistency of core identities and convictions that had been present throughout what was perceived as the band's postmodern phase. Second, it does not recognize how the band has grown because of that exploration of postmodern cultural theory and modes of music making. For example, Bono has abandoned his multiple, shifting personae, but he is now more playful, flexible, and self-reflexive in playing the roles of Bono: the heroic performer, the chummy Irish jokester, the Christian lyricist, and committed social activist. The band too, has found ways of channeling cultural currents and musical styles in shifting tones of irony, playfulness and earnestness. (The song "Vertigo," with its random bits of Spanish lyrics coupled with anthemic bombast is a good example of this new flexibility.) In effect, they have combined the modernist concept of artists as serious innovators and visionaries with the postmodern notion of the performers as of play-ful, sensitive conduits.

And most inspiringly, Bono has found a way to address con-structively these postmodern conundrums: What happens to personal integrity, faith, and purposeful moral action in a per-vasively ironic and detached postmodern culture? How does an individual commit to heroic ideas and action if identity is so elu-sive, shallow, and fragmented? If society so thoroughly rejects the authority of religious and political ideologies, and if the media environment sanctions ironic couch-potato criticism as a valid form of political engagement, how can one help to improve society and the world? In answering these dilemmas, Bono articulates the position of what could be labeled Postmodern Christian Pragmatism. To begin with, Bono does not reject the complexities and inherent skepticism of a post-modern worldview, but he does wed it to an ongoing devotion to stable pre-modern constructs such as the elevating effects of a faith in (or at least investment in the metaphor of) Christ as a cultural and individual savior (most recently and explicitly restated in the lyrics of the song "Yahweh") and an unshowy devotion to his family, his hometown of Dublin, and Irish her-itage. He has also shown that a heroic, earnest type of moral, political action can be pursued despite the seeming relativity of truth and morality in a cultural environment that emphasizes cultural difference, the slipperiness of truth and meaning, and the flux of identity. Moreover, in ways similar to Salman Rushdie, and the politician Vaclav Havel, Bono has found ways of championing humanistic visions and concepts of multicultur-alism with postcolonial, postnational, and anti-fundamentalist sophistication.

To clarify how these practices justify coining this new label, while other brands of postmodern thinking might settle for bleak nihilism, amoral relativism, or an existentialist-style effort to reframe morality outside of Christian theology, Bono's ongo-ing investment in basic Christian concepts of grace, redemption, universal morality, charity, love, and so on, grounds his post-modern musings. At the same time, his postmodern sensitivities prevent his Christianity from calcifying into the type of funda-mentalist dogmatism that would alienate listeners, create cultural barriers, or reinforce prejudices. The pragmatism described here is borrowed from the twentieth century school of philosophy

that describes the benefits of an intellectual exertion of something like faith—a belief in, and application of, a set of principles that results in positive individual and societal results. In
other words, rather than making extravagant claims about the
timelessness, stability, and universality of truths, it modestly
applies principles, looking for positive individual and social
results. As a result, positive social structures and moral action
can be achieved without appealing to the rigidity often associated with institutions that promote traditional moral values.

Bono's lyrics in the song "Stuck in a Moment" carry the fla-
vor of this mature, modest pragmatism:

> I'm not afraid of anything in this world
> There's nothing you can throw at me that I haven't already heard
> I'm just trying to find a decent melody
> A song that I can sing in my own company.

These are not the words of an angry, Old Testament prophet,
calling people to repentance, or of a zealous, Christian revolutionary; instead, they are the honest lyrics of a rock star who
uses the metaphor of lyric-writing to describe the ongoing, ultimately fruitful search for solid identity and moral action through
an exertion of both Christian and Pragmatic faith.

As if resurrecting and updating existentialist solutions for a
postmodern age, Bono emerges from the moral void seemingly
created by late-twentieth century traumas and theoretical complexities with a purposeful stride. As he does so, he identifies
and commits himself to foundational social causes based on
basic human rights and then proceeds to address them in pragmatic, purposeful ways. Chatting with George Bush in the White
House about African debt relief may not be as visually heroic as
draping oneself in a white flag and singing an anthem about
peace and equality, but in terms of practical, political value, it is
profoundly significant.

Bono, the pragmatic, postmodern Christian rock star is able
to be a self-reflexive, playful performer, an artistic innovator,
and an effective social activist. World politics and popular music
are the richer because Bono found ways to negotiate through
competing paradigms of identity construction and art-making,
borrowing useful tools and concepts along the way while
always being true to his religious convictions.

# 6

# "Even Better than the Real Thing"? Postmodernity, the Triumph of the Simulacra, and U2

IAIN THOMSON

Bono famously declared that U2 entered its "postmodern" phase with their 1991 album *Achtung Baby*. *Achtung*, of course, standardly translates as a command for "Attention!"—but it also literally connotes "respect" or "care" (for that to which one should have been moved to "attend" in the first place)—and in what follows I shall suggest how attending to and thinking carefully about some of the philosophical ideas and themes underlying U2's work from the "postmodern" period that begins with *Achtung Baby* can cast a mutually illuminating light on both U2 and "postmodernity."

## In Search of Postmodernity

What, then, does it mean to be *postmodern*? That's not intended to be a trick question, but it may sound like one (at least to those "already in the know"), because the very idea that we should be able to specify *the* meaning of a philosophical concept is a characteristically *modern* assumption, that is, just the sort of assumption *post*modernists seek to get *beyond*. The modern pursuit of *unambiguous* precision proved to be stunningly successful for the mathematical sciences, which extended and so reinforced modernity's defining project of gaining control over the objective world through knowledge, *via* the Copernican revolution in which, rather than observe the way nature behaves independently of us, we "strap nature to the rack and force her to yield up her secrets"—and Bacon's

73

notoriously misogynistic formulations of the modern project look, in retrospect, rather revealing.

For this "phallogocentric" modern project of "Tryin' to throw your arms around the world" (and so also "trying to throw his arms around a girl," a variation U2 nicely employs in the ninth song on *Achtung Baby*) continues to generate undeniable technological and medical advances, along with equally undeniable and unwanted side-effects (such as environmental devastation and the innumerable other inhumanities generated by the rapacious struggle to control and profit from this knowledge over nature) and real dangers (from the slow erosion of our sense of the meaningfulness of life to more dramatic threats of looming global catastrophe, whether nuclear, environmental, biogenetic, or even nanotechnological).

Our increasingly exact calculations allowed us to extend our technical mastery of the natural world so far that, to mention just two (not unrelated) examples, we have been able to construct buildings and planes that do not fall from the sky (without sufficient provocation) as well as an unmatched military-industrial arsenal capable of enforcing our supposed geopolitical dominance (which, in turn, provides our newest *others* with the "sufficient provocation" mentioned earlier . . .).[1] What such connections suggest is that even the best efforts of our modern mathematical sciences have not been able to master the natural world without generating *rebound effects*, in which the very world we seek to master at least partly escapes and then returns with a vengeance. We see these rebound (or "blowback") effects all around us, in our political headlines as well as in the mounting environment crisis more or less systematically excluded from these same headlines.

Seeking to draw our heads outside the lines that usually corral our thinking, postmodern theorists sometimes describe these effects as *the revenge of the real*, a scenario in which (as with those symptoms Freud called *the return of the repressed*) we are revisited by destructive effects ultimately attributable to our very

---

[1] This arsenal also reminds us of the other sense of U2's "Tryin' to throw your *arms* [my emphasis] around the world." Moreover, the fact that this supposed geopolitical dominance did not actually protect our planes and buildings (or the people within them!) raises the question of what, if anything, such dominance does protect, other than the most avaricious and destructive economic interests.

efforts to control, suppress, deny, or exclude in the first place. In response, postmodernists generally seek to isolate and overturn those usually unnoticed modern assumptions that function both to devastate our world and to pre-emptively neutralize our critiques of this destruction (rendering these critiques as ineffectual as protestors confined to predesignated "protest sites").

## Fantasies of Control

Surprisingly, however, some avowedly "postmodern" scientists (of which there are more than a few) seem to believe that the best way to eliminate such devastating rebound effects is *to master nature still more precisely*, for example, by employing non-monotonic logics that do not presume bivalence, using fractal models capable of predicting the behavior of extremely complex systems, and so on—in short, by giving us *more* precise mechanisms of control, *more* finely-grained conceptual mappings of the real, *better* predictive hypotheses, calibrated with such complex precision that, finally, nothing will exceed our grasp, our "arms" (conceptual and military—a fortuitous ambiguity nicely suggested by U2) thrown entirely "around the world." This sounds like a prescription for a more intense dosage of the very radiation that made us sick in the first place, but it is not immediately clear what other rational alternatives remain open to us, since our modern obsession with prediction and control seems to have painted us into a conceptual corner in which all we can think of that might help involves more prediction and control—as if we could get our *addiction to control* under control if we just had a bit *more* self-control.[2]

---

[2] And yet is it so obvious that we cannot do so? What is meditation, for example, if not a proven path whereby one may control one's way beyond control? The paradox, in Heideggerian terms, is that the subject must *decide* to learn *Gelassenheit*, the "releasement" or "letting be" that helps us transcend the "subjectivism" of modernity's subject-centered worldview by recognizing that the great sophist Protagoras was wrong: Humanity is not the measure of all things, and then helping us realize that we can be healed by experiencing our connection to a greater whole, a reality that transcends us and to which we belong, part to whole, organisms in an holistically interconnected environment. The holy, Heidegger suggests (and I shall develop this suggestion below), is whatever allows us to experience this connection to the whole that heals us and restores our health. For the crucial Heideggerian background to the ongoing renaissance of postmodern religious thinking, see my *Heidegger on Ontotheology: Technology and the Politics of Education* (Cambridge: Cambridge University Press, 2005).

The very persistence of such fantasies of control, moreover, suggests that, however disastrous some of the consequences of modernity's drive toward total control are proving to be, the source of this drive is to be found in the intrinsically limited nature of our own cognitive capacities and, indeed, in the generally laudable resistance to all such limits—a resistance sometimes called *freedom*, or even *life*, forces it makes little sense to stand *against* (especially because the struggle whereby we finite beings seek to achieve the impossible has also helped generate our most cherished scientific, medical, and technological advances, many of which we do not want to forfeit). So, if modernity has painted us into this conceptual corner historically, how might we go about getting out of it? That is one way of asking the *question* of *post*modernity.

In a brilliant analysis of September 11th, Derrida describes the way "repression in both its psychoanalytic sense and in its political sense—whether it be through the police, the military, or the economy—ends up producing, reproducing, and regenerating the very thing it seeks to disarm." (Does not U2, whose own work emerged internationally as a reflection on terrorism— remember "Sunday, Bloody Sunday"—draw our attention to the same problem in "Peace on Earth," for example, when Bono warns that "Where I grew up there weren't many trees / Where there was we'd tear them down / And use them on our enemies / They say that what you mock / Will surely overtake you / And you become a monster / So the monster will not break you / And it's already gone too far"?).

Theorizing such effects in terms of the logic of *autoimmunity*, in which the forces in us that seek to *keep out the other* grow so excessive that they begin to destroy the health of the system they are supposed to protect, Derrida calls for an "immuno-depressant" response by which we would seek to "limit the mechanisms of rejection and to facilitate toleration."[3] Derrida articulated an earlier version of this strategic response in terms of what he rather cleverly called "hauntology" (the logic of *being* haunted), suggesting that we must accept the fact that

---

[3] See Giovanna Borradori, ed., *Philosophy in a Time of Terror: Dialogues with Jürgen Habermas and Jacques Derrida* (Chicago: University of Chicago Press, 2003), pp. 99, 188 note 7.

every concept "is in advance contaminated, that is, pre-occu-
pied, inhabited, haunted by its other" and so stop attempting the
various exorcisms that in fact animate these specters and give
them a stage on which to appear. Instead, Derrida liked to say,
we should transform such *ghosts* into *guests* by offering our others our hospitality.[4] (U2 evokes the rebound effect in a particularly haunting way in "Until the End of the World" when Bono
sings: "In my dream I was drowning my sorrows / But my sorrows they learned to swim," and here Bono even seems to recommend the same response as Derrida, describing the
peace-making gesture in which: "I reached out for the one I
tried to destroy.")

Following Derrida (and so Heidegger, who Derrida himself
mostly follows), many postmodernists call for us to resist
extending the demand for unambiguous precision typical of
modern mathematical science into the domain of ordinary
human life. (The ironic lines of "Zooropa" similarly caution
against the unthinking techno-capitalist extension of modern
fantasies of control: "Zooropa . . . better by design / . . . /
Through appliance of science / We've got that ring of confidence," and U2 seems to offer comparable advice in "Zoo
Station," advocating being "Ready for the shuffle / Ready for the
deal / Ready to let go of the steering wheel.") Hence, instead of
embracing the modern drive toward control through unambiguous mathematical precision, most postmodernists echo the neo-
Heideggerian call for us to learn to develop, in our own lives, a
sensitivity to poetic *polysemy*, that is, an attunement to the experience of *multiple simultaneous meanings* known to all careful
readers of poetry (and probably experienced by aficionados of
all the other *poetic* arts, all the divine arts of "making" which,
like God, bring new things into existence).

If our modern bridges are going to stay up, a steel girder
must *either* be capable of bearing a certain weight *or* not. For a
poem to really work, however, it need not mean *either* one
thing *or* another, indeed, quite the opposite. (I shall show in the

---

[4] Derrida seems to thus articulate what is in effect an unreachable regulative ideal,
although that is a conclusion he himself resisted (believing that only the concrete realization of such unconditional "hospitality" is genuinely deserving of the name). See
Jacques Derrida, *Specters of Marx: The State of the Debt, the Work of Mourning, and the
New International* (New York: Routledge, 1994), p. 160.

conclusion that this is the case with U2's "Even Better than the Real Thing," but let us begin with a more traditional example of poetry.) The real, true, or genuine meaning of E.E. Cummings's "if you are glad / whatever's living will yourself become" is not that when we feel "glad" (that is, happy, willing, bright, *and* cheerful), *either* (A) we find ourselves identifying with whatever is most alive, *or* (B) we become attuned to the inner vitality of life, *or* (C) we identify our own wills with what enlivens rather than with what enervates in all that is, and so become willing agents actualizing the vitality of all that lives, *or* (D) we attune ourselves to the vital force within all things, including ourselves, and so actualize that life within us that allows us to grow along with all other living things.[5] An attunement to poetic polysemy suggests that, where poetry or the subtle density of everyday life are concerned, the question, *What does it really mean?* will not be answered with *either* A, B, C, *or* D but, rather, with *All of the above (and more).*

## Postmodern Polysemy

If this is true of a single line within a poem, how much more true will it be of the poem itself as a whole, let alone of the poet's entire poetic *oeuvre?* (Or of the relation of that *oeuvre* to its world, and ours?) And if it is also true of my experience of a single leaf falling through the sunlit morning onto the path before me, or a remark you utter that changes me in some indefinable yet irrevocable way, or the look on the face of a stranger I have not quite forgotten, each a single moment of a single day, how much more true will it be of the life in which those moments resonate together? (And of all the other lives that I, in turn, impact and subtly realign?) This exuberant insight, that mere existence is unspeakably deep, that meaning is inexhaustible, that "every atom of sunlight is a chance of blossoming fruit" (as Baudelaire wrote), seems to me to be one of the postmodern insights *par excellence*, and an insight in which we can recognize the postmodernists' neo-romantic refusal of the modern scientific rejection of romanticism, and so discern the pre-modern roots of postmodernism. The exuberance that

---

[5] See e.e. cummings, *Collected Poems* (New York: Harcourt, Brace, 1923), "New Poems," #315.

accompanies this insight is perhaps also the source of the post-modern movement's visionary fervor and hence its occasional, undeniable, evangelical excesses.

And yet, the minute we begin to imagine that we have placed our fingers on the living pulse of *the* postmodern, do we not risk betraying the polysemy of the very concept of *post-modernity*, as if mistakenly believing that the postmodern impulse could itself be defined and measured more or less precisely and unambiguously along a single axis of meaning? Or, to make the same point in another way (and so also note the first of several apparent *paradoxes of reflexivity* haunting the post-modern project): If postmodernity should be defined by its call for a sensitivity to polysemy, then presumably we should also understand postmodernity itself polysemically, as possessing *multiple meanings*, which would mean that postmodernity should mean *more* than just the call for polysemy—and, in fact, it does. Ironically, the postmodern is even in danger of meaning too much.

For we now use the adjective "postmodern" to describe not just philosophical ideas but the vast array of cultural "texts" embodying these ideas, texts found all along that increasingly obsolete continuum spanning "high" and "low" art, a distinction postmodernity nicely undermines by lavishing its theoretical attentions on objects previous generations rarely stooped to examine. As evidenced by this book and others like it, a new generation of "highbrow lowbrows" mobilize postmodern insights and theories to analyze everything from television (*"Lost* is the postmodern *Gilligan's Island"*), to comic books ("Alan Moore's *Watchmen* is a masterpiece of postmodern literature"), to Hollywood movies ("Quentin Tarantino's combination of non-linear narrative and pulp sensibility gives his films their post-modern texture"), to pop music ("U2 entered its postmodern phase with *Achtung Baby* and celebrated it with the *Zooropa* tour"—a claim to which we will soon return), to conceptual art ("There seems to be a mutual affinity between U2 and the post-modern artists Jeff Koons and Cindy Sherman"), to philosophy ("Baudrillard may be the greatest of the avowedly postmodern philosophers, but Lyotard is probably the most influential"), and even to religion ("Postmodern theologians heatedly debate whether God *is* humanity, non-appearance, or absence, but post-modern Christians could simply insist that *God is love"*).

Thus, if one tries to infer the meaning of postmodernism by induction from the disparate uses of term one overhears (even in the circles of the learned), one may begin to fear that the concept of the "postmodern" has become so saturated with different meanings that it risks collapsing under the weight of their competing pulls and so fracturing into a disordered multiplicity, the various facets of which only arbitrarily bear the same name. *Postmodern* begins to look like one of those words used so frequently, and in such a bewildering variety of ways, that it has lost all purchase and specificity. Overloaded with meanings, it loses all meaning; for, *if everything is postmodern, postmodernity means nothing.* This is the reflexive paradox mentioned above: Approached in its own terms, postmodernity risks suffering a kind of *death by polysemy*, its meaning drawn and quartered, again and again, until nothing remains.

## Three More Meanings of Postmodernity

It seems to me, then, that in order to understand postmodernity, we need to navigate carefully between the twin excesses of *modern singularity* and *postmodern multiplicity*, the Scylla of the only One and the Charybdis of the infinitely Many. I shall thus risk a more schematic approach, setting out what, to my ear at least, seem to be three more ways in which it makes good sense to describe something as *postmodern*. Of course, *postmodern polysemy* suggests that it is a bit arbitrary to discuss only three more senses of postmodernity. (Why stop at three?) Indeed, a great poem always means more than one thing at once and yet does not mean *everything*, for that latter would drown out all the poem's particular meanings in a dissonant cacophony (or, perhaps, a mystical harmony or fusion).[6]

---

[6] At least in the form of *song*, we may experience a poem that seems to mean *everything* (if only by presenting some aspect of experience so powerfully that we can sense everything else reflected in and so connected by it), a song that thus transports us beyond the mundane realm of differentiated human meaning in an ecstatic feeling of transpersonal, mystical union with the All. As Schopenhauer and, following him, the early Nietzsche realized, the medium of music more easily facilitates such a mystical experience that any of the other arts (hence the full title of Nietzsche's *The Birth of Tragedy from the Spirit of Music*); indeed, music may be more likely to facilitate such an experience of mystical union than any natural experience, with the possible exception

At the same time, however, a truly great poem always holds itself open to meaning more than I currently realize. (Thus, on explaining my sense of a poem as fully and carefully as I can, I will nevertheless be aware that I am far from exhausting its meaning; and hence someone else can say to me, "I think it means something else than what you've said, namely, the following...," and I will often be able to see just what she means.) Accordingly, in my view, the postmodern call for us to attend to *polysemy* is best taken as a hopeful request for a poetic sensitivity to the *inexhaustibility* of meaning rather than an insistence on the static *infinity* of meaning, an *always more* rather than an *everything at once*. (In such a postmodern attunement, as Bono suggests in "Zooropa," "I don't know the limit / The limit of what we got.")

This is to take postmodernity to be saying, in other words, that *the future is not here yet*, or it arrives only in the moment of moving (however incrementally) beyond where we were. The future is not simply implicit in the past but rather requires the creative efforts of those who would yet *invent* it (that is, literally, enter into it) in order to remain genuinely *futural*, open or yet to come. (And was not U2's attempt to remind us of this very *futurity* of the future one of the driving impulses of their avowedly *postmodern* "Zooropa" tour? Slogans like "It's your world, you can change it" flashed across the screens during performances, while songs like "Acrobat," "Zooropa," and "Always" exhorted the audience to "dream out loud." Perhaps this was even partly anticipated on *Rattle and Hum*, the album prior to *Achtung Baby*, where "Love Rescue Me" already celebrated that utopian, revolutionary moment when "I've conquered my past / The future is here at last / I stand at the entrance to a new world I can see. / The ruins to the right of me / Will soon have lost sight of me.") Without further apology, then, here are the three other main senses of postmodernity I hear when I direct the postmodern sensitivity to polysemy back upon the concept of *postmodernity* itself.

---

of sex itself, at least if it is understood in the transpersonal sense suggested by Plato's *Symposium*.

## Beyond Modernity

First, to be *post*modern means *to seek passage beyond modernity.*
In other words, "postmodernity" does not name a new historical
epoch, a new age that is already here and that came after modernity, as one trend might follow another, but, rather, the act of getting free of those modern assumptions that have been most
disastrous for our world and in the grip of which we remain so
stubbornly caught. To be postmodern, then, is to be *on the way*
or in transition *toward another way of existing,* one which not
only (1) *transcends* (in the Hegelian sense of negating while pre-
serving at a higher level, but without Hegel's modern assumption
that this dialectical *Aufhebung* ultimately serves the teleological
aim of generating an all-encompassing conceptual system) our
continuing *modern* obsession with extending the human subject's dominance and control of an objective world, but which
also (2) "twists free" (in what Heidegger called a *Verwindung*) of
our distinctive *late-modern self*-objectification, which increasingly reduces all entities, modernity's celebrated human subject
now included, to the ontological status of an intrinsically meaningless "resource" (*Bestand*) standing by merely to be optimized
and ordered with maximal efficiency for flexible use.

This sense of the *postmodern* also resonates nicely with the
work of such post-Heideggerian thinkers as Levinas, who
insists that "infinity" *is* only in the *act* of *infinition* (that is, the
ethico-poetic act of bringing something new into this finite
world), an act which must speak to the finite world in order to
be understood and so cannot radically break with the past
once and for all, and also, albeit in a more complicated way,
with Lyotard's thinking of our postmodern condition (as we
will see shortly).[7]

What is so misleading here, however, is that many self-
described postmodernists do use the term *postmodernity* not
simply as a handy label for the latest developments in their
field but, apparently hypostatizing and generalizing these
developments, instead treat *postmodernity* as if it referred to a
*new age,* an historical epoch into which these postmodernists
have already entered, as if all that needs to happen now is for

---

[7] See Emmanuel Levinas, *Totality and Infinity: An Essay on Exteriority* (Pittsburgh: Duquesne University Press, 1969).

the rest of us to catch up to where they already are. Such van-
guardism, despite its occasional nuggets of truth (for who
could deny the great poetic visionaries their defining experiences of a genuinely postmodern revelation?), nevertheless
risks degenerating into a naive and dangerously Pollyannish
optimism. For its rose-colored spectacles can blind us to the
uncomfortable yet undeniable fact that the modern assumptions we need to twist free of remain deeply and pervasively
entrenched in the fundamental but unnoticed ontotheological
principles of vision and division by which we go about making sense of our worlds. None of us lives permanently unaf-
fected by the *modern* subject-object divide or by the
*late-modern* reduction of everything to intrinsically-meaning-
less resources standing by for optimization.

None of us are postmodern saints, in this modern world and
yet not of it. Still, all of us remain capable of at least temporarily
achieving experiences in which the subject/object divide dis-
solves into a unified being-in-the-world (especially with the aid of
music, meditation, sport, or religion), and many of us do at least
occasionally have an experience of belonging to something that
genuinely matters independently of our own goals and desires.
(Whether we describe such experiences with names drawn from
poetry or religion might be irrelevant, were it not for the way theologians too often reinterpret such experiences so as falsely to
suggest that they remain beyond the reach of us mere mortals—
an important matter to which I shall return in the conclusion.)

Otherwise put, none of us is a postmodern island, but we do
have postmodern experiences, some subtle and some profound,
which means that there exist, here and there, postmodern arch-
ipelagoes jutting out from our modern past into a territory that
has yet to take the firm shape of a new land, a genuine "new
age" or widespread and relatively coherent historical *postmodernity*. Indeed, to many it is not even clear that such a
promised land ever could rise from the various mists now dark-
ening our future horizons.

Those who doubt that any such new postmodern world is
even in the offing find it most suggestive to emphasize the frequent identification of postmodernity with wandering and
nomadism, with deterritorialization and the sojourn (without
permanent homecoming), with Moses and all those who point
toward a utopia they know themselves unable to take up any

final residence within. Others of us welcome such fellow-travelers but wonder if they will be able to keep their good cheer indefinitely while underway toward a promised land they believe they can never reach. (If such worries get raised by the bleak portrait of "wandering" or "drifting" painted by U2's postmodern appropriation of Johnny Cash on *Zooropa*'s "The Wanderer," they may be partly assuaged by listening to "Kite" on *All That You Can't Leave Behind*.) We thus think it important, if only to keep hope alive long enough for it to become more than hope, not simply to elevate means above ends, not to permanentize a holding-pattern, not to substitute Nietzsche's "constant overcoming" for the possible arrival of Heidegger's "last God" (this being one of the names Heidegger used, mostly in his private notebooks, to try to help us envision our collective entrance into a *genuine* historical postmodernity, which for him meant an historical age in which we—or our descendents—transcend our late-modern reduction of reality to resource by, to take only the most likely example, coming together to recognize and celebrate our belonging to the *earth*).[8]

## Incredulity

Let us turn to the second sense. Postmodernism is usually taken to mean an "incredulity toward metanarratives," as Lyotard famously put it in *The Postmodern Condition*, the most influential book explicitly written about postmodernity.[9] If *narratives* are the stories we tell ourselves and each other in order to make sense of our lives (by bestowing meaning on the historical trajectory of existence), then a *metanarrative* would be a perspective from which to adjudicate between the different and competing narratives that struggle with one another (tacitly or actively) to tell us our story the most authoritatively. This, moreover, is why one so often hears that *postmodernists are relativists*: If we cannot believe in any standpoint from which we

---

[8] I develop these ideas in "Ontology and Ethics at the Intersection of Phenomenology and Environmental Philosophy," *Inquiry* 47:4 (2004), pp. 380–412; and "The Philosophical Fugue: Understanding the Structure and Goal of Heidegger's Beiträge," *Journal of the British Society for Phenomenology* 34:1 (2003), pp. 57–73.

[9] See Jean-François Lyotard, *The Postmodern Condition: A Report on Knowledge* (Minneapolis: University of Minnesota Press, 1984), p. xxiv.

might reasonably adjudicate between competing interpretations of our historical situation, then we are indeed consigned to relativism (and its ethico-political bedfellows, cynicism and interest-driven *Realpolitik*). Fortunately, so the received view goes, postmodernism thus understood immediately undermines itself (in a second paradox of reflexivity). For what is Lyotard's historical claim that we no longer believe in metanarratives but itself another metanarrative? If Lyotard offers us a metanarrative about the end of metanarratives, then, as on the liar's paradox (the most straightforward example of which is "This sentence is false," a statement which, if true, must be false, but then, if false, must be true, and so on, in an endless circle or Möbius strip), *if Lyotard were right, then we would not believe him.*[10] This is how Lyotard is commonly understood, and so quickly dismissed. Yet, this dismissal of Lyotard as self-undermining is much too quick; it commits what philosophers call the straw-man fallacy, rejecting a simplified caricature so as not to have to grapple with an idea in all its complexity and force. In fact, Lyotard's considered view is much more specific than his early definition of postmodernism, taken out of context and treated as a perfectly general thesis, leads readers to conclude.[11]

As the subtitle of *The Postmodern Condition: A Report on Knowledge* suggests, Lyotard's focus is on *knowledge* as it is embodied and transmitted by contemporary institutions of higher education. The important question he asks is, *What justifies knowledge and the institutions responsible for embodying and transmitting it?* Lyotard argues that we can no longer answer this question the way the original founders of the modern university did. On Lyotard's reading of the German idealists who were largely responsible for founding the University of Berlin at the dawn of the nineteenth century, the point of the modern *University* was either (1) to *unify* the disparate domains of knowledge or (2) to progressively *emancipate* humanity. In the two intervening centuries, however, we have witnessed both

---

[10] "The [Cretan] liar's paradox" takes its name from the story of a man from Crete who asserts that "All Cretans are liars." U2 provided audiences with a provocative example of the liar's paradox on the Zooropa tour by flashing across their screens the message that: "Everything you know is wrong."

[11] See for instance Gianni Vattimo, *Nihilism and Emancipation: Ethics, Politics, and Law* (New York: Columbia University Press, 2004), pp. 5–6.

(1) the increasing specialization and consequent fragmentation of the various fields of knowledge (undermining our modern faith that knowledge would justify itself by eventually giving rise to a *unified* understanding of all reality) as well as (2) the uncoupling of scientific progress from the advance of human freedom (which has led us to lose the optimistic modern enlightenment belief that knowledge inherently serves human freedom).

Lyotard's thesis concerning our "incredulity toward metanarratives" is in fact limited to these two specific examples. We can no longer believe in the metanarratives of *unity* and *emancipation* by which modernity sought to justify knowledge, and it is in precisely this sense that we are in a *post*modern condition. There is thus nothing self-undermining in saying so, nor even in Lyotard's further argument that these two modern metanarratives have now been supplanted historically by the "postmodern" *metanarrative of optimization*, in which all "legitimation . . . is based on its optimizing the system's performance"—although I do think it would be less confusing to refer here to our "late-modern" condition because these developments emerged from the way we turned the techniques and procedures devised for controlling the objective world back upon the modern subject, leading, as we will see, to a dissolution of this modern subject and its historical self-understanding without yet putting any new, substantive historical self-understanding in its place—and thereby yielding the historical situation U2 aptly describes in *Zooropa*'s "Numb," in which "Too much is not enough" (see *The Postmodern Condition*, p. xxiv).

Nor does Lyotard simply accept (what he calls) "the postmodern condition" *cynically*, as critics often allege. Rather, he advocates a Trojan horse strategy according to which we should recognize—and *provisionally* appeal to—this dominant logic of optimization in order to transcend it from within. (This Trojan horse strategy, I would suggest, also nicely characterizes the "postmodern" spirit of "Zooropa," which seeks to move through the banality of corporate slogans into the "guiding light" of "uncertainty" in order to encourage us to "dream out loud" and so "dream up the world [we want] to live in.") Lyotard's crucial claims here are that knowledge domains are finite and so will eventually become exhausted unless we encourage "paralogy," that is, paradigm-altering transformations of the fundamental assumptions (or "metaprescriptives") underlying and guiding the various domains of knowledge, and that such transformations are the most likely source for the emergence of any new historical logic other than the empty optimization imperative (*The Postmodern Condition*, p. 65).

The hegemonic knowledge system will accept paralogy precisely because paralogy promises to optimize knowledge (by allowing us to transcend the finite resources of any fixed knowledge domain). Yet, Lyotard suggests, paralogy will also work from within the optimization economy to encourage paradigm-shifting developments that may emerge like some metastatic growth from a particularly fecund region of knowledge (ecology, let us hope, rather than cybernetics). In this way, Lyotard believes we might successfully generate a new justification for knowledge in general (and for institutions responsible for embodying and transmitting such knowledge), a justification that would eventually supplant the empty optimization imperative that itself displaced the modern metanarratives of unity and emancipation (and only then, *pace* Lyotard, would we enter into a genuine *postmodernity*). Thus, although many details of Lyotard's analysis remain questionable (and certainly call for much further thought), he is basically offering a neo-Heideggerian vision for how we might actually go about transcending our current historical self-understanding, the nihilistic reduction of all knowledge and meaning to "optimal input/output matrices" that Lyotard calls (in a somewhat misleading overgeneralization) *the postmodern condition*.[12] Lyotard is at most only a *strategic postmodernist*, then, one who suggests that we must face up to our historical predicament clearly and so provisionally accept its terms if we are ever to discover a path leading through and beyond it.

## Fragmentation

Third, and finally, postmodernism is often taken to connote *the fragmentation of the subject*. The "unholy trinity" of Marx, Nietzsche, and Freud developed their *hermeneutics of suspicion*

---

[12] See Lyotard, *The Postmodern Condition*, p. xxiv. For an explanation and defense of Heidegger's remarkably similar views, see Chapters 3 and 4 of my *Heidegger on Ontotheology*.

suggesting, each in a different way, that the heroic modern conception of an autonomous subject firmly in control of an objective world was an illusion, a surface appearance or projected
fantasy concealing the deeper truth that subjectivity is a battle-
ground for forces of which we often remain unaware. These
great critics of modern subjectivity focused on experiences we
normally overlook in order to argue that the subject is a prod-
uct of more or less unconscious drives for respect (Marx, following Hegel), power (Nietzsche, generalizing Darwin), and
erotic fulfillment (Freud, developing Plato). Compared to these
critical analyses, which broke down the modern subject into its
component forces, the positive visions of Marx, Nietzsche, and
Freud were notoriously underdeveloped, but each did at least
try to imagine how a *post*modern epoch might be built up from
the fragments of modern subjectivity.

Marx envisioned a socialist utopia of mutual respect, in which
advances in technology would eliminate the need for the alienating labor that estranges us from ourselves (and so prevents the
formation of any satisfying self-understanding), thereby allowing
each of us to cultivate (and be *recognized* by others for) his or
her unique contributions (hence Marx's famous formula for
socialism: "From each according to his ability, to each according
to his needs"). Nietzsche, playing his part in the postmodern
drama, not only announced the death of the God who had guar-
anteed the privilege of human subjectivity but also predicted the
emergence of a "higher type" of human being who would face
up to the death of God, embrace the dangerous truth that life is
will-to-power, and so set out to reshape human beings the way
artists sculpt clay (hence *Thus Spoke Zarathustra*'s notorious doctrine of "the *superman*: Humanity is something that should be
*superceded*").[13]

Finally, and with comparative modesty, Freud called for the
achievement of a new and more austere autonomy, in which the
widespread practice of psychoanalysis would enable us to transmute our neurotic misery into ordinary unhappiness by helping
us relinquish our (paradigmatically modern) subject-centered

---

[13] I develop these points in "Deconstructing the Hero," in Jeff McLaughlin, ed., *Comics
as Philosophy* (Jackson: University of Mississippi, 2005), pp. 100–129. See also
Nietzsche, *Writings from the Late Notebooks* (Cambridge: Cambridge University Press,
2003), p. 71.

fantasies, reconcile ourselves to the unfulfillable desires that drive us (by acknowledging and then finding socially acceptable ways to sublimate and express these drives), and thereby reclaim and reintegrate the self (hence Freud's well-known slogan, "Where *id* was, *ego* shall be"). One would thus need at least two axes to measure the influence of these positive visions, because the considerable influence each exerted historically seems to have been met by an at least equal and opposite reaction (due in no small measure to the way the Nazi and Communist appropriations of Nietzsche and Marx distorted their teachings).

Even if the postmodern visions of Marx, Nietzsche, and Freud worked like powerful magnets, repelling as much as they attracted, the influence of their different ways of analyzing subjectivity into its component forces has been immense, leaving an indelible imprint on the self-understanding of our current historical epoch. For what emerged historically from this three-fronted dissolution of modern subjectivity was that even broader fragmentation and fracturing of *identity* we now see expressed in the common claim that postmodernity is an age without an integral style, one which—lacking any robust sense of its own positive identity—borrows freely from all other styles in its *postmodern pastiche*, famously employing such hospitable techniques as bricolage, *détournement*, and sampling. Not surprisingly, the initial resistance to this underlying fragmentation of the robust modern self was considerable, perhaps most prominently visible in Kierkegaard's appropriation of the idea that "purity of heart is to will one thing" (hence Kierkegaard's own passionate belief that he could not be *both* a writer *and* a husband, and his famous call for the decisiveness of an *either/or*) as well as in Heidegger's neo-Kierkegaardian appeal in *Being and Time* for each of us to resolutely choose a defining life project (or "ultimate for the sake of which") that will allow us to integrate our various senses of self in the achievement of an *authentic* identity (a vision not so different from Freud's, as the existential psychoanalytic movement noted enthusiastically).

Yet, more contemporary post-Heideggerian thinkers—many of whom came of age in post-War France during a time when the influence of Marx, Nietzsche, and Freud were powerfully reinforced by (what Gutting nicely describes as) "the structuralist decentering of the subject"—almost unanimously advise us to abandon this quest for a unified identity as, at best, an illusory nostalgia for something we never really possessed and, at worst, a neurotic reaction to the vertiginous anxiety of freedom that leads us (as some might suggest it led Heidegger himself) to rush into the arms of an awaiting authoritarian regime, one promising us the final reassurance of its one true answer.[14] These French neo-Heideggerians thus led the call for us to transcend modern subjectivity (and even its echo in the early Heidegger's valorization of the robust, *authentic* self), for example, in Foucault's prediction of the passing of the era of modern subjectivity ("the end of man"), Derrida's tireless deconstructions of the myths of full "self-presence," Lacan's neo-Freudian analysis of subjectivity as an ultimately hollow construction, Deleuze and Guattari's "schizoanalysis" celebrating the divided self, and even in Baudrillard's post-Marxist diagnosis of our late capitalist "triumph of the simulacra," the victory of an age in which our strange and estranging preference for artificiality comes to eclipse our relation to *anything* real, including ourselves. This last phenomenon especially, I shall now suggest, brings us directly into the sphere of U2's own distinctive postmodern experiment, and so requires us recognize and confront the real dangers of their postmodern venture ("I'm ready," *Achtung Baby* begins by resolutely repeating), asking whether U2 has shown these risks to be worth taking—and, if so, how?

## U2 and Postmodernity: *Et tu*, Bono?

U2 has been blessed with a long and influential musical career, the various stages of which other philosophers in this volume chronicle and address. The task I have been charged with here is to facilitate further thinking about U2's famous experiment with postmodernity, the "postmodern phase" they self-consciously entered into with *Achtung Baby* and celebrated in the complex and almost overwhelming pop-cultural pastiche of the

---

[14] For a suggestive development of the latter critique, see *Nihilism and Emancipation*, p. 20. On the former point, see Gary Gutting, *French Philosophy in the Twentieth Century* (Cambridge: Cambridge University Press, 2001), p. 261. Bono too recognizes fascism as a reaction to the anxiety-provoking truth of uncertainty; as he put it: "The fascists at least recognize the void, their pseudo-strong leadership a reaction to what feels like *no* leadership . . . Fascism is about control. They know what we won't admit: that things are out of control." Bill Flanagan, *U2 at the End of the World* (New York: Delta, 1995), p. 172.

*Zooropa* tour. The obvious question, then, is: Which of the senses of postmodernity we have explored best allows us to understand the meaning and significance of U2's own distinctive *postmodernity?* As you may not be surprised to hear, I think the answer is, *All of the above.*

It's very tempting to understand U2's exemplary postmodern song (on which, in good postmodern fashion, I shall isolate and focus on here), "Even Better than the Real Thing," as a celebration of the very postmodern condition Baudrillard characterizes as *the triumph of the simulacra.* How else are we to understand this song's oft-repeated, eponymous chorus— "Even better than the real thing"—than as an embrace (whether ironic or not) of a world in which *we come to prefer surfaces to depths, images to reality, sex to love, the fake to the genuine?* Worse, insofar as U2's famous song does celebrate this postmodern triumph of the simulacra, then must we not suspect that its great popularity worked to reify that terrible triumph, thereby making U2 into agents, willing or (if the song is meant ironically and that is lost on most listeners) unwilling, of the most nihilistic aspects of postmodernity? Whatever their intentions (and many other good deeds), would we not then feel moved to castigate U2 for spreading this triumphant postmodernity around the world, like a virus embedded in a catchy hook?

There is no way around it: That is precisely the uncircumventable risk U2 took with "Even Better than the Real Thing," and some superficial listeners may have taken the song in exactly this way and never gone any further, a fact with which U2 and their fans will have to come to terms in order to take responsibility for this postmodern venture. At the same time, however, I think we can see that this gamble was a worthy one. For, if we think about what has been said thus far, we can begin to recognize that there is something else going on in "Even Better than the Real Thing" than a simple capitulation to superficiality and the allure of the artificial. Indeed, I know of no sophisticated proponents of such an allegedly "postmodern" celebration of glittering surfaces over mute depths. (Some thinkers, following Nietzsche, deny the very existence of such depths, but in so doing they banish the contrast between surface and depth on which this portrait of postmodernism depends.)

This common picture of "postmodernity" thus appears to be a caricature advanced by superficial critics seeking to portray themselves, by contrast, as sober defenders of tradition and common sense, who thereby fail to notice that the very "common sense" we inherit from the tradition is shaped by the prejudices of modernity, and so functions indiscriminately to reinforce our internalization of even the most nihilistic and destructive aspects of the modern worldview. To move beyond such brutal simplifications, then, let us remember where we began: The postmodern call for a sensitivity to *polysemy* suggests that, if U2's "Even Better than the Real Thing" is genuinely postmodern, then its meaning cannot be reduced to any straightforward embrace of a single axis of postmodernity, including the nihilistic phenomena Baudrillard describes as the triumph of the simulacra. If what else I said was right, moreover, this song should also suggest an attempt to forge a path *through* and beyond the problematic aspects of our historical age by attuning us to a more genuinely redemptive experience, and to do so even while it resists being reduced to any single meaning or simple self-identity. So, does it? The Devil—or God—is in the details.

## Sex, Love, and God: The Spiritual Politics of the Postmodern U2

The lyrics of "Even Better than the Real Thing" are clearly written to a lover, perhaps originating as a poetic appeal to a specific lover for another chance (or two, suggesting a certain recidivist repetition of the pattern). If that was its inspiration, however, its meaning quickly changes. For, as a song, it is also clearly addressed to a *broader* audience, and thereby seeks to transform this entire audience into the beloved. In so doing, however, it loses its force as an appeal to a particular lost love for a second (or third) chance and becomes an affirmation of the very powerful communal experience that, we can easily imagine, would repeatedly pull Bono (or any member of U2) away from the arms of any particular lover.

If one insists on hearing the song as addressed to a specific lover, then it seems to celebrate sex above love: With its singer promising an ecstatic experience of sliding "down the surface of things" (and the like), "Even better than the real thing" implies that sexual ecstasy is better than the experience of genuine love.

Notice, however, that when these same lyrics are heard as addressed to an audience, especially a live audience, the meaning of these words is subtly but radically realigned: Now the implication is that U2's relation to this audience is "Even better than the real thing" not in the simulacra-triumphant sense that mainstream Western culture does in fact seem to prefer sex to love; instead, the song seeks to evoke and celebrate the experience of a profound feeling of communal love that is "even better" than genuine personal love, an experience in which we can all be taken "higher" and "higher" and "higher" without ever reaching that fatal point (what the French call *la petit mort*) where, like Icarus, our wings "melt" and we fall back down to earth.

Heard in this communal register, the erotic meaning that "I'm gonna make you sing" has when addressed to a particular lover becomes transformed, elevated into a celebration of communal singing as an ecstatic experience that transcends even the feeling of real love between two individuals. (This universalization of love—by which U2 seeks to transmute the entire audience into a beloved—works, as Plato observed in the *Symposium*, by generalizing from the particular; it is thus striking that Bono sometimes performs the same gesture in reverse, bringing a particular audience member onto stage in order to sing to her personally, as a particularization of the general audience he seeks to reach *through* her.)

With the very idea of an ecstatic experience transcending personal love, we tread, I would suggest, into the territory of the *holy*, that which heals us by making us feel whole, raising us up by allowing us to feel ourselves a part of a greater whole to which we genuinely belong. "Even Better than the Real Thing," then, would be less a celebration of the real pleasures of erotic sexuality than of the communal experience of universal love, a love transcending the bounds even of the community in which it is experienced, and so working (ethically, spiritually, erotically, politically) to both reinforce and expand the bounds of those communal bonds by extending the feelings of unity, sympathy, and belonging beyond the contingent limits of a group—toward that universe experienced in love which both inspires and beckons for such an unlimited embrace.

Does the embrace and demand (*Achtung, Baby!*) at the heart of that experience of universal love include and call upon me as

well? Yes, and *you, too*. That is perhaps the deepest message of
the *postmodern* U2, which is, at the same time, the *Christ-ian*
U2, where by "Christ-ian" I mean Christ-emulating rather than
"Christian theology" following, in other words, striving to live—
and live up to—Christ's own teachings of universal love rather
than the more narrowly circumscribed doctrines of some particular church.

What is more, if I am right that Christianity itself was born
out of such a fundamental attunement of universal love, born,
that is, in Christ's own powerful experience of and subsequent
call for us too to experience what it is like genuinely *to love
everyone and everything*, without imposing borders or distinctions (and in this way Christianity represents a significant ethical modification of Judaism, which seems to me to have
emerged from an importantly different fundamental attunement,
namely, that awesome experience of wonder before the mere
fact that reality exists, that *there is something* rather than nothing at all, an experience Christ transforms simply by seeing this
reality through the eyes of unlimited love), then understanding
U2's postmodernity in these terms allows us to recognize that
their postmodern experiment is in fact continuous with, and so
not some bizarre deviation from, the consistent artistic trajectory
U2 has followed all along.

For U2's postmodern swerve can be seen as another switch-
back on the mountainous path they follow as they continue
seeking a way to express effectively (and so let be felt in our
late- or post-modern world) their enduring commitment to the
immeasurable and uncontainable ethical, aesthetic, spiritual, and
political implications of that genuinely polysemic experience
postmodernists and Christians (or at least Christ-ians) might yet
agree to call *love, charity*, or *peace* (no single element of which
can long exist without the others—the words and actions of
many prominent, self-described "Christians" notwithstanding).

If I express a certain caution here by predicting that postmodernists and Christ-ians "*might* yet agree," even as Rorty and
Vattimo seem to be leading the way toward just such a post-
modern-Christian alliance, this is not only because *post*modernity (as a movement seeking *transition beyond*) reminds us not
to foreclose the *futurity* of the future (the unpredictability in
virtue of which the future remains yet *to come*)—a reminder
reinforced by U2's Christ-ian teaching, *apropos* of "love," that:

"She moves in mysterious ways."[15] My caution also stems from respect for another "postmodern" strand of anti-theological religious thinking, that heritage running from Kierkegaard through Derrida (and beyond), which valorizes social *alienation* and the radical *individuation* it facilitates as an alternative and at least equally genuine and important dimension of religious experience. It thus seems appropriate, by way of conclusion, to suggest that U2's own postmodern Christ-ianity helps us see how we might fruitfully combine postmodernity's competing spiritual pulls toward both the universal and the particular. In this spirit, I end with the inspired and, I hope, inspiring words from U2's "One": "One life / But we're not the same / We've got to carry each other / Carry each other . . ."[16]

---

[15] See the essays by Rorty and Vattimo in Mark Wrathall, ed., *Religion After Metaphysics* (Cambridge: Cambridge University Press, 2003) and their subsequent interview in Santiago Zabala, ed., *The Future of Religion* (New York: Columbia University Press, 2005).

[16] Thanks to Mark Wrathall for the enthusiastic invitation to write this essay and many valuable suggestions, and to Francisco Gallegos, Christian Wood, and especially Sara Amber Rawls for very helpful insights.

# PART II

# I Don't Mean to Bug Ya

## The Philosophical Basis of U2's Ethics and Politics

Am I bugging you?
I don't mean to bug ya.
Okay, Edge, play the blues.

—"SILVER AND GOLD,"
*Rattle and Hum*

# 7

# U2 and the Problem of Evil

TRENTON MERRICKS

The world is full of glorious and wonderful things. On some days, laughing children and happy reunions and healthy bodies seem to be around every corner. At the same time, the world is full of very bad things. Cruel people damage and abuse those under their control. Poverty-stricken children die of easily treatable conditions like diarrhea and malnourishment. There are moments when suffering and pain and injustice seem to be around every corner.

Given all the evil—and despite all the good—the world does not look as you would probably expect a world ruled by an all-powerful and good and loving God to look. Our world doesn't look like we would probably expect God's world to look. For this reason, the existence of evil threatens to undermine belief in God. Philosophers call this *the problem of evil.*

One way for evil to undermine belief in God would be by way of a proof, by way of an airtight chain of logical reasoning that gets from the starting point of *there is evil* to the conclusion *there is no good and all-powerful God.* I mention this way just to set it aside. For, while evil does pose a challenge to belief in God, virtually all philosophers working in this area these days agree that we cannot prove that God does not exist (or is not good or is not all-powerful) from the bare existence of evil.[1]

---

[1] For an excellent discussion of why the existence of evil does not prove that there is no God, see Daniel Howard-Snyder's "God, Evil, and Suffering" in Michael J. Murray, ed., *Reason for the Hope Within* (Grand Rapids: Eerdmans, 1999).

The failure of such a proof is not, however, my main reason for setting it aside. (So you can read on, even if you don't believe me when I say it fails.) My main reason is that I think that most who reject belief in God on account of evil do not do so because of a supposed proof or indeed because of any explicitly formulated argument at all. If I am right, then most who reject belief in God on account of evil will not feel that, for example, criticizing the logic in such arguments gets to the heart of the matter. Instead, I imagine that most of them—upon considering the evil around us—are *just struck* with the conviction that our world is not in the hands of a loving and all-powerful God.

These atheists do not have what philosophers would call an *argument* from evil against God's existence. Rather, they have a *reaction* to evil. With this in mind, consider the closing lyrics of XTC's song "Dear God":

> I won't believe in heaven and hell.
> No saints, no sinners, no devil as well.
> No pearly gates, no thorny crown.
> You're always letting us humans down.
> The wars you bring, the babes you drown.
> Those lost at sea and never found,
> and it's the same the whole world 'round.
> The hurt I see helps to compound
> that Father, Son and Holy Ghost
> is just somebody's unholy hoax,
> and if you're up there you'd perceive
> that my heart's here upon my sleeve.
> If there's one thing I don't believe in it's you . . .
> Dear God.

This song contains no argument against God's existence. XTC does not offer premises, and then—by way of careful logic—generate the conclusion that there is no God. This song presents, instead, a way to *react* to all the evil in the world. Look at the evil, the song seems to say, and you can just tell there is no God.

Is XTC's reaction the best one? Is it the most sensible, reasonable, plausible reaction? Is it a reaction we should share? It would be unwise to answer these questions without first comparing XTC's reaction to other reactions. And this brings us to U2.

## U2, XTC, and the Psalmist

U2 sometimes presents the problem of evil in a way that would do XTC proud. "Wake Up Dead Man" opens with: "Jesus, Jesus help me / I'm alone in this world / And a fucked up world it is too." In this same song, U2 wonders aloud if Jesus's hands "aren't free." And the song asks Jesus: "Did you think to try and warn her? / Or are you working on something new?"

U2's "Peace on Earth" also emphasizes the seeming tension between a good God and the state of the world. It proclaims being sick of both sorrow and pain, sick of hearing "again and again" that there's "gonna be Peace on Earth." Bono asks Jesus if he can "take the time to throw a drowning man a line." And the song concludes with: "So what's it worth? / This peace on Earth."

These songs shove the problem of evil right in your face. The simplest reaction to this problem is to conclude that God (or Jesus) is powerless or unconcerned or even non-existent. But U2 does not react in the simplest way.

A clue to U2's more nuanced reaction comes from some of Bono's remarks on the Psalms:

> Abandonment, displacement, is the stuff of my favourite psalms. The Psalter may be a font of gospel music, but for me it's in his despair that the psalmist really reveals the nature of his special relationship with God. Honesty, even to the point of anger. "How long, Lord? Wilt thou hide thyself forever?" (Psalm 89) or "Answer me when I call" (Psalm 5).
>
> That's what a lot of the psalms feel like to me, the blues. Man shouting at God—"My God, my God, why hast thou forsaken me? Why art thou so far from helping me?" (Psalm 22).[2]

XTC, U2, and the psalmist all have something in common. All react to evil with frustration and anger and a look of despair toward heaven. But then XTC parts ways with the psalmist and concludes that there is no one in heaven to be seen. What does U2 conclude?

---

[2] From Bono's introduction to *Selections from the Book of Psalms* (New York: Grove Press, 1999), p. viii.

## U2's Reaction to Evil

U2's reaction to evil includes—in addition to anger—a longing for heaven, a yearning for the time when God will make all right. We've already considered the first three lines of "Wake Up Dead Man." Here is what follows: "Tell me, tell me the story/The one about eternity/And the way it's all gonna be." In this song, U2 reacts to evil with anger and frustration. But— as the lines just quoted suggest—U2 also reacts with hope, reaching for the promise of the next life, a life free of evil.

Then comes the refrain, which says over and over: "Wake up, wake up dead man." The refrain (and so the song's title) can be understood in at least two different ways. First, it can be understood as asking Jesus to wake up and *do something*. Calling him a "dead man" suggests his apparent inaction and indifference and even that he may not have risen from the dead at all, and so may not be God. On the first way of understanding it, the refrain expresses the already familiar anger and doubt.

But there's a second way to understand it. A central teaching of Christianity is that, at some point in the future, Jesus Christ will come again and raise the dead. At this resurrection of all people Jesus will rule and his kingdom will be fully established and there will be no more tears and no more suffering. At least part of the answer to the problem of evil—part of the promise that God is indeed good—is this promised resurrection. When Christ calls out to each in his or her grave, "*Wake up, dead man!*" death will be conquered and evil will be no more. This is the story about eternity, and the way it's all gonna be. This is peace on Earth.

So we find hints of hope even in the middle of U2's most anguished lament about evil. And other U2 songs give more than just hints. It's no stretch to assume that the Grace of "Grace" personifies the grace of God. Grace, according to this song, takes the blame, covers the shame, and removes the stain. And Bono sings: "She carries a pearl in perfect condition[3] / What once was hurt / What once was friction / What left a mark / No longer stings / Because Grace makes beauty / Out of ugly things."

---

[3] "Again, the kingdom of heaven is like a merchant in search of fine pearls; on finding one pearl of great value, he went and sold all that he had and bought it" Matthew 13:45-46 (Jesus speaking).

It would be an oversimplification to say that the U2 songs here discussed clearly and unambiguously express only two reactions to evil. For we could find in them a wide range of reactions, voiced with varying degrees of confidence. Nevertheless, among the many reactions we can find in these songs, we should find the following. First, there is anger at God. Second, there is belief and yearning: belief that God will make all right and yearning for the time when he does.

These two reactions might seem opposed to one another—one a reaction of doubt, the other a reaction of faith. But I think both spring from a single root, outrage. Innocent children are murdered; women are raped; young men are beaten senseless just for being in the wrong place at the wrong time . . . and on it goes. The world, as it is now, is absolutely unacceptable. We should not be comfortable with the general run of things; we should not find the world more or less pleasing, merely in need of a minor tweak here and a small adjustment there. We should, instead, be outraged.

Such outrage can naturally lead to anger toward God, since God could prevent evil though, for reasons unknown to us, does not. But it should also make us hunger for when things will be better, to yearn and thirst for something beyond this time of darkness and suffering. And so Bono says:

> "40" became the closing song at U2 shows and on hundreds of occasions, literally hundreds of thousands of people of every size and shape t-shirt have shouted back the refrain, pinched from "Psalm 6": "'How long' (to sing this song)." I had thought of it as a nagging question—pulling at the hem of an invisible deity whose presence we glimpse only when we act in love. How long . . . hunger? How long . . . hatred? How long until creation grows up and the chaos of its precocious, hell-bent adolescence has been discarded? I thought it odd that the vocalising of such questions could bring such comfort; to me too. (*Selections from the Book of Psalms*, pp. xi–xii)

In reflecting on U2's yearning for God to make things right, we find something surprising: Sometimes experiencing evil does not undermine faith, but instead strengthens it. For many of us with comparatively comfortable lives, the real threat to genuine faith is complacency—complacency with the world more or less as it is. I find myself hoping, not for the day when Christ will return to end wars and reunite divided families and set those in slavery free, but rather for the day when I will make more money. Desire for God and his kingdom gets pushed aside in the scramble for the petty and immediate. We settle for new shoes while the Lord wants to give us himself and peace on earth.

My point here is *not* that God permits horrible suffering so I can get a wake-up call. (Indeed, I don't think any of us knows why God permits horrendous evil.) I would never accuse God of permitting genocide and natural disaster just to give middle-class professors a more meaningful spiritual life. Nevertheless, it is undeniable that a hard look at pain and suffering can snap us out of soul-numbing complacency. Facing evil reminds us that things are not made right by a nice car or a better jump shot. Focusing on the evil all around us causes us to long for, to hunger for, to crave with all we have the Lord's coming and his kingdom. Pain and suffering drive us to yearn for a time when God, by his grace, makes beauty out of ugly things.

## What Makes a Reaction Reasonable?

U2 acts as well as hopes—and presumably acts in part *because* it hopes. They joined other artists in opposing South African Apartheid. They worked to bring world attention to the suffering in Sarajevo (during the Yugoslavian civil war). The most impressive and visible example along these lines is Bono's work to help poor countries shed their debt and to address AIDS in Africa.[4] This all illustrates a third aspect of U2's reaction to evil: active participation in God's work of making things right, a work which, though it won't be completed in this life, has already begun.

So how should we evaluate U2's reaction to evil, a reaction that includes anger at God, hope for heaven, and laboring to set things right? Specifically, how does it compare to that of XTC, which concludes that there is no God? Which reaction is more reasonable, sensible, and appropriate?

I shall not consider anger, which both XTC's and U2's reactions share. After all, since they react alike in this way, there is no question—in this regard—of which reaction is more reasonable than the other. Likewise, I'll set aside U2's humanitarian

---

[4] See the *Time* cover story "Can Bono Save the World?" (4th March, 2002)

efforts. For everyone should agree that such a reaction to evil is reasonable. Besides, there is no reason why XTC couldn't work against evil too (and, for all I know, maybe XTC already does).

Let's focus on the part of XTC's reaction that includes the belief that God does not exist. And let's focus on the part of U2's reaction that includes the belief that God does exist and will redeem evil and will make things right one day. This is the fundamental difference between their two reactions. And thus the fundamental question here is which of these beliefs is a more reasonable reaction to evil.

Perhaps someone's atheism is reasonable for reasons having nothing to do with evil. And perhaps this atheist is reminded of her atheism by evil. A similar point holds for someone who believes in God. Both could then reasonably react to evil by being reminded of their already held, and already reasonable, convictions. But none of this touches on the point I want to consider. For I want to ask not whether experiencing evil brings to mind an already reasonable atheism or an already reasonable trust in God. I want to ask, instead, whether being confronted with evil can all by itself *make* such a belief reasonable in the first place (or more reasonable than it was to begin with).

We cannot answer this question until we say a bit about what makes beliefs reasonable. For example, some beliefs are made reasonable by *other beliefs*. You ask me why I believe that Paul Hewson is inside a mirrorball lemon. I reply that *I believe that Bono is inside a mirrorball lemon* and also that *I believe that Paul Hewson is identical with Bono*. These two beliefs, assuming they are themselves reasonable, render reasonable my belief that Paul Hewson is inside a mirrorball lemon.

But not all reasonable beliefs are made reasonable by other beliefs. Sometimes a belief is made reasonable by an *experience*. You hear some music (and so have a particular experience); that experience causes you to believe that someone is playing U2's *War* and also makes that belief reasonable. You recognize a face at a party (again, have an experience) and you find yourself with the reasonable belief that here is an old friend. You have the visual sensation of seeming to see a tree; you end up with the reasonable belief that there is a tree in front of you.

Let's examine this last example. This is, of course, not a case of a belief's being made reasonable by other beliefs. And so it is not a case of your giving an argument that starts with the belief that you had a certain visual experience and ends with the conclusion that there is a tree in front of you. Rather, your belief *there is a tree in front of me* is made reasonable, in large part, by your *having the experience* of seeming to see a tree. Your believing that there is a tree in front of you is a *reasonable reaction* to that experience.

Not all beliefs produced by experiences are like those just considered. Not all beliefs produced by experiences are reasonable. My three-year-old son has the experience of my refusing to let him play with the lawn mower. Alas, his reaction to this experience is to believe that I am mean. He is wrong. Moreover, there is an important way in which his reaction is not reasonable. For he does not form the belief that I am mean by way of a trustworthy faculty like vision. Instead, that belief is, in large part, a result of his ignorance and his jumping to hasty conclusions.

## Which Reaction Is More Reasonable?

In the atheistic reaction to evil we have an experience (such as being horrified by evil) that results in a belief (the belief that there is no God). Is this like the belief, produced by visual experience, that there is a tree in front of you? Or is it, instead, like my three-year-old son's belief that I am mean, produced by his experience of not being allowed to play with the lawn mower? That is, is the atheistic reaction to evil a case in which experience produces a *reasonable* belief?

The belief about the tree is made reasonable by a faculty or way of knowing—namely, vision. Our minds or brains can take visual experiences and turn them into reasonable beliefs about our environment. With this in mind, I say that the atheistic reaction would be reasonable only if our minds or brains could somehow turn the awareness of (or emotional reactions to) evil into the reasonable belief that God does not exist. If we are not constructed in that way—if we don't have a way of producing reasonable beliefs like that—then the atheistic reaction is not reasonable.

I do *not* say that atheism is reasonable only if we are made so that the awareness of evil generates a reasonable belief that God does not exist. There are lots of ways atheism might be made reasonable, none of which rely on our being made like that. For example, you could have a compelling argument for atheism. Or you could be reasonable in taking things on your parents' say-so and they might say "there is no God." And so on. So I am not saying that atheists must have some "special faculty" to be reasonable.

What then am I saying? I am saying that the *atheistic reaction to evil* is reasonable only if we are constructed in such a way that the awareness of evil produces the belief that God does not exist and also makes that belief reasonable. I am saying that forming the belief "God does not exist" *simply in reaction to how evil strikes you* is reasonable only if we have some mechanism that makes such beliefs reasonable.

And I deny we have any such mechanism. Where would it come from? If there is a God, our mental abilities ultimately come from him. But presumably he would not have constructed us so that the mere awareness of evil produces the reasonable belief that God does not exist. If there is no God, then all of our belief-producing mechanisms are constructed by naturalistic evolution—evolution in which blind forces work, unguided by the hand of God. Given this story of our development, it is not plausible that we have evolved with a special ability, when confronted with evil, to *just see* that there is no God. To insist that we did evolve with this ability would be like insisting that we evolved with an ability, when confronted with evil, to *just see* that there is no plant life on Mars!

So, whether or not God exists, it is not plausible that we have the ability to just see, in reaction to evil, that there is no God. And so the atheistic reaction is not produced by anything analogous to our faculty of vision, a faculty that allows us to just see, in reaction to certain visual experiences, that there is a tree in front of us. Thus I think the atheist should not accord any weight at all to her reaction to evil; she should not think that her reaction to evil makes it reasonable to deny God's existence. In this way, I take the atheistic reaction to evil to be unreasonable.

How does U2's reaction fare? It depends. Suppose, first of all, that atheism is true. Suppose there is no God. Then it seems like we are not able, in the face of evil, to produce reasonable beliefs about heaven. If atheism is true, then it seems that U2's reaction is instead a coping mechanism, a turning to comforting fantasy when the real world is too awful to face. If atheism is true, then I say that U2's reaction is unreasonable.

But suppose atheism is false. Suppose God exists. Suppose also that God has created us with the ability to know various things. (Whether he used evolution to create us, or some other means, is not relevant.) For example, God made us so that, when we experience the visual sensation of a tree in front of us, we form the belief that there is a tree there. Because this is how we are made, and because God did a good job in making us, our belief that there is a tree is reasonable.

Suppose, further, that God does not merely want us to know about trees. Suppose that God loves us and wants us to know about him. As a result, suppose that God has created us so that certain circumstances give rise to convictions about God. For example, suppose that God has made us so that when we hold a newborn baby, some of us are just struck with the conviction that God is good. Or consider what Bono says to God in "All Because of You": "I saw you in the curve of the moon / In the shadow cast across my room / You heard me in my tune / When I just heard confusion."

## Seeing God in Evil

Our question is not primarily whether we can see God in a baby or in the curve of the moon. It is whether we can see God in evil. So suppose that God has created us so that when outraged by the evil in this world we sometimes find ourselves believing that God will someday make all right. Because this is how we are made, and because God did a good job in making us, this belief—no less than beliefs produced by vision—is reasonable. In this way, the experience of evil becomes not a road to atheism, but instead a kind of religious experience in which God draws us closer to himself. And we are drawn even closer when we act in love to oppose evil.

XTC reacts to evil in one way, U2 in another. There is an important way in which XTC's reaction—the atheistic reaction—is not reasonable. For the atheistic reaction to evil has no independent force in making atheism reasonable. On the other hand, U2's reaction might be reasonable. If God really does exist and has made us to know him, then the most reasonable reaction to evil includes the conviction that God will one day heal all the sick, feed all the hungry, and raise all the dead.

# 8
# U2, Feminism, and Ethics of Care

JENNIFER McCLINTON-TEMPLE and
ABIGAIL MYERS

"If I could, through myself, set your spirit free / I'd lead your heart away / See you break, break away / Into the light and to the day:" these lines from "Bad" tell of a soul trapped in addiction and the speaker's pain in being unable to save that soul himself. He is, as philosopher Nel Noddings would say, "one-caring." In other words, the speaker is not working from an egocentric position, he is clearly thinking of others first. Nor is he simply projecting outwards from himself. He is instead, receiving the other into himself, placing the connection between himself and the other person at the center of his ethical decision making process. He recognizes the pull of temptation, however, by acknowledging that to resist he must remain "wide awake" himself.

There is no condemnation here, only commiseration and compassion. The impression could even be called maternal, as the speaker's evident pain upon the addict's destruction is certainly comparable to that a mother has for her child. But "maternal" implies "woman," doesn't it? And Noddings's "Ethics of Care" is a feminine approach to ethics. Are U2 feminine? Are they feminists? In this chapter, we'll look at the philosophical and political implications of the label "feminist," in our consideration of U2's ethical stance.

## Rock 'n' Roll, Feminism, and U2

In "Tryin' to Throw your Arms Around the World," U2 repeats Australian philosopher Irina Dunn's famous quote, "A woman needs a man like a fish needs a bicycle." Can we take this to mean that U2, through its music, supports feminism? Could we say that they, again through their music, actually *are* feminists? Rock music does not have a very good track record where feminism and feminist issues are concerned. Rock 'n' roll, or so we have been told, goes hand in hand with sex and drugs. Rock stars (the male ones at least), with their recreational drugs and their flocks of nubile groupies, certainly seem unlikely feminists. In general, rock music has not been a vehicle for breaking down traditional gender roles—though people like Freddie Mercury and David Bowie certainly broke down barriers, they were the exceptions. Nor has rock 'n' roll been an especially friendly place for a feminine point of view. On the contrary, with all those phallic guitars, driving beats, and suggestive songs about women, rock music is more often than not, a man's world.

From the beginning, however, U2 was different in this respect. Even with their first professional performances in Dublin in 1980, the crowd sensed that something was different about this band's view point. They inadvertently developed a large following among the gay community, who felt drawn to rock lyrics about adolescence, sex, and confusion that were, for once, not from an overtly masculine point of view. As their career moved forward, U2 would continue to sing in a non-gender specific way that would speak to many people all at once. When they did sing about women, as in "Two Hearts Beat as One," from *War*, the result is far from rock cliché. Neither explicitly sexual nor sentimental, "Two Hearts" has a quick tempo and although it seeks a funky feel, it never quite gets there. The song soars in the stratosphere, far away from the earthy sexiness one might expect of an ode penned to a new wife on honeymoon. Lyrically, it speaks of how he "can't stop the dance," and how he feels stymied and confused, but not by her, by everything else. Their relationship, he is sure about. In the twenty-five years that U2 has been recording, very few of their songs have addressed a woman, or a relationship with a woman so unambiguously.

In general, then, U2 do not address women in their songs, nor do they sing about women in a way that is either objectifying or idealizing. This does put them against the grain in the rock tradition. It's hard to find a song that *isn't* about women in the early Beatles catalog, and even with their more lyrically sophisticated later works, women are still very much present ("I

Want You (She's So Heavy)," "Something," "Oh! Darling"). The Rolling Stones's proclivity for singing about women can probably go without saying.[1] U2's contemporaries continue the pattern. In the Top 100 Singles of 1987, the year *The Joshua Tree* was released, "With or Without You" (which some have argued is about a woman and some have argued is about God; with lyrics like "see the thorn twist in your side," either is possible) and "I Still Haven't Found What I'm Looking For," are nestled in with "I Want Your Sex" (George Michael), "The Lady in Red" (Chris De Burgh), "(I Just) Died in Your Arms Tonight" (The Cutting Crew), and "U Got the Look" (Prince). So U2 does not typically write about women—and that's fairly unusual in the world of rock and roll. Is this because they are feminists?

This question isn't a philosophical question, it's a political one. When someone is labeled "a feminist," it usually means that they support certain causes, most prominently equal rights and the specific changes that go along with that such as equal representation, equal pay, and equal treatment on the job. "Feminists" are typically thought to be unconcerned with the domestic sphere, with what goes on in the home. They want not, as Hillary Rodham Clinton famously said, to stay home and "bake cookies." But this is simply a stereotype. Feminism is, to be sure, concerned with equality—but not just on the job, and not just for women, and this is where we would like to turn the question of U2's feminism from a political into a philosophical one. Politically, the members of U2 are not overtly feminist. There are no speeches from the stage defending women's rights or damning the patriarchy. Philosophically, however, they are indeed feminists. Consider how the music of U2 portrays the world and the responsibilities of human beings within that world.

In the book *Women's Ways of Knowing*, Mary Belenky and her co-authors examine how women gather, process, and impart knowledge, and whether or not one can claim there is a female or feminine epistemology. In other words, they wanted to know if women's ways of knowing are significantly different from men's. The authors of this text are careful not to essentialize, or

---

[1] The Who, a band U2 has often claimed as an important influence, did not sing often about women either, but perhaps that is one of the reasons U2 counts them as such an influence.

to claim that particular ways of thinking are essential to being female, but they do identify certain ways of understanding the world that seem to, at least, lean toward the feminine. One that is especially important to this discussion is "connected knowing." Belenky and her colleagues claim that those who are "separate knowers" rely upon external, impersonal procedures for establishing the truth, whereas for "connected knowers," truth emerges through care.[2] The way connected knowers arrive at the truth, how they know what they know, has to do with their relationship with the object of knowing, which may or may not be a person. The lyrics of "One Step Closer," from *How to Dismantle an Atomic Bomb* make clear the speaker's search to know, or his search for the truth. He speaks in multiple metaphors that highlight how difficult it is for human beings ever to grasp meaning, and to know for certain that meaning represents a universal truth. He laments being "under a bridge in a rip tide / that's taken everything I call my own." His relationships with those that he may call his own give his life meaning. The speaker seems to imply that isolation is akin to death, and only when he is connected, whether that connection be positive or negative, does he feel alive. He says, "The heart that hurts / is a heart that beats."

Other songs, especially three from *All that You Can't Leave Behind*, emphasize the importance of connection in terms of how one sees the world. "When I Look at the World," and "Kite," both have the speaker finding meaning by looking through the eyes of others, and "Beautiful Day" extols the connectedness of all of us in our search for happiness. "Connected knowing," is an important component of the ethics of care, for how we *know* helps us develop our ethics and make decisions based on those ethics. Connected knowing points us toward ethics of care, and not toward other ethical systems, because it helps us resist universality and abstraction. For instance, "Beautiful Day," was written in response to the Jubilee 2000 effort to cancel the unpayable debt of the world's poorest countries. The United States had recently committed to the cancellation of $435 million dollars of debt, and Bono was celebrating

---

[2] Mary Field Belenky, Blythe McVicker Clinchy, Nancy Rule Goldberger, and Jill Mattuck Tarule, *Women's Ways of Knowing* (New York: Basic Books, 1986), p. 102.

that fact in this song.[3] But the way he chooses to extol the virtues of debt relief is significant. He speaks of finding someone to whom you can "lend a hand / in return for grace." We should cancel the debt because we are all connected, not because, as a utilitarian might say, because it would mean the greater good for the greatest number of people.

Utilitarianism, like other ethical systems, relies on a litmus test for making moral decisions. Ethics of care, on the other hand, is a method for making moral decisions which places particular emphasis upon the principle that people should look out for and protect one another, given the *particulars* of relationships between persons involved in a given situation and the feelings of those *particular* persons. These concerns, a care ethicist[4] would argue, have pre-eminence over rules, laws, and universal principles of justice. Other ethical theories do, of course, consider feelings, concerns, and relationships between human beings, but only care ethics both makes these concerns central and eschews universality and abstraction. Care ethics began as a descriptive system of ethics (a system that attempts to explain how and why people act), and not as a prescriptive system of ethics (a system which sets out to recommend how people should act), such as utilitarianism. It was born not from philosophy, but from the cultural psychology in Carol Gilligan's groundbreaking 1982 study, *In a Different Voice,* which, through Gilligan's study of abortion, examined how thousands of women made moral decisions.[5] Yet other feminist thinkers and philosophers took up the cause of the ethic of care to formulate

---

[3] Niall Stokes, *U2 into the Heart: The Stories Behind Every Song* (New York: Thunder's Mouth, 2001), p. 147.

[4] Here a "care ethicist" is not only an ethicist oriented in the tradition of care, but is also any individual who employs principles of care in making ethical decisions. The term "care thinker" is sometimes similarly used.

[5] Gilligan's *In a Different Voice* (Cambridge, Massachusetts: Harvard University Press, 1993), the touchstone for any work in the field of care ethics that came after it, was born from Gilligan's dissatisfaction with the moral development theories of Kohlberg and Erikson, which had both been formulated from studies examining only men. Gilligan's study found that women's motivations for moral decisions were based less in laws and societal conventions, but in their personal relationships and the emotions attached. Gilligan was careful to point out that the ethical theory she presented, which came to be known as "care ethics," was not *necessarily* gendered; although women more frequently employed it, men could and did employ it as women sometimes employed more masculine ethics.

an alternative to other ethics, which were seen as analytical, cold, and detached from real relationships and ethical situations. Most other ethical systems fall roughly into two categories: they prescribe adhering to independent moral rules or duties or they attempt to focus on the consequences of an action in an objective way.[6]

Care ethics from its outset outraged as many feminists as it delighted because it seemed to reinforce the notion that most women are "nurturers," perhaps even essentially so, and seemed to deny women the impartiality and rationality that accompany ethics of justice and utilitarian ethics. Carol Gilligan herself refuted this charge later, saying, "My critics equate care with feelings, which they oppose to thought, and imagine caring as passive or confined to some separate sphere. . . . The title of my book was deliberate; it reads, 'in a *different* [emphasis Gilligan's] voice', not 'in a woman's voice'" ("Reply," p. 209). This crucial distinction between "care ethics" and "women's ethics" has a direct impact on our discussion of the ethics of U2, as this (admittedly predominantly *feminine*) ethic is, ultimately, gender-blind.

Gilligan's work was a direct response to the moral theory of Lawrence Kohlberg, who, in the early 1970s, developed a famous theory of moral development which borrowed from the work of American philosopher John Dewey and Swiss psychologist Jean Piaget. Kohlberg's classifications proceed in this manner: preconventional morality (which contains Stage 1, obedience and punishment orientation, and Stage 2, instrumentalism/exchange); conventional morality (which contains Stage 3, "good boy/good girl" orientation, and Stage 4, law and order orientation); and post-conventional morality (which contains Stage 5, social contract orientation, and Stage 6, principled conscience orientation).[7]

Gilligan suspected this description of moral development might not be all-encompassing, and was particularly interested

---

[6] Ethics systems that prescribe adhering to independent moral rules or duties can be called deontological. An example is Immanuel Kant's "categorical imperative," which states that we should act only accordance with what we believe should be universal. In other words, if an action can only be counted as ethical if it would still be acceptable for everyone, in every situation. Ethics systems that focus on consequence are teleological; utilitarianism, as described above, is an example.

[7] Quoted in Barger, "A Summary of Lawrence Kohlberg's Stages of Moral Development." http://www.nd.edu/~rbarger/kohlberg.html.

in Kohlberg's third stage—what Robert Barger calls the "good boy/girl" stage—as Kohlberg interpreted it as seeking approval for one's actions and attempting to make everyone involved in a particular situation happy. She doubted that many women, particularly the ones involved in her study, followed Kohlberg's stages (*Voice*, p. 11). She theorized instead that the women in her study seemed to undergo three main stages of moral development, beginning with stage one (characterized by caring exclusively for the self and concentrating on survival), continuing through stage two (judging stage one behavior to be selfish and caring only for others) and reaching fruition in stage three (in which care becomes a self-chosen principle and one realizes the interdependency between the self and others). "The fact of interconnection," Gilligan observes about stage three, "informs the central, recurring recognition that just as the incidence of violence is in the end destructive to all, so the activity of care enhances both others and self" (*Voice*, p. 74).

Nel Noddings says that in ethics of care, "at the foundation of moral behavior is feeling or sentiment" and that further, there is a "committment to remain open" to that feeling or sentiment.[8] Unlike other ethical systems, ethics of care will not justify itself by invoking an abstract concept such as justice or duty, nor will it ever choose the lesser of two evils because that would produce the best consequences for the most people. Instead, a care ethicist demands that we justify "not caring," and believes that we are obliged to see everyone, everywhere as "one-caring" before judging his or her actions.

## So What Does This Have to Do with U2?

Is it possible that the songs written and performed by U2 demonstrate the ethics of care? Gender is a flexible category for U2, as the band has flirted with the feminine from its earliest days. It seems likely that U2 could embrace a more traditionally feminine take on ethics.

The group's work on behalf of the sick, poor, and forgotten of the world might come immediately to mind. The average

---

[8] Nel Noddings, *Caring: A Feminine Approach to Ethics and Moral Education* (Berkeley: University of California Press, 1984) p. 92.

person's idea of U2 might boil down to "I Still Haven't Found What I'm Looking For" and a mental picture of an unsmiling, sunglassed Bono rambling on about debt relief and AIDS in Africa. This alone makes the band unique among its contemporaries (although other artists and bands have occasionally come along for the ride, and Coldplay's Chris Martin is quickly becoming one of the better-known advocates of debt relief in the music world).

But what interests us here is not the efforts the band members undertake *outside* the music, but rather the way U2's *songs* demonstrate this ethics of care. One way U2 do this is by writing and performing songs that deal with the lives, and deaths, of real people. Perhaps growing up in a war-torn Ireland has something to do with this; perhaps the members of U2 have known and seen too many people whose lives have been destroyed by blind adherence to the grand notions that many care ethicists reject. One obvious example of this is in "Peace on Earth":

> They're reading names out over the radio
> All the folks the rest of us won't get to know:
> Sean and Julia, Gareth, Ann, and Breda
> Their lives are bigger than any big idea.

Bono commented on this song:

> ["Peace on Earth"] was written literally on the day the Omagh bomb [a car bomb planted by an Irish paramilitary group that killed twenty-nine people in August 1998] went off, right then. . . . In Ireland, when they read out the names of the people who died on the six o'clock news, the city just came to a complete standstill. . . . People were just weeping in cars, on O'Connell Street, all over the place. It was really a trauma for most people—because not only was it the destruction of lives, it was the destruction of the peace process. . . . It was certainly the lowest day of my life, outside of personal losses. I couldn't believe it, that people could do that.[9]

How does this single instance, a mention of a few names within a song that laments centuries of violence and conflict in the

---

[9] Niall Stokes, *U2 into the Heart: The Stories Behind Every Song* (New York: Thunder's Mouth, 2001), p. 156.

name of nationalism, convey an orientation in an ethic of care? The names in and of itself—the pause to reflect on individual lives—encourages the listener to understand this senseless tragedy in terms that are inescapably personal, unavoidably intimate. In the spaces between the names, the listener imagines the individuals as parents, siblings, children, friends. Recall Gilligan's comments about interconnection between persons: an understanding of interconnection helps people to avoid violence and encourages them to care for each other, enriching both the self and the others for whom one cares. Names do not arise organically for individuals; they are chosen by parents, godparents, clergy, or friends. The mere naming of a name calls forth recognition of caring relationships. The pain that Bono mentions, at hearing the names of the individuals killed, reflects an intimate understanding of interconnection and a feeling of repugnance toward violence—indispensable for any care ethicist.

U2 personalize war, violence, and nationalist conflict similarly in "Van Diemen's Land," one of the few U2 songs that Bono did not have a hand in writing. The song is an ode to John Boyle O'Reilly, an Irish poet deported to Australia (then a penal colony) in 1848 for his part in an attempt to rebel against the British rulers of Ireland. This attempted uprising came at the climax of the Great Famine, in which potato crops in Ireland failed for several years in a row while the British continued to export the plentiful crops being grown in Irish fields. Over a million Irish died and many more emigrated. "Van Dieman's Land," as written and sung by The Edge, is not, however, an anti-British ode. It speaks instead of intimacy and connectedness, of the elements closest to the poet's heart: "It's a bitter pill I swallow here / to be rent from one so dear." But the last verse best illuminates the song's care ethics: "Still the gunman rules and widows pay / A scarlet coat now a black beret / They thought that blood and sacrifice / Could out of death bring forth a life."

The speaker notes that the scarlet coats worn by the Fenian rebels in the nineteenth century have merely been traded for the berets of the modern-day Irish Republican Army and ends the song with the point that no amount of justice or sense of duty can justify violence and intimidation. Other schools of ethics might allow for the events described in "Van Dieman's Land." For instance, one could easily argue from a utilitarian perspective that transporting criminals from England to Australia was ethical, because it was from the greater good of England. In addition, while a Kantian perspective would condemn the bombing itself, it might allow support of the position of the IRA, that Ireland be a free and united country. Kant's categorical imperative only asks that we act in such a way that we could rationally support everyone acting, without exception. Members of the IRA would, one presumes, support this kind of nationalism in any organization. U2, however, in "Van Dieman's Land," "Please," and their most famous song directed at the conflict in Northern Ireland, "Sunday Bloody Sunday," will not take sides. This latter song is, as Bono used to say when introducing it in concert, "not a rebel song."

U2 will not praise the IRA (or any other perpetrators of violence) as "rebels with a cause." That doesn't mean they don't extol the virtues of others we might consider rebellious. *The Unforgettable Fire* memorably and eloquently eulogizes the Reverend Dr. Martin Luther King, Jr. in "Pride (In the Name of Love)" and "MLK." Bono praises the work of Bishop Desmond Tutu, an anti-apartheid activist in South Africa and recipient of the Nobel Peace Prize, in the live version of "Silver and Gold" from *Rattle and Hum*. "Walk On," from *All that You Can't Leave Behind*, is dedicated to Aung San Suu Kyi, the Burmese activist who worked steadily for peace and reconciliation in her homeland even while under house arrest by a military junta. "New Year's Day" was inspired by the Polish Solidarity movement, and "Mothers of the Disappeared," from *The Joshua Tree*, empathizes with the mothers of the victims of "disappearances" in El Salvador.

U2 grew up confronted by the very personal ravages of war and nationalist conflict, but there are other influences on the ethic behind many of U2's songs. Bono, the band's primary lyricist, lost his mother at a young age, and has expressed the grief from the loss in several songs. Most obviously and from the band's outset, Bono says in "I Will Follow":

> A boy tries hard to be a man
> His mother takes him by his hand
> When he stops to think, he starts to cry
> Oh, why?

It may be waxing a bit too psychological to speculate that the band's many quests to save the world from various evils all stem from the loss of Bono's mother. But it may not be entirely use-less, either, to wonder if perhaps the image of "following" his mother might not have more than one implication. After all, care ethics is, though perhaps not a "woman's" ethic, nevertheless a somewhat more traditionally feminine ethic, at least in the way most of us are accustomed to conceiving femininity (though certainly femininity is, at least partially, a socially constructed notion). Most notably, Sara Ruddick has pointed out[10] that care ethics is tightly linked to motherhood. All by itself, this excerpt from "I Will Follow" is, like many U2 lyrics, probably deliberately vague. But when placed in the context of the band's body of work and the context of Bono's biography, it is plausible to suggest that the longing for a mother might inspire one to emulate, or at least possess great esteem for, in some ways, a mother-figure.

The absence of a mother figure pops up often in U2's song catalog,[11] but it is one of their most recent songs, always explicitly dedicated to Bono's father, that perhaps best shows ethics of care at work. In "Sometimes You Can't Make It on Your Own," Bono speaks of caring for his ailing father, of "tak[ing] some of the punches" for him as he battled cancer. The song is not a sweet ode to a great dad. Anger and resentment surface throughout, with lines such as "it's you when I don't pick up the phone," "a house doesn't make a home." But Bono speaks consistently as one-caring. He wants his father to know he is not alone, and that above all, he will be there to care for him. In the stirring bridge to the song, Bono sings,

> I know that we don't talk
> I'm sick of it all
> Can you hear me when I sing?
> You're the reason I sing

Each word of the line "Can you hear me when I sing?" is emphasized as he gradually sings higher and higher notes, ending in a stunning final word, "sing," followed by the claim that his father is the reason why he sings. What makes this passage so powerful, and what makes it exemplary of a care ethic, is

---

[10] *Maternal Thinking: Towards a Politics of Peace* (New York: Ballantine, 1989).
[11] "I Will Follow," "Lemon," and "Mofo," are a few obvious examples.

that this passage resists universalization, by eschewing the usual metaphors employed by songwriters. It simply speaks of this relationship, at this moment in time. This song is not open to interpretation, at least not in the way other songs about fathers and sons might be. It is a literal depiction of Bono's relationship with his father, and because it is so literal and so honest, it highlights the importance of that relationship, putting care above all else, above anger, above Bono's persona as a singer, and above the fans. He refuses to allow us to sing along with him, both because of the content of the lyrics and the range of the notes, and thereby demonstrates an ethic of care.

Other ethical systems would most likely arrive at the same conclusion here: that Bono should take care of his dying father. However, other systems would have different reasons, abstract, universally applied reasons, for reaching this conclusion. For instance, Christian ethics would tell us that it is our duty to "Honor thy Father and Mother," the Fourth Commandment. A Utilitarian perspective might advise Bono that for the sake of his own children, kindness and care given at the end of his father's life will set a good example. Only ethics of care foregrounds the individual, particular relationship between the two men as the basis for action and decision.

Obviously, U2 isn't a collective of feminist ethicists playing sold-out arenas just to pay the bills. But U2's status as *bona fide* "rock stars" makes this evident commitment to an ethic of care in the band's music and life even more engaging. They reject the classical trappings of the rock life, eschewing the meaningless sex and rampant drug use in favor of messages that a Carol Gilligan or a Nel Noddings could get behind: *War's worst wounds are reserved for the innocent. There is no excuse for extreme poverty, for starvation, for death from treatable disease. Women are to be treated with respect and love.*

It's a testament to how care ethics can compel anyone and everyone that the tenets of care ethics can be embraced, sung about, and even lived by wealthy, successful white men. In this way, U2 are great spokesmen for care ethics by weaving compassion, gentleness, and connected knowing into the fabric of rock and roll. They make maternal thinking and feminine ways of thinking loud, rhythmic, catchy, even *cool*. They very clearly suggest that caring is responsible and significant in and of itself, not because it satisfies an obligation or duty or because it helps us follow a preset rule. This is unmistakably a principle rooted in feminist philosophy. Maybe, with these messages in their music, U2 plant in their audience the seeds of new ethical thought in line with what care ethicists have had in mind all along. If it takes a rock band to do it, well, ethics, too, can move in mysterious ways.

# 9
# Why Listen to U2?

CRAIG DELANCEY

Because you like their music, of course. But my question—and perhaps your question, as you pick up this book and wonder, what could U2 tell me about *philosophy,* or what could philosophy tell me about *U2?*—is also: why listen to what they have to sing about and what they have to say? Why listen to their concerns about Irish warfare or African debt or American civil rights? There's the rub.

The answer, I'm about to argue, is that there is no special reason why you should listen to U2—but there's no special reason why you shouldn't, either. In fact, all things weighed properly, you may find you have, for some issues, more reason to listen to U2 than you have to listen to most other people trying to convince you of one thing or other. U2 may be less susceptible to some kinds of corruption, and they may be more visionary, than most of what you hear and see. To make this clear, we need to consider for a moment the nature of corruption and vision and passion and—most importantly—the nature of reason.

## Reason

Practical reason is about making the right decisions in order to accomplish the goals that you have. It probably is, or at least should be, also about having the right goals. Having reason in part amounts to knowing what to believe, and what not to believe. It also in part amounts to feeling the right feelings.

But, perhaps, in our time practical reason should be most concerned with evaluating the reports that surround and over-

whelm us. We hear or read many kinds of claims, and sometimes it's obvious how to evaluate them, how to decide whether
they deserve our attention or belief. We can check scientific
claims with science, mathematical claims with mathematics,
arguments with logic. But sometimes we do not have any obvious way to evaluate a claim. Many claims are simply reports—
observations about things others claim to have seen and that we
have no way to check. Then we are left wondering about the
source. U2 made it clear in a song like "Mothers of the
Disappeared" that they believed things were bad in Latin
America, where the mothers of the song observe:

> Midnight, our sons and daughters
> Were cut down and taken from us
> Hear their heartbeat
> We hear their heartbeat[1]

But about the same time many newspapers told us things in
Chile or Argentina or Columbia were getting better, if they were
not already grand. Whom should we have believed? If Bono
suggests in an interview that third world debt is killing people,
but The World Bank insists their loans are doing good, whom
should we believe?

Deciding whom to believe is a pressing question in our time.
Today in America, a handful of large corporations, each controlled by a handful of little-known, extremely wealthy individuals, determines both directly and indirectly the vast majority of
what appears on television, on radio, or in the newspaper, and
has say over most of the books that get published. A very few
other corporations control what gets distributed. In the many situations where these corporations share a bias, all of the most
readily available sources of information in the United States will
echo that bias. The situation is little better in Europe, and
quickly becoming worse everywhere in the world. We are
drowning in two-hundred-plus TV channels and an army of gas-
bagging pundits and shockjock howlers and fifty-point upper-
case font catastrophic headlines, but most of these voices are
singing an identical tune. The "dissent" that appears on television or the newspaper is not a different melody, but an orches-

---

[1] "Mothers of the Disappeared," on *The Joshua Tree*.

trated counterpoint to the dominant theme. When we get swept up into that song, when it's the only thing we hear in our own heads even after the television is turned off, we are being not only deceived, but even in some sense reduced. We are made inauthentic.

This dire assessment is true of what claims to be fact. The situation of course is far worse for the majority of the claims we encounter, that are made by advertisers and by the ever-multiplying PR storm troopers. These two industries produce claims that are known to be lies by everyone, are crafted as lies explicitly by the people who create them, and yet, through some miraculous rebirth in our subcortical brains, come to have some strange power over us. U2 tried to satirize this with their album and tour *Pop,* and the failure of their humor to stick is an indicator of how hard it is to satirize commercialism: our cynicism is so deep that even mocking commercials and commercialism can be a kind of commercial. The band's observation that

> It's who you know that gets you through
> The gates of the playboy mansion.
> Then will there be no time for sorrow
> Then will there be no time for shame . . .
> Then will there be no time for pain.[2]

is earnestly critical, but at the same time one can easily imagine this being the advertising copy for a new reality show.

Knowing that a person has some motivation other than the dissemination of truth does not, of course, prove that what they say is wrong. To conclude that would be to commit what philosophers call the *genetic fallacy.* Whether a claim is true or false must be evaluated as best you can in light of the evidence you can gather. But, when your only or primary source of evidence is the reports of others, then a known bias should lead you to recognize that you should doubt that source. In fact, you should doubt as much as you can, since it is the omissions, and not distortions or lies, that are the most misleading factors, and only a very radical, and broad, critical sense can help protect you from manipulation via ignorance.

---

[2] "The Playboy Mansion" on *Pop.*

## **Authenticity**

I have said that the many claims that surround us are over-
whelmingly inauthentic. The philosopher Martin Heidegger had
a description for the kind of inauthenticity that comes from
adopting the superficial world view that our mass culture
repeats to us.[3] This mass tune, which has no singer but is sung
by all of us, is the voice of *Das Man,* or "The They." Heidegger
recognized that we want to relinquish responsibility to others, to
the spirit of our time. Life is easier this way: confronted with difficult and often painful questions like, "What should I believe?
What should I do? What should I be?" It is easiest to avoid these
questions altogether by adopting the answers that no one in particular but everyone in general seems to be offering. Answers
like, you should believe one of the two sides you see debated
before you, you should act like that person you see in that beer
commercial on TV, you should be a patriot. Or, sometimes, that
you should just be numb:

> Don't move
> Don't talk out of time . . .
> Don't think . . .
> Everything's just fine.[4]

Relinquishing these questions and concerns means you live
only inauthentically. In simplest terms, living inauthentically
means that there is some dishonesty at the core of the choices
that we make. The lie at the center may be so simple as to tell
yourself that these choices are yours. You cannot authentically
just follow along because you cannot escape these fundamental questions, you must answer them or you must lie to yourself in order to avoid a struggle with them. Heidegger thought
that inauthenticity, and our subservience to The They, was
something we naturally lapse into, something it is hard to
avoid and which we cannot always avoid. It seems a fair
assessment that Heidegger could not have foreseen how very
unified and global The They would grow to be (or, then again,
maybe he did: one of Heidegger's last public statements was,

---

[3] See Martin Heidegger, *Being and Time* (New York: Harper and Row, 1962).
[4] "Numb," on *Zooropa.*

"Only a god can save us"[5]). It becomes harder and harder to be authentic as our global economy homogenizes culture.

In this environment, this world of aggressive and over-whelming reduction of vision and voice, few things are more important to our own souls, and even to our long term safety, than finding authentic voices. Even a mistaken voice can serve us well, by making us see and confront our assumptions, and investigate which of these are well kept, which well discarded. You need to find that novelist whose independent publisher cannot afford to pay to have the book put out front by the door of the megalobookstore and that Walmart refuses to stock. You need to read that news journal from the other side of the ocean. You need to read those Spiegelman comics that the *New Yorker* was too afraid to publish. And you need to listen to those musicians who are trying to keep themselves sincere.

Thus we arrive at the odd observation that some Rock artists—the Clash, Bruce Cockburn, Billy Bragg, Ani DiFranco, U2—may be some of the most authentic voices you can find. They may not have special knowledge about what they sing about, but, at their best, they've both thought about and they believe what they sing about for their *own* reasons. You can't say that of any advertiser or PR spokesperson or TV pundit, and you can say it of very few of the rest of those making noise or pictures out there. Rock 'n' roll has a tradition of a kind of inde-pendence. Sometimes this manifests as childish opposition to everything conventional, resulting in a kind of conventional pose of unconventionality (wake me up when that guy is done smashing his guitar . . .). But sometimes Rock and Roll just means that you were paid to sing, but not paid to sing what you sing—in the best cases, you started singing it before you had any hope of being paid for it.

I'd like to think U2 is one of the best of these voices. I'm con-fident none of these four men knows much about political eco-nomics, about civil rights history, or labor history, about AIDS vectors or conflict resolution. But I'm also confident that the people I see talking about those things on TV don't know much about them either, and those people on TV are being paid a

---

[5] "'Only a God Can Save Us': *Der Spiegel*'s Interview with Martin Heidegger", in *Philosophy Today* 20, pp. 267–285. (The interview was conducted in 1966 and origi-nally published in 1976.)

wage to say what they say, or often, implicitly, through self-censorship and the creation of the acceptable dimensions of public discourse, are paid to not say what they don't say. So, you've got at least as much reason, and probably more reason, to listen to Bono and the Edge and Larry and Adam as you do to listen to those shriekers on Fox "News."

We should note, of course, that the authenticity of Rock is doomed. Part of what allowed Rock to be authentic was that it began as a grass-roots movement—it started as a bunch of theys, not as The They. Another thing that allowed Rock to be authentic is that often people in positions to squash it didn't think Rock needed to be taken seriously. Like King Lear's fool, Rock once got away with singing the truth because it was dressed in a jester's clothes. Now, of course, truth's a dog that must to kennel. Rock Incorporated has become an extension of the same few corporations that control TV, radio, newspapers, and publishing. A rock star who expresses politically unacceptable sentiments on disk or in concert or even just home in an interview can be banned from the three-hundred-plus station Cumulus Broadcasting radio conglomonsterate, or have her CDs pulled off the shelf at the distribution-channel-choking Walmart, or face a PR-orchestrated record burning. That's the kind of pressure that you get in corporate news and publishing, and the flattening it causes there can only happen even more quickly and more effectively in Rock, where, let us be honest now, getting chicks and getting your face on MTV, not saving the Palestinians, are the primary motivations. To paraphrase Bono Vox, you should not trust rock stars, they are people who became rock stars because they were obsessed with watching themselves sing in the mirror. Even the most sincere rock star could at times honestly observe that "I must be an Acrobat to talk like this and act like that."[6]

Nonetheless, there are still some special moments of authenticity in Rock. And, given that pundits and newscasters are people who became pundits or newscasters because they were obsessed with watching themselves talk in mirrors, and the owners of news stations are people who are obsessed with watching their empires and their wallets grow, this sin of rock

---

[6] "Acrobat," on *Achtung Baby.*

stars is not one that singles them out for damnation. But it is important to be aware that authenticity is under threat in Rock at least as much as it is under threat in the other mass media and mass arts. One effect is that artists grow quiet about what they feel and believe. Another effect is that some artists become esoteric—they shroud their meaning behind double entendres. U2 has increasingly taken this latter course. A song like "Crumbs From Your Table" can be interpreted as a lament about a relationship gone sour, or a profound disappointment with the fearful selfishness of the United States after 9/11, after people around the globe rallied in support of its citizens: "I was there for you baby / When you needed my help / Would you deny for others / What you demand for yourself . . . ?" Such a double reading can get you past the corporate filter but simultaneously be a gesture of solidarity to the sentiments of those who feel the same but feel alone.

## Passion and Practicality

If you're not a graduate student in philosophy, you should well be thinking right now, *What is this guy on about? I don't listen to this stuff because I'm looking for another news source—I like the sound of it, man. I like the way it makes me feel.*

Exactly right. We philosophers would put that in a slightly different way. We might phrase it as a question: how does authentic insight—what we might call practical wisdom, or at least practical encouragement—come to have some purposefulness for us? How does it come to mean anything? Ultimately, how does it change us, and translate into action?

Practical reason is concerned with evaluating what we should believe. I have discussed some doubts we may have about sources, and also the crisis in authenticity. But these may not be the whole of reason. From the earliest beginnings of our efforts to struggle with these problems, many philosophers have recognized also that reasoning must be coupled with the right emotions or sentiments in order for intelligence to become practical wisdom. To lack emotions, to be numb, is to be unmoved. But one must also have the right emotions to be moved in the right way. A sentiment captured in one of U2's most famous lyrics: "One man come in the name of love / One man come and go / One come he to justify / One man to overthrow." This is a recognition that for King's political victory, it was love that mattered most, that moved King and his followers to do the right thing.

Plato thought of the soul of a human as a kind of thing we can see as having three parts or aspects: desires, passions, and reason. Desires and passions are essential, but they also must be in harmony, and must be managed by reason. In his great work, *The Republic,* Plato pictures a chariot with two horses and one driver: one horse is desire, the other passion, and the driver is reason.[7] Reason is pulled along and made effective by desire and passion, but without reason these horses may run wild, and run nowhere or to places that will do them or others harm. Plato's student Aristotle developed a different view but with a shared belief in the importance of our passions and desires.[8] For Aristotle, the good person is a person who fulfills his capabilities well, in the appropriate ways, and never to excess. Thus, anger may be a virtue when had in moderation and for the appropriate reasons. If you witness great injustice, you should feel angry, and this should drive you to right that wrong. Too little and rare anger makes you cold-hearted, and too much and too frequent anger makes you temperamental. The virtuous person strikes a mean in her capabilities, avoiding too little or too much.

Surely Aristotle was correct to observe that righteous anger is both righteous, and necessary. The bitter sentiments of *War*'s "Sunday Bloody Sunday" — that "I won't heed the battle call, It puts my back up, puts my back up against the wall" — may be the right and even best response to a terrorism that loses sight of what it fights for. These words give us a visceral feel for the stupidity of war, and the inevitable terrorism of occupation. Consider the furious observations of cruelty in "Silver and Gold" on *Rattle and Hum*: "Broken back to the ceiling / Broken nose to the floor / I scream at the silence, it's crawling, / It crawls under the door." Such anger and horror may be the only sane response to the horrors that were perpetrated to maintain apartheid.

Rock seems also profoundly successful at evoking the mixture of anger and contempt that can keep you going in the face

---

[7] See Plato, *The Republic* (Indianapolis: Hackett, 1992).
[8] See Aristotle, *Nicomachean Ethics* (Indianapolis: Hackett, 2000).

of seemingly overwhelming opposition. "Walk On," from *All that You Can't Leave Behind*—the song which U2 wisely chose to sing at the support concert that followed 9/11—is one of the great examples:

> Walk on, walk on
> What you've got they can't deny it
> Can't sell it, or buy it.

A song like this, or the powerful closing sentiments of *Achtung Baby*'s "Acrobat," can help us feel motivated and empowered in the face of powers that want us to feel powerless. That is no small gift.

## Democracy and Utopia

Passions especially matter when we live together in a democracy. Not just democracy in the sense of finding your own authenticity in a monomaniacal commercial vision, but the good old practical sense of voting and bureaucracy and making laws. In *The Republic,* Plato describes an ideal city state—perhaps a place where the streets have no name. Plato does this because he is trying to answer the question, "What is justice?" He believes that justice is partly a political matter, and he also believes that it is easier to see justice in the relationships between people than it is to see it in any one person's soul, and so he concludes he can best describe and explore justice by describing a utopian political system. Plato's perfect state is one where a small group of wise kings lies to the people of the city in order to lead them most directly to a good life. All inappropriate art is censored, and a person's position in the city is partly determined by her aptitudes, as the kings discern them. These kings are unselfish rulers focussed upon the welfare of their city, and use their wisdom to defend and guide the city.

Yeah, right. Perhaps in Plato's time such a story could seem plausible. Plato's contemporaries were slave-owning plutocrats well convinced of their own superiority, and though Plato was as harsh a critic of his peers as anyone (albeit indirectly), he may have inherited an aristocrat's faith in the possibility of good dictatorship. Today, every American thinks he is an above average driver, of above average intelligence, and is more well liked than most people. Just so, each aristocrat has always believed that he was a model of good government. Perhaps this is a kind of inauthenticity, or lack of imagination, arising from the fact that rarely does one, like the boy confronting loss in "A Day without Me," have to see himself and what he's done from the outside. Such a view can be liberating but painful: "I started a landslide in my ego / Look from the outside / To the world I left behind."[9]

History—and statistics—teaches unequivocally that no one has the kind of wisdom Plato imagined for his rulers, and that no one should be trusted with that kind of power. The brilliance of the Enlightenment was the discovery that the safest way to avoid tyranny was to encourage each person to think— that is, to think well, with good reasoning—for herself. The brilliance of the birth of modern democracy, exemplified in the spirit of 1776, was that a government should be formed with checks and balances that ensure no one can become the "philosopher" king.

Some of us still believe in utopia, but utopia now becomes an ideal, something to measure against and strive for, and not a complete and incorrigible program to be enforced as soon as possible and at any cost. In fact, one essential difference between conservatism (in the classical sense—and, alas, classical conservatives are now as rare as Florida panthers) and the various historical movements that have been loosely labeled "the left," is that classical conservatives traditionally were anti-utopian, on the grounds that a very much better society is impossible, and utopianism encouraged impractical but potentially very dangerous political motivations. The political philosopher Edmund Burke, looking at the French Revolution, saw what he interpreted to be utopianism fostering chaos and violence, followed by disastrous dictatorship.[10] Those of us on the left take a different lesson from France of the 1790s: utopia cannot be enforced, but only fostered, and any vision of utopia may have to be revised. We ask, rhetorically, as U2 does in the eponymous song, "Is that all?"

---

[9] "A Day Without Me," on *Boy*.
[10] See Edmund Burke, *Reflections on the Revolution in France* (New York, Oxford University Press, 1999).

So, left or right, there is some consensus that democracy is our best method of governance. There are no noble lies, since lying is only motivated by a goal to acquire unjust power. There should be no or minimal coercion, since that too is often motivated by a goal to acquire unjust power. So, how do we change things? How do we make them better? We must share with people a vision, perhaps even a utopian vision, of a better world, and try to motivate them—try to make them feel as we do about that goal—to help us make it real. Or, sometimes, we want to share with them a vision of outrage or sorrow, to motivate them to oppose injustice. We must persuade others to see something that we believe that we see. We do this justly only when we are authentic and sincere. Put briefly: in a democracy, if you want to change the world, you may just have to sing to people.

U2 shares with us a vision of compassion and hope, and occasionally of fear and outrage. Songs like "Pride (In the Name of Love)" remind us of MLK's heroism and foster in us a desire to continue his mission. "Is that All?" and "I Still Haven't Found What I'm Looking For" share an honest spiritual longing that should shore up those who feel it too but are oppressed by the smug theoplutocracism of the 700 Club or the cult of violence of Timothy LaHaye. "Bullet the Blue Sky" betrays doubt about a nation that is loved. If you are pulled into these songs then you not only enjoy them, you are changed by them: you may find the strength to do something differently. In other words, because the craft of U2 is good, it can provide for us a vision, but also it can persuade us to feel as they do about that vision. They are important both because they are good artists and because their vision is different from the inauthentic visions we received from nearly everywhere else.

That is why you should listen to U2.

# 10

# "Until the End of the World": U2, Eschatology, and Heidegger's "Being-toward-Death"

V.S. BENFELL III

One of the fundamental questions, indeed the most fundamental question, of existential philosophy concerns death. How do we deal with the finiteness or the limitations of our existence; how do we confront the insuperable fact of our own mortality? Many of U2's songs address this very question, though they typically do so not by overtly discussing death but by evoking the language of Christian eschatology with its imagery of an "end time" and a millennial reign of peace. These songs, though, rather than encouraging us to seek some kind of clearly defined eschatology or doctrine about the end of the world—to predict, say, the battle of Armageddon or to warn us of an impending final judgment—instead push us to confront our own mortality and thus consider the nature of our own existence.

## Inauthentic and Authentic Existence

The German philosopher Martin Heidegger's understanding of how we as human beings should confront death provides a compelling context in which to consider U2's songs that concern the end. Heidegger (1889–1976) sought to create a revolution in philosophy by concentrating his philosophical inquiries on the central elements of ontology—the study of Being. Heidegger contended that philosophers had forgotten about this most central of all philosophical questions, and he was determined to revive it. The way into the question of Being, according to Heidegger, was through a consideration of human existence. Through a painstaking analysis of the way that a human being (or, to use Heidegger's German term, *Dasein*) exists, Heidegger came to a new understanding of human existence.

Heidegger insisted that as human beings we find ourselves *thrown* into our existence. That is, we have never known a moment when we were not part of a "world"; we have always found ourselves living in a particular moment in history, in a particular place, and in relationships with other human beings. We don't begin our lives with a blank slate, free to create our lives only as we desire, but we are constrained by the network of relationships and places rooted in a particular moment that defines our existence. This sense of always belonging to a given context is what Heidegger refers to as *thrownness.*

This state is aptly illustrated in Wim Wenders's movie, *Wings of Desire.* (*City of Angels*, a bad Hollywood remake, was done a few years later.) Wenders, a close friend and collaborator of Bono (he directed Bono's screenplay for *Million Dollar Hotel*), has frequently used U2's songs in his movies. This film concerns a group of angels who operate in Berlin, watching over the men and women in the city, reading their thoughts and trying to influence them. Their lack of rootedness in the world, however, prohibits them from exercising any direct influence, and they often appear frustrated by their impotence. Finally, one angel decides to become human, and his "fall" into humanity is portrayed quite literally, as he plummets to the earth. U2 refers to this event in their song, "Stay," which was written for the Wenders film *Faraway, So Close*, the sequel to *Wings of Desire*: "Three o'clock in the morning / It's quiet and there's no one around / Just the bang and the clatter as an angel runs to ground." When the angel finds himself on the earth, thrown, so to speak, into a given historical place and time, he learns to navigate his human life within the constraints of that moment. Whereas as an angel he was free to move from place to place, uninhibited by his physical and historical constraints, he is now defined by his place and time. Literally thrown into existence, he must operate within the possibilities offered by where he finds himself.

In a different manner, the song "Some Days are Better than Others" registers the fact of thrownness in an almost matter-of-fact way, describing the constraints of a day-to-day existence defined by our place in time and space. One verse thus notes, "Some days you wake up with her complaining / Some sunny days you wish it was raining," while a later verse notes, "Some days you wake up in the army." Other verses recount the limitations imposed by the situations in which we find ourselves: "Your skin is white but you think you're a brother / Some days are better than others."

This condition is inescapable, but it can have both positive and negative consequences. One possible negative consequence is that when we examine our lives carefully, we find that in our day-to-day existence, in what Heidegger calls our "average everydayness," we tend to forget ourselves in the preoccupations of our daily lives. U2 seems to allude to this process in "Gone": "You wanted to get somewhere so badly / You had to lose yourself along the way." But more than that, in forgetting ourselves we also abandon our selves over to others, showing an all too ready willingness to let others determine who we are, what we value, and how we live our lives. These "others" for Heidegger form a kind of impersonal, public self that absorbs us in our "average everydayness," and he refers to this public self with the impersonal the "they." This phrase sounds odd, but it accurately characterizes the way that we talk much of the time, when we want to cite an authority for something we say. *They* say that this movie is great. *They* have done studies that show that Vitamin C reduces the frequency of colds. This state of "average everydayness," in which we typically find ourselves, he labels *fallenness*.

> This "absorption in . . ." has mostly the character of Being-lost in the publicness of the "they." Dasein has, in the first instance, fallen away from itself as an authentic potentiality for Being its Self, and has fallen into the 'world.' "Fallenness" into the 'world' means an absorption in Being-with-one-another, in so far as the latter is guided by idle talk, curiosity, and ambiguity.[1]

Heidegger, then, sees our average, everyday existence as *inauthentic*—marked by a forgetfulness of our selves that manifests itself in our absorption in "idle talk" (a kind of chattering that fails to seek for truth), "curiosity" (an idle inquisitiveness that moves from one object to another with concern only for novelty), and "ambiguity" (the inability to distinguish between genuine and superficial understanding).

---

[1] Martin Heidegger, *Being and Time* (New York: Harper and Row, 1962), p. 220.

The first verse of the song "The Playboy Mansion" provides an apt illustration of this kind of inauthentic, fallen existence. In this song, the speaker associates the superficial aspects of modern consumerism with the most profound aspects of human existence, thus manifesting ambiguity. The speaker, it should be noted, is not the person Bono, but the fictional character created in the song: "If Coke is a mystery / And Michael Jackson, history / If beauty is truth and / Surgery, the fountain of youth . . . "

Coke is a "mystery" (presumably because of its secret formula), Michael Jackson is "history," and talk shows have replaced "confession." This song portrays consumerism as defining the ultimate truth for our culture, though the speaker seems both to want to embrace that culture and to stand outside of it from an ironic, mocking distance. This ironic portrayal of the inauthenticity of public existence is continued in the subsequent verses, where we learn that banks and casinos have replaced cathedrals, and chance has become the meaning of existence; it's a "kind of religion / Where you're damned for plain hard luck." In this song, then, public culture, of which the speaker both is and is not a part, embodies curiosity in Heidegger's sense—a continuous seeking for novelty without profundity. Furthermore, it shows ambiguity, as individuals seem unable to distinguish a talk show that appeals to our idle curiosity from a genuine religious confession, or Michael Jackson from the deeper meanings of human history. "The Playboy Mansion," shows us a culture where individuals are absorbed in the public self, "lost in the publicness of the 'they,'" and hence living an inauthentic life.

## The Being-toward-Death

What is Heidegger's answer for our common inauthenticity? He considers this question at length, proposing a way for us to pull ourselves out of our "average everydayness" through a realization of our own "finitude." That is, by coming face to face with our own death, we are forced to recognize the fact that we are limited beings, caught in time, indeed defined by time, and that we are responsible for our own existence. For Heidegger, death is "that *possibility which is one's ownmost, which is non-relational, and which is not to be outstripped*" (*Being and Time*, p. 294; all italics are Heidegger's). That is, I must come to the realization that my death is my own, that no one can die for me, and that I can never escape my death. Of course, we are all aware of this fact of death, but in our average everydayness, we tend to forget this fact about our lives, to cover it up, or to flee from it. "As falling, everyday Being-towards-death is a constant *fleeing in the face of death*" (p. 298). Generally, in fact, the "*'they' does not permit us the courage for anxiety in the face of death.*" Instead, the "they" helps us to flee by imagining some other end for our existence.

Again, "The Playboy Mansion" illustrates this process beautifully. In this song, the "end" envisioned is not death, but getting "through / The gates of that mansion" where there will be "no time" for "sorrow" or "shame," a kind of consumerist version of the Christian paradise. "The Playboy Mansion," that is, portrays a possible end for our existence. It is, however, an inauthentic end proposed to us by the "they" through television and other media, one that encourages us to flee from the fact of our own death. It is an infinite future in which existence is imagined as a beer commercial—a continuous experience of pleasure without care or anxiety, the very emotions that, it turns out, can help us on the way to authenticity.

What, then, is the answer for Heidegger to our fallenness or our being lost in the "they"? How can we move toward authenticity? For Heidegger, it is through an authentic "Being-toward-death," which requires an authentic notion of temporality, one that recognizes that, unlike the future imagined by "The Playboy Mansion," when there will be *no time* for sorrow or shame, an authentic future "reveals itself *as finite*" (*Being and Time*, p. 378). That is, when I realize not that everyone will die, but that *I* will die, that *my* existence is finite, then I can begin to break out of the complacency of the "they."

Heidegger describes this process as one that reveals itself through our "moods." Key to our awaking from our average everydayness is the mood Heidegger calls "anxiety." This mood involves my realization of both my own possibilities and my own finitude. While I usually float along through my existence, fleeing death, and displacing my freedom to choose onto the "they," there may come a time when I come to understand the fact of my own death and realize that I do not have to follow the "they." Although I find myself thrown into a given context, I nevertheless am able to choose. Indeed, my thrownness obliges me to choose, as the situation into which I have been thrown confronts me with clearly defined choices. For most of us, this realization, though, is not a comfortable one. It induces anxiety because I now come to the realization that not only can I choose to direct myself toward certain possibilities rather than others, but I *must* choose. In this sense, "anxiety individualizes. This individualization brings Dasein back from its falling, and makes manifest to it that authenticity and inauthenticity are possibilities of its Being" (p. 235).

The speaker in "Playboy Mansion" provides us with a good example of this anxiety. He experiences this anxiety, but the public "they" attempt to force him to repress it so that he does not come face to face with the fact of his own death. He admits, for example, that he senses that the "they" do not adequately speak for him, since he feels "damned for plain hard luck"; he also feels out of place since he "never did see that movie / Never did read that book." Nevertheless, the "they" push him to accept their image of an inauthentic end the "they" propagate, even though he "can't say why." The "they," furthermore, do not adequately account for his "pain"—the anxiety that keeps pushing him to break out of his inauthentic existence.

Let's imagine, then, that like the speaker of the "Playboy Mansion," I sense the inadequacy of the "they's" view of mortality and that this anxiety about my place within the world allows me to gain the sense that I am a finite creature who nevertheless has possibilities for which I am responsible, and leads me to the realization that I cannot escape either my responsibility or my place within the world. I must take actions and these actions will impact the human beings and the other entities that I encounter in the world. I must deal with the world, and I am responsible for how I deal with it. That is, we realize that we are ineluctably guilty, which is a fundamental condition of our thrown existence. Heidegger does not use "guilt" in its traditional sense. Rather, it refers to the emotion we experience when we come to the realization of our own finitude and our own responsibility. A reference to Heidegger's original German word may help us here. The word translated as "guilt," is "die Schulde," which can be rendered as either "guilt" or "debt." One way of thinking of Heidegger's guilt, then, is that in some sense we have a debt to the world and to other people who live in it. If we return again to U2's song

"Gone," we can see a reference to this condition: "You get to feel so guilty got so much for so little / Then you find that feeling just won't go away." The guilt in this song does not seem to arise from something that "you" did, but from the very fact of existence. The point here is not to overcome our guilt (an impossibility) but to become anxiously guilty, not repressing our guilt but willingly accepting it. In "Sunday Bloody Sunday," we see the kind of abdication of guilt that attends an inauthentic existence. We are "immune" from guilt or our debt to others since we do not even take the time to understand the situation in which we find ourselves. Instead, "fact is fiction and T.V. reality / And today the millions cry / We eat and drink while tomorrow they die."

As we seek, then, to become more authentic, Heidegger tells us that we must learn to cultivate an authentic "Being-toward-death," a genuinely finite understanding of the future that will enable us to liberate ourselves from the "they" and "their" inauthentic conception of the infinite future. Heidegger names this authentic attitude toward the future "anticipatory resoluteness," in that we are no longer simply abandoning ourselves to the "they," passing off our own responsibilities to the public self. Instead, we take an active stance of anticipation. Indeed, this authentic "future must first win itself, not from a Present, but from the inauthentic future" (*Being and Time*, p. 386). The winning of an authentic future seems to happen for Heidegger through the call of conscience, which brings us to a knowledge of our own guilt. We come to recognize that we are limited and thrown into the world and that we must take responsibility for that thrownness.

In "Last Night on Earth," U2 describes a woman who seems to gain an authentic temporality because of anxiety. She lives "like it's the last night on earth," because "She feels the ground is giving way / But she thinks we're better off that way." Anxiety is necessary for Heidegger because we are unable to "ground" our decisions on anything transcendent, since the transcendent (as embodied in a moral code that is true in all circumstances) is not available to us. Thus, as the woman in the song, we may begin to feel that the ground is giving way. If we come to an accurate assessment of our condition, though, we too will realize that this anxiety can help us to live authentically and not try to impose our responsibility on something transcendent. Thus, the woman living like it's the last night on earth is "not waiting on a Savior to come." She is instead fully aware of how limited her existence is, since "time is slipping / Slipping away." Once I accept how limited I am, I feel anxious, but this anxiety should lead me to accept that we are guilty; that is, I am responsible for the suffering I impose on the world, and I can no longer hide that responsibility from myself. I can no longer simply be born along by the "they," but I must confront my own individuality. In order for me to have an authentic Being-toward-death, I must, in Heidegger's terms, be "released from the Illusions of the "they" (p. 311). The call of conscience that brings all of this about must ultimately come from within me, but it may triggered by something outside of me, such as another person, someone authentic who is already resolute in his or her own Being-toward-death.

## Until the End of the World

U2's most overtly apocalyptic song can best be understood within this philosophical context. "Until the End of the World" evokes this very process of becoming authentic by liberating oneself from the "they" and winning an authentic future through a resolute Being-toward-death. Let's take a look at the song, verse by verse.

It opens with the reunion of friends. Someone ("I") addresses a long-lost friend ("you") and begins to reminisce about previous experiences together.

> Haven't seen you in quite a while
> I was down the hold, just passing time
> Last time we met it was a low-lit room
> We were as close together as a bride and groom
> We ate the food, we drank the wine
> Everybody having a good time
> Except you
> You were talking about the end of the world.

Typically, this song is seen as a soliloquy spoken by Judas to Christ, with this verse referring to the last supper.[2] One of the

---

[2] See, for example, the postings on the web site devoted to the meaning of U2's lyrics, http://hem.bredband.net/steverud/U2MoL/AB/endofworld.html, many of which interpret the song as referring to Judas and Christ.

reasons that U2's songs are so philosophically interesting, however, is that they are suggestive enough to exceed a reference to any one particular scenario. This song, that is, finds broader application than the existential situation of Judas.

This first verse evokes a party atmosphere in a "low-lit room" where everyone is "having a good time," seemingly caught up in the public self of the "they." The "I" also reveals himself as a part of this world of the "they"; since he last saw "you," he has been simply "passing time," certainly not resolute in anticipation of the future. The one exception to the public unity of the crowd at the party, however, is "you," who interrupts everyone's "good time" by "talking about the end of the world." On the one hand, we could begin to think that "you" is simply a spoilsport, a religious fanatic who insists on ruining everyone's fun by talking about a final judgment. Another possibility, though, and one that is borne out by the rest of the song, is that "you" is resolute in an authentic Being-toward-death and is trying to wake up the voice of the conscience of "I" so that he can free himself from simply losing his individuality within the public self of the "they."

In the second verse, though, we see that "I" remains in an inauthentic mode, failing to take responsibility for his own choices: "I took the money, I spiked your drink / You miss too much these days if you stop to think / You led me on with those innocent eyes / And you know I love the element of surprise / In the garden I was playing the tart / I kissed your lips and broke your heart / You, you were acting like it was the end of the world."

The allusions to the role of Judas are most overt in this verse, with the reference to a "garden" where "I kissed your lips" and thus betrayed "you" (though the claim that "I spiked your drink" seems out of place in that context), but again the song's deliberate lack of specificity makes its application much more general. The speaker's actions and his manner of acting, explicitly disclaiming responsibility for taking the money and spiking "your" drink because "you miss too much these days if you stop to think" shows someone caught up in the "they" self, unable or unwilling even to consider that he has responsibility for his actions. In the garden, he "plays" the tart, adopting a role that allows him to avoid confronting his own guilt and his own responsibility for the decisions he makes. Instead, he claims that his actions that resulted in breaking "your heart" were just a part of that role and thus unimportant. As listeners, we can all see ourselves in the speaker, floating along, passing time, playing roles, but without realizing that we should become more authentic and deliberately choose and thus take responsibility for our actions. "You," however, reacts like "it was the end of the world," demonstrating an authentic temporality by reacting in a way that may induce "I" to consider what he is doing in the context of an authentic Being-toward-death.

In the final verse, in fact, the "I" has recognized that his inauthenticity can no longer continue: "In my dream I was drowning my sorrows / But my sorrows they learned to swim / Surrounding me, going down on me . . . / I reached out for the one I tried to destroy."

The final verse reports one of "I"'s dreams, where he comes up against the fact that he can no longer continue as he has. He tries to "drown his sorrows," that is to avoid confronting them in the inauthentic manner of the "they," drinking so as to forget, to flee in the face of his own finitude. He finds, however, that he is no longer able to deal with his sorrows in this way, since they have "learned to swim." He has reached a crisis where he is ready to listen to the call of conscience, and he begins to think of someone in his past whose authentic existence calls to him now. In addition, he recognizes that his actions have harmed "you," and so he begins also to recognize his responsibility for having tried to destroy "you." He reaches out, therefore, for this authentic one, whose actions and existence have been defined by an authentic future, a resolute Being-toward-death that manifests itself in a resolute anticipation or a kind of active waiting. We must assume, that is, that "you" is not waiting passively, in the manner of the "they" who does not take an active choice in anything; instead, we must assume, because "you said you'd wait until the end of the world," that "you" has deliberately chosen to wait in resolute anticipation.

The song, in other words, has little or nothing to do with traditional eschatology; we nowhere hear about an apocalyptic scenario or final judgment of world history. Instead, the "end of the world" gains meaning solely in an individual, existentialist sense. The speaker is confronted not with the imminent end of world history, but with a heightened sense of anxiety in his sorrows that cannot be dismissed. The end of the world, that is, is the end of his own world, which, when he gets sight of it in an authentic way, disposes him for change. His new-found anxious guiltiness prepares him to accept his finitude and become an authentic individual. In this and other songs, then, U2 evokes apocalyptic, eschatological themes not to warn us of the end of the world or of an impending judgment but to call us toward a more authentic existence.

# PART III

# Three Chords and the Truth

## Meaning, Knowledge, and the Power of Music

# 11

# "This Music Changed the Shape of the World": U2 and the Phenomenological Understanding of Music

BÉATRICE HAN-PILE

Bono once recalled an experience of listening to music in the following way: "this music changed the shape of the room. It changed the shape of the world outside the room; the way you looked out the window and what you were looking at."[1] This is a remarkable way of describing music—one which challenges the main ways that philosophers have typically explained music. The philosophical analysis of music traditionally has been approached from three principal angles. First, music can be understood in a rationalist fashion, focusing on the relationship of music to numbers, measure, and calculation. Second, music can be understood according to its effects on the emotions and human feelings; that is, on "sentiments." Third, philosophers have often taken a metaphysical approach, which attributes a universal, metaphysical meaning to music by referring it to a hidden worldly essence that music would supposedly express in a better way than any representative art—and better than philosophy itself.

There is some merit to each of these approaches, and traces of them can be found in U2's own music and understanding of their music. But there are also weaknesses with all of them. The rationalist approach seems to miss what's crucial about music— the effect it has on the listener. The subjectivist approach falls back unduly on the interiority of consciousness and its passions, and seems to reduce all thought about music to a questioning of its effects on the subject. The metaphysical approach

---

[1] "Bono: The *Rolling Stone* Interview," *Rolling Stone* 986 (3rd November, 2005), p. 52.

rests on extravagant presuppositions about the musical nature of ultimate reality. So we will consider, in the conclusion, another philosophical approach to thinking about music, one that seems to fit better with U2's own understanding of the role their music plays. We can call this approach the phenomenological approach.

## "Maybe You Could Educate My Mind": The Rationalist Approach to Music

It is obvious that music can be defined by reference to numbers, through an analysis of the mathematical relationships that regulate the different intervals among sounds. René Descartes (1596–1650), for example, does not define music by melody, which only addresses sentiments and thus escapes any strict regulating principle. Instead he characterizes it by harmony, for the latter is the only element that can be the object of a calculation of proportions, thereby lending itself to a mathematical understanding.[2] Similarly, in his famous definition of music as "an unconscious exercise of arithmetic [done by] a spirit that knows not that it is counting," Gottfried Leibniz (1646–1716) privileges the rational and mathematical structure of harmony over the emotional impact of melody ("Letter 154 to Goldbuch"). More precisely, he asserts that musical pleasure derives from a sort of isomorphism tying together musical harmony and the mathematical order that regulates nature as a whole. Leibniz says that consonances secure an agreeable sentiment while dissonances create an impression of annoyance. The reason is that the former is the sensible reflection of the universal harmony desired by God, and the latter its contradiction.[3] This conception of music as calculation, illustrated notably by J.S. Bach in his use of counterpoints, especially in his fugues, probably finds its most complete theoretical development in Jean-Philippe Rameau (1683–1764), for whom "music is a science which should have definite rules. These rules should be drawn from an evident principle [harmony as "a natural and universal princi-

---

[2] See Descartes, *Compendium of Music* (Rome: American Institute of Musicology, 1961).
[3] See "Principles of Nature and Grace, Based on Reason," in Gottfried Leibniz, *Philosophical Essays* (Indianapolis: Hackett, 1989).

ple"], and this principle cannot really be known to us without the aid of mathematics."[4]

Recently, researchers have developed a computer program called "Hit Song Science" or HSS which, they claim, can predict hit songs by statistically analyzing the "underlying mathematical patterns" of a song, including chord progression, beat, tempo, and pitch. According to the program's analysis, U2's music bears some mathematical-statistical similarity to Beethoven's.[5] Of course, that fact might point to the limitations of the mathematical analysis of music. Whatever structural similarities a U2 song has to a Beethoven symphony, the *experience* of the two is surely very different.

As Arthur Schopenhauer (1788-1860) observed regarding Leibniz's mathematical definition of music, such views consider only "the immediate apparent, external sense of the musical, or to say its 'skin' or 'peel'."[6] This "external" and "empirical" conception, although correct, reduces music to a "means of grasping, immediately and in the concrete, larger numbers and more complex numerical ratios." But the Leibnizian definition misses the "aesthetic or inner significance" of music (*World as Will and Representation*, p. 265). For it is only by noting its effect on our sentiments that one can grasp music in its true sense, that is, as "a great and exceedingly fine art" with a "powerful" "effect on man's innermost nature" (p. 256), and able to disclose in this way "the deepest secrets of human willing and feeling" (p. 260).

This leads us to the second view of music:

## "The Opera Is in Me": Music as Subjective Expression

The most famous definition of music along subjectivist lines is probably that of Georg Hegel (1770–1831), who in his *Aesthetics* understands music as the art whose "essential element is interiority as such, sentiment deprived of form."[7] A little later, he adds

---

[4] Jean-Philippe Rameau, *Treatise on Harmony* (New York: Dover, 1971), p. xxxv.
[5] "Together in Electric Dreams," *The Guardian* (17th January, 2005).
[6] Schopenhauer, *The World as Will and Representation* (New York: Dover, 1969), Volume 1, p. 256, translation revised.
[7] G.W.F. Hegel, *Aesthetics* (Oxford: Clarendon, 1975), p. 18

152 Béatrice Han-Pile

that music draws its material from the human soul, from sentiment as such (p. 18). Musical sound, transient and ever changing, is, for Hegel, the sensible expression of the emotional life of the soul But before Hegel, the artists of the *Sturm und Drang* ("Storm and Stress") especially Wackenroder, had already characterized music as "a comprehensive and flexible mechanism for the portrayal of human emotions."[8] According to Wackenroder, music possesses this expressive potential because it appears as the increasingly refined thematization of "shapeless emotions" primitively expressed by screams and the rolling of drums. Born of the necessity of bringing "the external world into balance with their inner spiritual excitement" (*Confessions and Fantasies*, p. 188), music was constituted as an "ingenious system" of sounds through which an "inexplicable sympathy" is revealed " between the individual, mathematical, tonal relationships and the individual fibers of the human heart." Wackenroder's romantic view of language describes well U2's own approach to musical composition. Bono describes it in this way: "I try to put into words what I felt from the music. We spend most of our time working on the arrangements and the melodies, and then at the last minute, I try to articulate the feeling we found while we were improvising."[9]

Conversely, if musical art owes its birth to the violent eruptions of human sentiments, it articulates them in return by giving the subject the means of understanding his or her passions. Therefore, "the human heart becomes acquainted with itself in the mirror of musical sounds; it is they through which we learn to feel emotion" (*Confessions and Fantasies*, p. 191). To take up Schopenhauer's expression, if sentiment can be said to be the "*ratio essendi*" of music (that in virtue of which music exists), then music is the *ratio cognoscendi* of sentiment (that in virtue of which the sentiments can be known). Therefore, music reveals itself as a mysterious form of expression, obviously nonverbal, but infinitely more powerful than any articulated words, an "originary language" that exceeds the elucidating capacity of human language in power and truth. Or, as Bono explains, "pop lyrics, in a way, are just a rough direc-

---

[8] Wilhelm Heinrich Wackenroder, *Confessions and Fantasies* (University Park: Pennsylvania State University Press, 1971), p. 188.
[9] Hank Bordowitz, ed., *The U2 Reader* (New York: Hal Leonard, 2003), p. 133.

tion that you sketch for where the listener must think toward. That's it, the rest is left up to you. . . . Feelings travel better than thoughts" (*The U2 Reader*, p. 195). The power of music inheres in the immediacy of its relationship with sentiment: while language achieves only the representation of the passions, music is, by essence, their direct presentation, and thus infinitely more true and powerful than any speech. In his *Conversations with Eckerman*, Goethe (1749–1832) expresses a similar view by asserting that "music has an innate strength that is superior to anything else, and that no one can explain."[10]

By way of this fundamental link to sentiment, music is understood in terms of subjectivity, considered both as its source and its point of application. Because it expresses the "innermost heart" of the musician, it supposedly translates and addresses what is most profound in humankind. Robert Schumann (1810–1856) says, for example, that music is the expression of the artist's "inner states" and personality, which fully reappear in the emotions, sentiments, and passions created by his works. Thus, "masters like Beethoven and Schubert . . . have translated almost every possible condition of life into the language of tone."[11] Bono similarly acknowledges that his music refers to things which "are quite personal—but they wouldn't be in there if they were just personal" (*U2: Into the Heart*, p. 131). Take for example his own experience of losing his mother at a very young age (an experience he shared with Larry). Different aspects of this personal experience are taken up in number of U2 songs—"I will follow," "Mofo," "Lemon," to name a few. But each time it appears, it is expressed in a way that all of us can relate to—the feelings of loss, emptiness, longing, despair that the songs express are not unique to Bono.

Thus Schopenhauer interprets the relation between music and sentiment in the following way:

> music does not express this or that particular and definite pleasure, this or that affliction, pain, sorrow, horror, gaiety, merriment, or peace of mind, but joy, pain, sorrow, horror, gaiety, merriment, peace of mind themselves, to a certain extent in the abstract. *It*

---

[10] Johann Wolfgang von Goethe, *Conversations with Eckerman* (New York: Dutton, 1930), p. 534, translation revised.

[11] Schumann, *On Music and Musicians* (New York: Norton, 1969), p. 57.

*gives us their essence without any embellishments.* (*World as Will and Representation*, p. 261, translation modified, my emphasis)

Sentiments expressed in this way are not "subjective" in the sense that they are peculiar to this or that particular person. Instead, they are subjective in that they show us what is essential to any subject: they show us the subtle "quintessence" of passion, or, so to speak, sentiments-in-themselves. In music, the most particular (human individuality) and the most general (the will) are fused together through the mediation of the composer, who "reveals the innermost nature of the world, and expresses the profoundest wisdom in a language that his reasoning faculty does not understand" (*World as Will and Representation*, p. 260). In this, music again differs deeply from the plastic arts that owe their existence to a disincarnation process through which the painter or sculptor loses his or her individual characteristics and becomes "the impersonal eye of the world," thus gaining access to the ideas. In contrast to the plastic arts, music dwells upon the individuality of the musician it transfigures by giving it a "magical" capacity to express the universal by means of the particular. Therefore, the musician's sentiments (Schopenhauer mentions Rossini) take on an exemplary value, a paradoxically individual generality that, although it belongs but to one person, can nevertheless be reappropriated by each and every human being.

But recognizing this points us beyond a purely subjectivist view of music and, for Schopenhauer, helps support the next philosophical approach to music:

## "Listen Over the Rhythm that's Confusing You": Music as Showing Us Metaphysical Truths

The third approach takes up and systematizes various aspects of the previous two into a metaphysics, a theory of ultimate reality. From the beginning, the Pythagorean tradition (it's founder, Pythagoras, lived in the sixth century B.C.) distinguishes between terrestrial music and the "music of the spheres": the former is the sensible echo of its celestial counterpart which, although it is inaudible to human ears, expresses the mathematical relations on which the harmony of the world is grounded. In his *On the Heavens*, Aristotle (384–322 B.C.) evokes "those who, taking as their hypothesis that the speeds of the stars, judged by their distances, are in the ratios of the musical harmony they affirm that the sound of the stars as they revolve is harmonious."[12] Understood in the etymological sense of harmony (originally the Greek word *harmozein* meant "to adjust," "to hold together"), music forms the metaphysical framework of the world. This ontological characterization of music is taken up by Plotinus (third century A.D.), for whom sensible music arises out of suprasensible music, "the terrestrial representation, of the music that exists in the rhythm of the ideal realm" (*Enneads* V, 9, 11). It's also found in Boethius's medieval distinction between *musica mundana, musica humana,* and *musica instrumentalis*—the harmony or mathematical structure of the cosmic spheres, the harmony or mathematical structure of humans and their world, and instrumental music (the music performed by human beings).

The relationships between these different kinds of "music" is a constant theme in U2. When Bono reflects in "Gloria" on his fumbling efforts "to sing this song," or when he asks despairingly in "Sunday bloody Sunday" "how long must we sing this song?", he's pointing to the existence of a *musica mundana,* God's divine order, as well as commenting on the harmony between our music and God's order for the universe. The music of the human world is also the theme of songs like "Wake Up Dead Man" where, in the face of the evil of the world, Bono voices the doubt that "there's an order in all of this disorder." The answer to the doubt, sung by the Edge when performed in concert, comes in the instruction that we need to learn to listen beyond the harmony of the human world—the *musica humana*—to detect the deeper structure of the universe—the *musica mundana*: "Listen over the rhythm that's confusing you / Listen to the reed in the saxophone / Listen over the hum of the radio / Listen over the sounds of blades in rotation / Listen through the traffic and circulation / Listen as hope and peace try to rhyme / Listen over marching bands playing out their time." If hope and peace could rhyme (or hope and history in "Peace on Earth"), it would amount to a harmony between the *musica mundana* and the *musica humana.*

---

[12] Lines 290b20–23. See equally his *Metaphysics* A, 5, 985b.

The metaphysical understanding of music often aims at achieving a correspondence between the *musica mundana* and the *musica instrumentalis*, and culminates in the desire to "withdraw quietly into the land of music as into the land of belief" (Wackenroder, *Confessions and Fantasies*, p. 179) and in the idea that music, because of its sublime nature (it "portrays human feelings in a *superhuman* way") (*Confessions and Fantasies*, p. 180, my italics), touches through its essence the divine, to the point of being transformed into "a veritable divinity for the human heart" ("L'essence intime" p. 377; English, p. 194). More than one critic has noted the similarities between a rock fan's passion for his music and religious faith. Bono takes this idea quite seriously, observing in a kind of biographical reflection: "I stopped going to churches and got myself into a different kind of religion. Don't laugh, that's what being in a rock 'n' roll band is, not pseudo-religion either . . . Show-business is Shamanism: Music is Worship, whether it's worship of women or their designer, the world or its destroyer, whether it comes from that ancient place we call soul or simply the spinal cortex, whether the prayers are on fire with a dumb rage or dove-like desire . . . the smoke goes upwards . . . to God or something you replace God with."[13]

The nineteenth century saw in Schopenhauer's philosophy the most extreme attempt to fuse the rational, subjective, and metaphysical views of music. As we've already noted, Schopenhauer connects the numerical features of music to its effects on sentiment. Both the rational and subjective views of music are subsumed under a metaphysical definition according to which music "is directly a copy of the will itself, and therefore *expresses the metaphysical of everything physical in the world*, the thing-in-itself of every phenomenon" (*World as Will and Representation*, p. 262, translation modified, my emphasis). The arts of representation, such as painting and sculpture can only give us a view of ultimate reality mediated by ideas. Yet, in doing so, they remain subject to the "general principle of representation" (that is, time, space, and causality). But music constitutes a direct representation of "the world's essence" and

<hr/>

[13] Bono, "Introduction," to *Selections from the Book of* Psalms (New York: Grove Press, 1999), pp. x–xi.

operates without the mediation of the principle of sufficient reason. Its metaphysical will that is expressed so well that music and the thing-in-itself are sometimes fused together in Schopenhauer's text. Thus, "we could just as well call the world embodied music as embodied will" (*World as Will and Representation*, pp. 262–63). Hence, music and philosophy appear as parallel yet complementary activities: both are trying to help us grasp the deep, underlying truth about the world of appearances. Music presents the noumenal essence of the world in a non-conceptual form that philosophy seeks to make explicit. This is why Schopenhauer comes back a second time to Leibniz's definition and modifies it as follows: "If we situate ourselves from a infinitely higher point of view, we will be able to modify the quote and say that music is an unconscious exercise of metaphysics in which the spirit does not know that it is doing philosophy" (*World as Will and Representation*, p. 264, translation modified).

It is, however, hard to take seriously Schopenhauer's metaphysical view that the world is "an incarnation of music," while music is an "immediate reproduction of the will itself." Philosophers like Friedrich Nietzsche (1844–1900) have rejected the idea of an underlying essence of the world which music would be reproducing. And although believers might take seriously the idea of a divine order (a celestial music), few any longer would believe that our human music can really express this—and certainly not rock music, let alone the Schopenhauerian music of Wagner. Nietzsche's critique of Wagner's music probably applies just as well to rock music: "It is simply bad music—'Sentiment,' 'passion,' as surrogates when one no longer knows how to achieve an exalted spirituality is the happiness that attends it. Technically, 'sentiment' and 'passion' are easier—they presuppose much poorer artists"[14] Nietzsche thought Wagner's art is one of poverty because it lacks style, it has "lost his own law" and attempts to overcompensate this deficiency through an excess of romanticism, that is, by multiplying its effects through a "perfecting of the medium of expression" that only ends up in an unhealthy exacerbation of passions (*Will to Power*, p. 441, translation modified). Nietzsche's critique is aimed at the over-empha-

---

[14] Nietzsche, *The Will to Power* (New York: Vintage, 1967), p. 440, translation modified.

sis of the feelings and sentiments—one might perhaps think that he would say the same of most rock music as well.

But, in the end, Nietzsche's critique of Wagner and Schopenhauer is directed primarily at their pessimism—their rejection of the world. Nietzsche himself writes expectantly of an ideal character, the "musician of the future": "Who will sing a song for us, a morning song, so sunny, so light, so fledged that it will not chase away the blues but invite them instead to join in the singing and dancing? Mr. Hermit and Musician of the Future! No! No such tones! Let us strike up more agreeable, more joyous tones!"[15] Seen from this perspective, Nietzsche would surely approve of the fact that U2, unlike most rock bands, aim to produce what Bono describes as "ecstatic music": "It has a sense of wonder and a joy about it. And joy is the hardest thing. You can create anger. You can achieve drama easily. But joy . . ." (*The U2 Reader*, p. 164).

It's not sentimentality *per se*, then, that Nietzsche rejects, but a certain kind of appeal to sentiment—a hysterical music that reeks with pathetic hyperbole and exaggerated sentiment. When Nietzsche objects to Wagner and other pessimistic, life-repudiating forms of music, then, he needs to find a way to cast his objection that does not altogether negate the relationship between music and the passions. He needs a philosophical concept that distinguishes between mere sentimentality on the one hand, and a genuine connection to our moods on the other. With such a concept in hand, we could then distinguish two different ways of critiquing music. First of all, we could evaluate music with regard to how successful it is in producing a genuine effect on our moods or dispositions for the world (instead of merely playing superficially with our emotions). Secondly, we could evaluate music with regard to the *way* it affects our moods—whether it makes us more pessimistic, or whether it genuinely succeeds in "chasing away the blues."

We can find just such a philosophical concept in Martin Heidegger's (1889–1976) account of "mood" (Heidegger's German term is "*Stimmung*"). This leads to a fourth approach to music—what we could call a phenomenological approach to music that is neither metaphysical nor subjective.

------

[14] Nietzsche, *The Gay Science* (New York: Vintage, 1974), p. 348.

## "As the Music Played I Saw My Life Turn Around": Music as Attuning Our Mood for the World

Heidegger's phenomenology explores things in terms of the effect they have in shaping and structuring our experience of the world. On the phenomenological view, music transforms our way of being in the world by acting on the moods specific to each situation. Unlike sentiments, moods are not private, but can be shared. One problem with understanding music in terms of private sentiments is that it fails to capture the way that music puts us into a mood that we all share. Moreover, moods are not mere feelings because they concern the way things and human beings show themselves to us, even before they can be reinvested in the framework of passionate relationships. A mood is more like an "atmosphere" (which is one of the meanings of "*Stimmung*" in German), a "climate," or an "ambiance" than a sentiment, which can only be determined on the background of mood itself and in reference to the ego. As we all have experienced, when the sun shines it creates a joyful climate in which the world itself appears more lively while, conversely, fog inclines toward melancholy—which is perfectly illustrated, for example, by the closing scenes of the video for "Stay (Far Away, So Close)".[16] On the background of this joy or this melancholy, certain feelings will be accordingly amplified or minimized: the sadness that I feel at the death of someone dear to me will be exacerbated by a melancholy mood, whereas a more joyful disposition would probably alleviate it. Mood is broader and less specific than sentiment insofar as it is a nonsubjective opening to the world that is prior to the our making the nature and object of our passion explicit.

The action of music can be described exactly in these terms. Of course, music can give rise to violent passions—think, for example, of the rage communicated by Edge's guitar in "Bullet the Blue Sky," the angry frustration of Larry's drum line in "Sunday Bloody Sunday," or the intense desire expressed by Adam's sensuous bass line in "If You Wear that Velvet Dress." Bono's tender performance of "Sometimes You Can't Make It on Your Own" builds an intensely nostalgic climate. "Beautiful Day" or "All Because of You" engender an atmosphere of gaiety, of

---

[16] Also "All I Want Is You" and "Love Is Blindness."

joyous energy, while a songs like "Promenade" or "4th of July" plunge the listener into an indeterminate reverie. In each of these cases, our opening onto the world is colored differently, but without our necessarily finding ourselves with a specific sentiment directed toward a precise object. This deep affinity between mood and music is conveyed by the fact that metaphors used to describe moods and dispositions ("tonality," "accord," "resonance") all belong to the musical domain. As film-makers know well, comparable scenes disclosed by different music will be perceived very differently. Think of the way that "In God's Country" turns the closing scene of *Three Kings*—a scene where the protagonists are arrested and threatened with courts martial—into a moment of moral triumph. Compare this with the scene from *In the Name of the Father* in which Gerry Conlan is arrested by the military. The music in that scene helps create a very different mood—a sense of suffocating fear.

Thinking of music in terms of mood allows us to deal with Nietzsche's critique of music. A successful piece of music doesn't merely toy with our sentiments. Instead, it changes our mood, allowing us to see or experience things that we wouldn't otherwise. U2's lyrics themselves allude to this disclosive dimension of music. In "The First Time," Bono sings of a lover who "teach[es] me how to sing / shows me colours when there's none to see / gives me hope when I can't believe." Bono once described the artist's task as follows: "to tell our stories, to play them out, to paint pictures, moving and still, but above all *to glimpse another way of being.*"[17]

"When Love Comes to Town" ties that experience of glimpsing a new way of being to the disclosive power of musical mood: "I ran into a juke-joint when I heard a guitar scream / The notes were turning blue, I was dazed and in a dream. / As the music played I saw my life turn around / That was the day before love came to town."

The recognition that different kinds of music support a different range of moods also allows us to understand Nietzsche's critique of Wagner and romantic music generally

---

[17] In Bill Flanagan, *U2 at the End of the World* (New York: Delacorte, 1995), p. 171; emphasis in the original.

as decadent art forms. In his later writings, Heidegger adopted an historical understanding of moods as basic dispositions— *Grundstimmungen*. If music can be understood in terms of its role in shaping our experience of the world, one might expect to find a correspondence between basic moods and the different historical epochs of music. In *What Is Philosophy?*, Heidegger refers to three fundamental dispositions: astonishment, characteristic of the being-in-world of the Greeks, continually surprised by the fact that there are entities; the certainty and rational evidence (*Richtigkeit*) of Cartesianism, and more generally characteristic of modern times, as well as the impression of mastery that it engenders;[18] and finally, the anguish of the contemporary epoch, anguish in the face of the abyss arising out of the collapse of metaphysical certainty. At the same time, this anguish (Michel Haar states while quoting Adorno), tends to be hidden by the fading of all disposition, "distress at the absence of distress."[19]

It seems probable that contemporary music's dominant tonality actually is anguish. U2 suggests as much in "Zooropa," when our nihilistic cultures is described as a place with "no particular song," or in "Numb" where the prevailing mood of our age is described as numbness to everything that goes on around us. It requires no particular insight to see much of popular music as grounded in a sense of despair or of anxiety. Even the apparent light-heartedness of much popular music seems an effort to evade the gnawing feeling that, to again quote "Zooropa,"

> I have no compass / And I have no map / And I have no reasons / No reasons to get back. / And I have no religion / And I don't know what's what / And I don't know the limit / The limit of what we've got.

The disquietude of the song's introduction and verses gives way to the transparently forced happiness of the chorus: "Don't worry baby, it'll be alright / You got the right shoes / To get you through the night." In an interview, Bono puts the conclusion bluntly: "Partying is a disguise, isn't it?" (*The U2 Reader*, p. 48).

---

[18] Michel Haar, *La fracture de l'histoire* (Grenoble: Éditions Jérôme Millon, 1994), pp. 221–22. See equally "The Age of the World Picture" in *The Question Concerning Technology and Other Essays* (New York: Harper and Row, 1977).

For U2, the rock musician's responsibility is to use the power of music to help transform the prevailing mood of our age—to help us to recover our ability to feel and care, without the need for overstimulation. The concluding chorus of "Zooropa" points us in this direction: "Don't worry baby, it's gonna be alright / Uncertainty can be a guiding light / I hear voices, ridiculous voices / In the slipstream. / Let's go, let's go overground / Take your head out of the mud baby / She's gonna dream up / The world she wants to live in / She's gonna dream out loud."

U2 calls for a music to wake us up to the emptiness, the ridiculousness of the pop culture that seeks to numb us to our situation. And they envision an art that would attune us to love, to moral obligation, to compassion. In Bono's words:

> as much as we need to describe the kind of world we do live in, we need to *dream up the kind of world we want to live in*. In the case of a rock 'n' roll band that is to dream out loud, at high volume, to turn it up to eleven. Because we have fallen asleep in the comfort of our freedom. Rock 'n' roll is for some of us a kind of alarm clock.[19]

---

[19] *U2 at the End of the World*, pp. 172–73. Portions of this chapter were drawn from my article, "Beyond Metaphysics and Subjectivity: Music and *Stimmung*," *Epoché* 5 (1997), pp. 39–69.

# 12

# To Find a Song that I Can Sing: What Philosophy of Language Can Tell Us about Popular Success

THEODORE GRACYK

It struck me again and again when we were making the record [*All that You Can't Leave Behind*]. A song about a specific time, a particular person or incident would suddenly sound like it was written about Africa or some great global theme, which, of course, as a writer, you must never try or you'll burst through sheer pretentiousness.

—Bono, 2004[1]

## Some Days Are Better than Others

In 1997, U2 appeared to have rendered themselves irrelevant. The *Pop* album and subsequent tour failed to connect with anyone beyond their core fan base. After four months, album sales evaporated with just one million copies sold. Their 1997 network television special, *A Year in Pop*, was a ratings disaster. Few of their live performances sold out during a summer tour of the United States, and low sales forced them to cancel shows in New York and Philadelphia. The costs of mounting and running the tour threatened U2 with financial ruin.

Three years later, in 2000, U2 released *All that You Can't Leave Behind*. The song "Beautiful Day" won three Grammy Awards in 2001. The album remained a best seller until the summer of 2001, when it finally fell out of the top fifty albums. The big surprise was that U2 dominated the radio again in the last three months of 2001, particularly the song "Stuck In a Moment

---

[1] Quoted in Adrian Deevoy, "U2 Walk on Water," *Blender* (November 2004), p. 116.

You Can't Get Out Of," which won the 2002 Grammy Award for best performance by a duo or a group. "Walk On" won the 2002 award for Record of the Year. U2 had not received such public acclaim since 1988, when "I Still Haven't Found What I'm Looking For" and *The Joshua Tree* received three Grammy Awards.

What accounts for this vast difference in popular and critical reception? Why did *All that You Can't Leave Behind* return U2 to the level of popularity first attained by *The Joshua Tree*, which had been their first number one album in most markets? *Pop* was not a bad album. Compared with most of its competition that year, *Pop* was an interesting and attractive set of songs. As a work of social commentary, it certainly achieves its goal of reflecting pop culture itself, thereby satisfying nineteenth-century poet Percy Bysshe Shelley's demand that art should express the spirit of its times. Shiny and loud and disposable, *Pop*'s design and sound display the shallow heart of late twentieth-century consumerism.

Like so many popular artists, U2 became popular but could not sustain that level of popularity. U2 is remarkable for the way that success has visited them twice. Released thirteen years apart, both *The Joshua Tree* and *All that You Can't Leave Behind* dramatically broadened U2's appeal. While many musicians have hit records in different decades, no other musicians have attained *this* level of success twice in a long career. But why do some U2 songs suddenly move millions of people, while others barely register? And why is it so difficult to predict which will be which? (Paul McGuinness, U2's manager, did not believe that "With or Without You" would succeed on the radio and he argued against releasing it as a single.) In dealing with these questions, we begin to address the broader philosophical issues of what popular musicians offer to a mass audience and why musicians and the music industry so often fail to predict what will succeed. In other words, U2 offers a fascinating test case for explaining mass popularity. U2 reminds us that a successful explanation of musical popularity must explain why particular songs simultaneously move large masses of people. But we should also explain why popular success is so unpredictable. Most philosophers who've discussed these topics have worked in aesthetics, a traditional branch of philosophy that investigates beauty and art.

My hunch is that U2's popularity soured with *Pop* and soared with *All That You Can't Leave Behind* because *Pop* talks *to* its audience. In contrast, both *The Joshua Tree* and *All That You Can't Leave Behind* encourage the audience to talk *through* their most popular songs. This distinction between talking *to* and talking *through* draws on philosophical ideas developed about fifty years ago in the area of philosophy of language. In many fields, a theory that's fifty years old is merely quaint. But philosophers still debate ideas that predate Christianity. At fifty, a philosophical theory is still in its infancy.

Delivered as a series of lectures and posthumously published as *How to Do Things with Words*, philosopher J.L. Austin's theory of speech acts has been a rich source for reflecting on meaning in art. Austin's philosophy of language provides a powerful alternative approach to understanding the power of popular music.

## A Feeling on My Mind: The Expression Theory

What view is speech act theory an alternative to? One common explanation of U2's success is the expression theory, which assumes that people respond to emotional honesty. At least one book about U2, Niall Stokes's *Into the Heart*, operates on that premise. Examining their career song by song, Stokes tries to identify the events in Bono's life that explain each song. Like so many writers, Stokes assumes that rock music reflects the lives of its performers, and rock fans respond to honest, heartfelt self-exposure.[2] We respond most strongly to songs of autobiographical honesty, songs that reflect the real emotions of the writers and performers. Rock musicians fail when they offer trite, "fake" emotions that provide no basis for real empathy. So the most personally revealing rock music will be the most powerful, and will be the key to a band's success.

Sometimes Bono seems to endorse this idea. He once said, "'I Will Follow' has both anger, *real* anger, and an enormous

---

[2] Leo Tolstoy, the famous writer, defends this theory in *What Is Art?* (Indianapolis: Hackett, 1996). Keir Keightley argues that a claim to "sincere expressions of genuine feeling" distinguishes rock music from the artificiality of "pop" music. Keightley, "Reconsidering Rock," in Simon Frith, Will Straw, and John Street, eds., *The Cambridge Companion to Pop and Rock* (Cambridge: Cambridge University Press, 2001), p. 130.

sense of yearning." The anger and yearning are, presumably, *his* feelings.[3] Sensing this, we respond to the song's honesty. On this theory, U2's success has everything to do with Bono. The Edge, Larry Mullen Jr., and Adam Clayton are only important for their ability to provide Bono the platform he needs for successful self-expression.

## Faith Needs a Doubt: Questioning Expression Theory

But U2's emotional honesty cannot adequately explain their power and appeal. Did *The Joshua Tree* really make them superstars because it was emotionally clearer or more honest than any of the previous four albums?

Expression theory insists that a song's origins and reception are intimately related. But how? The obvious link would be that a song would be successful when the audience is clear about its meaning and can determine how sincere it is. But doesn't this get the whole story backwards? If songs move us because we know that they reflect the singer's life, our ability to evaluate the authenticity of the expressive gesture must precede our being moved. But then why does the mass audience respond to emotional outpourings from unknowns? How does a band ever get an initial hit record? We certainly don't want to explain U2's increased appeal at the time of *The Joshua Tree* and then again with *All that You Can't Leave Behind* by assuming that the audience suddenly somehow knew more about Bono at those moments in time. Because otherwise unknown rock bands do have huge hits—"one hit wonders"—and established bands suddenly change their levels of popularity with new releases, it is unlikely that the audience's response to a song is directed at *verifiable* sincerity.

At least one other factor challenges expression theory's ability to explain popularity or appeal. If I find myself moved because a song is a sincere personal expression (even if I don't know why), shouldn't I care just as much about every other song with a similar expressive pedigree? I find "I Will Follow" to

---

[3] Quoted in Niall Stokes, *Into the Heart: The Stories Behind Every U2 Song* (London: Carlton Omnibus, 1996), p. 9.

be a powerful song, both in the version on *Boy* and the version on *Under a Blood Red Sky*. None of the other songs from *Boy* move me in the same way. Yet one critic assures us that all the songs on *Boy* succeed expressively because they come from the same source: "sometimes a little too simplistic in language, but they work—perhaps because the group were still young enough to know the feelings they were dealing with."[4] Shouldn't I respond to all of them in the same way?

Likewise, I've recently learned that *October*'s "Tomorrow" is, like "I Will Follow," a song that Bono wrote in memory of his mother, who died during his early adolescence. "Sometimes You Can't Make It on Your Own" was inspired by the death of Bono's father. Shouldn't those songs move me just the same way that "I Will Follow" does? For I have no reason to think that those songs are less sincere or personally expressive than "I Will Follow." Yet neither engages me to the degree that "I Will Follow" does. A song's power to move the audience depends on something more than the expressive sincerity of the singer's communicative act. But if it requires something more, is personal expression necessary at all?

So although I don't deny that Bono's charisma is part of U2's power, Bono's capacity for self-expression does not explain the variability in U2's reception and popularity. The lyrics of their songs may have an important basis in Bono's experiences, emotions, and thoughts. But an appeal to this source cannot explain the *reception* of U2. The expressive origins of a song and performance may have nothing to do with its power as music, and need play no role in explaining why audiences prefer one song to another, or prefer one rock band to another.

## When I Look at the World: Meaning in Context

The context in which a song is created can be very different from the context of its reception. Historical events can have a dramatic effect on these contexts.

I live in the United States. I was scheduled to take a commercial airline flight on September 13th, 2001. Anyone who

---

[4] Neil McCormick, "The Making of a Legend," in Niall Stokes and the editors of *Hot Press* magazine, *U2: Three Chords and the Truth* (New York: Harmony, 1989), p. 14.

places that date in its historical context will know that my flight was canceled. Due to the terrorist attacks of September 11th, every commercial flight in the United States was canceled. Those cancellations, together with the closing of the financial markets, were highly visible government interventions in response to September 11th. But the government did not mandate most of the other sudden changes in daily life. For music fans, one of the most obvious changes was that radio immediately sounded different. Hundreds of familiar songs were no longer played. They were simply too painful, or radio programmers feared that hearing them would disturb or anger listeners. Rock music is saturated with rebellion. But in the wake of September 11th, songs of adolescent anger and partying felt shallow, callous, petty, or dumb. They temporarily vanished from the airwaves. Artists who got little or no time on mainstream radio suddenly dominated the airwaves. Two of the most widely played songs were Enya's "Only Time" and Five for Fighting's "Superman (It's Not Easy)."

During this period, U2's "Stuck in a Moment" emerged as one of the songs that expressed the American mood. The song was everywhere! But if we believe in the explanatory power of expression theory, we should wonder about the success of this song at this time. Bono has confirmed that the song was inspired by the 1997 suicide of his friend Michael Hutchence. It reflects Bono's feelings and thoughts about the futility of that act, "slapping him around the head" for it.[5] If expression theory is correct, then "Stuck in a Moment" succeeded either because millions of Americans were contemplating suicide and wanted Bono's advice, or people didn't take it as a song about suicide. I think the second alternative is obviously correct. But here is a puzzle. Did the song succeed because millions misunderstood or ignored its meaning?[6]

---

[5] Bono quoted in Chris Heath, "U2: Band of the Year," *Rolling Stone* 860 (January 18, 2001), p. 68. In the same segment of the interview, Bono suggests one element of the theory that I propose, that songs do not succeed if kept "specific" to their emotional inspiration.

[6] Notice that the same question arises about other songs. Am I moved by "I Will Follow" because I care about the death of Iris Hewson, or because I ignore the fact that it's about her? The latter option seems correct, but then expression theory must explain why the audience is moved apart from an interest in specifics, such as the fact that Bono's emotions involve his mother and her untimely death. For an appropriately complex version of the

Bono has addressed this very question:

> Songs that meant one thing before September 11th, for most bands I think, meant another thing after September 11th. But oddly enough our music meant the same thing. It's just that the events brought the subject matter closer into focus. And a lot of the themes and the moods of *All that You Can't Leave Behind* seemed to just make more sense. I don't think they changed.[7]

Setting aside the idea that some songs change meaning over time, Bono proposes that events made people understand what certain songs meant. Events in listeners' lives *focused their perception* of the songs. In the context of grief, they made "more sense."

Can we clarify what is Bono saying here? We need an account that assigns meanings that don't require knowledge of the private lives of rock musicians. Only hard-core fans care if the emotions are deeply personal in relation to the singer's life. At the same time, our explanation should agree with Bono that people got the "sense" of "Stuck in a Moment" in the wake of September 11th. They did not misunderstand it.

Sociology and psychology might help to explain why certain songs move millions of strangers. But as I suggested earlier, I think that a specific philosophical theory about meaning is useful for understanding the power of "With or Without You" and "Stuck in a Moment." Ever since Plato wrote about the topic twenty-four centuries ago, philosophers have debated how arbitrary combinations of sounds can mean anything. Many theories of meaning have been advanced, defended, and criticized. Among these, core ideas of speech act theory are promising candidates for clarifying Bono's insights about U2's songs in relation to events that the band cannot control.

## Somebody Try Something: Performing Actions

The central idea about speech acts is that speaking is a mode of action. This proposal has two important aspects. First, actions

---

expression theory, see R.G. Collingwood, *The Principles of Art* (Oxford: Oxford University Press, 1958).

[7] Bono quoted in Niall Stokes, "Matter of Life and Death—Part 1," *Hot Press Annual 2002* (1st December, 2001) at http://www.atu2.com/news/article.src?ID=2081, accessed 29th December, 2004.

are goal-directed behaviors. Second, most actions are guided by multiple goals, as when the act of lifting a light switch constitutes the additional act of turning on a light. When Bono sings, "I threw a brick through a window," anyone who comprehends English understands that he is describing the act of throwing a brick. But suppose we take this to be an autobiographical remark, and someone asks you what Bono said he did. We interpret complex actions by identifying how an immediate act is the means to some further end. Since the brick went through the window, you might say, "He broke the window." The breaking of the window is more than a mere *consequence* of throwing the brick. He threw the brick *in order to* break the window. We can have two actions in the same event when one (breaking the window) is accomplished *by means of* the other (throwing the brick at it).

Apart from exceptions like talking in your sleep or shouting expletives because you suffer from Tourette's Syndrome, most words are uttered to initiate a more complex action (as a means to some further end). Just as Bono selects a brick and not a sponge or wad of paper when he wants to break a window, he chooses words based on their suitability for doing what he is trying to do. Generally, people choose words in order to do things in addition to communicating their literal meaning.

The power to perform actions with words and other sounds depends on the total speech act in the total speech situation.[8] The point of stressing the "total speech act" is that each utterance typically performs three different acts: a locutionary act, an illocutionary act, and a perlocutionary act. The locutionary action is the production of meaningful sounds or other signs, such as Bono's ability to articulate the three sounds that form the two words "walk away" during the chorus of "I Will Follow." The illocutionary act involves doing something further in performing this first act. According to expression theory, Bono's illocutionary act is to express his feelings about his mother. The perlocutionary act is the production of consequences by means of the successful illocutionary act, such as the act of getting listeners to pay attention to the theme of mothers and sons. Many of U2's overtly political songs seem to be offered with the per-

---

[8] J.L. Austin, *How to Do Things with Words* (Cambridge, Massachusetts: Harvard University Press, 1975 [1962]), p. 148.

locutionary intention of getting the audience to think about politics, such as getting listeners to think about American imperialism by means of the words and music of "Bullet the Blue Sky."[9]

The point of noting that we must consider the "total speech situation" is that different situations will attach different illocutionary and perlocutionary acts to identical locutionary acts. As Austin puts it, "the occasion of an utterance matters seriously" (*How to Do Things with Words*, p. 100). During a game of hide and seek, the words "I see you" allow the person who's "it" to eliminate another player. Saying "I see you" in a poker game keeps the speaker in the hand, avoiding elimination from that round of betting. The words "I see you" do not have any *one* meaning that is the same on all occasions. The philosopher Ludwig Wittgenstein emphasizes that the "meaning" of each utterance depends on "the actions into which it is woven." Wittgenstein also warns that the only way to know whether the same actions are consistently associated with the same words is to look and see.[10]

## They Want You to Sing Along

If we look more closely at speech acts, one of the things we'll see is that the audience must complete each speech act. Knowledgeable speakers have significant control over their locutionary and illocutionary acts. But speakers have limited control over perlocutionary acts. Throwing a brick at a window, one has significant control over what is thrown, with what force, and in which direction. But the brick may or may not go through the window. *Rattle and Hum* documents Bono lecturing the audience about apartheid during "Silver and Gold," concluding, "Am I buggin' you? I don't mean to bug ya." Bono wants to inspire the crowd to think about apartheid, but he knows that the illocutionary act of preaching may commit a perlocutionary act that he did not intend, such as alienating the mass audience.

---

[9] "People always ask us if we think our songs can really change anything," The Edge said in 1988. "I think it would be too much to expect that. But they might make people think for a second, in the same way that we stop and think." Quoted in James Henke, "The Edge: The Rolling Stone Interview," *U2: The Rolling Stone Files*, p. 174.

[10] Ludwig Wittgenstein, *Philosophical Investigations*, third edition (New York: Macmillan, 1958), pp. 5e and 31e, respectively.

So the perlocutionary speech act depends on how the audience responds to the illocutionary act. To account for these transitions from illocutionary act to perlocutionary act, speech act theory proposes that a set of cooperative principles govern meaningful communication. Several principles have been identified, but three are important here: a communication should be as informative as required, it shouldn't be more informative than required, and it should be relevant.

These co-operative principles are of particular importance for understanding the intelligibility of indirect speech acts. We can agree with The Edge that "You write a song because that's the way you feel," but I propose that *performing* those songs for an audience is normally an indirect speech act.[11]

Suppose, during a meal, someone asks, "Can you reach the salt?" Taken at face value, the illocutionary act consists of asking a question, requesting information. Asking a question normally falls into the directive category of speech acts, because they direct hearers to make a response. But to answer "Yes" in this case, merely answering the question without additional response or action, is either rude or a misunderstanding. In order to be relevant to the situation, asking *about* the salt indirectly performs a second illocutionary act, also directive—the indirect act of asking *for* the salt. (In a slightly different situation, uttered just after a doctor has warned you to reduce your salt intake, the act might not be directive. It might be the indirect action of providing a humorous reminder about your health and eating habits.) With indirect speech acts, the speaker's perlocutionary intention assumes that the audience will see the irrelevance of taking the speech act at face value, and will make it relevant to their own situation. The trick is to say just enough, after which everything depends on audience cooperation in relating the utterance to its context.

"Stuck in a Moment" may be based on Bono's friendship with Michael Hutchence, but that cannot be the reason most people respond to the song. Its power is a mystery if we take it to be the speech act it pretends to be, namely the directive act of admonishing someone contemplating suicide. Admonishment is useless to Hutchence now, and Bono accomplishes nothing by

---

[11] The Edge quoted in Niall Stokes and Bill Graham, "The World about Us," in *U2: Three Chords and the Truth* (New York: Harmony, 1989), p. 78.

telling strangers to get over suicidal thoughts when most listeners won't be having such thoughts while hearing the song. Bono's act of sharing his thoughts and feelings about Hutchence must have an ulterior purpose.

So even if the words and emotions have a genuine source in the singer's own life, the act of *singing them* indicates that typical illocutionary commitments are being suspended. When a performer sings to an audience and the audience knows that the singer is intentionally doing so, what seems to be one act must be a springboard to something else. Bono thinks so, too. "When you're singing songs, people think you are like the songs you sing about," he said in 1987. "I think we need to let some air out of that balloon."[12] Yet this suspension of the overt illocutionary act doesn't strip Bono's words of communicative force. By singing, performers perform various illocutionary acts. In a great many circumstances, those acts just aren't the ones that would normally fit that combination of words. Generally, singing to an audience is the directive illocutionary act of inviting the audience to find some "fit" between the song and their own circumstances. To sing is to issue an invitation to listeners to make the song relevant, to make the song (but not the singer's own life) one's own.

Bono says that the emotional peak of "With or Without You"—the line "You give yourself away"—expresses his own role within the band U2. The Edge says that the songs on *The Joshua Tree* were an attempt to provide something "more straightforward, focused and concise," less "open-ended" than *The Unforgettable Fire* (*Into the Heart*, p. 66). But the beauty of "With or Without You" is that it is simultaneously focused and open-ended. Apart from Bono's saying so in interviews, none of the words tie it to his role in U2. Seeking relevance, almost everyone recognizes it to be about the vulnerability at the heart of every love relationship. *The Joshua Tree* and *All that You Can't Leave Behind* were breakthroughs based on songs that non-fans did not have to hear as messages from Bono to listeners. (Notice how "With or Without You" takes the last line of "Indian Summer Sky" and, by altering the surrounding words, shifts the "you" from having Bono

---

[12] Bono quoted in David Breskin, "Bono: The *Rolling Stone* Interview," *U2: The Rolling Stone Files*, p. 115.

talking to someone to the possibility that we are addressing ourselves.)

Larry Mullen Jr. apparently agrees that songs can furnish invitations to find personal, contemporary relevance. Discussing Irish politics in 1983, Mullen criticizes the Irish Republican Army by pointing to a song. "They call it a 'religious war,' but it has nothing to do with religion. It's like the Dylan song 'With God on Our Side.'"[13] Dylan's song opens with autobiographical references ("The country I come from / Is called the Midwest") before cataloguing barbarous acts that Americans justified by invoking God. Mullen points to a song by an American about American politics and history as making precisely his own point about Ireland. Dylan has succeeded because he has created a song that Mullen can fit to his own situation. To do so, Mullen ignores aspects that make it an expression of Dylan's life. Under the theory that singing normally signals an indirect speech act, Mullen has not changed Dylan's meaning. Instead, Mullen understands Dylan and cooperates with Dylan's speech act by making it relevant.

We can now explore a problem that I mentioned but did not pursue. Bono suggests that songs can change their meaning. Yet he thinks that when he sings "Stuck in a Moment," it means what it always meant. Speech act theory allows us to see that Bono is confusing two perspectives on the same activity. As a singer, he experiences no difference regarding his own illocutionary act, which is consistently directive. But when he thinks about songs he *hears*, he regards them from the point of view of the audience. The literal meanings of the words of all the songs are just as they were. But if Bono hears older songs immediately after September 11th and accepts the illocutionary invitation to make them relevant to his own life, he will make them relevant in new ways. Context will alter their effect, altering the perlocutionary act attributed to their writers and performers. The songs seem different to him because he has given them a new "focus" in his own life. Bono simply lacks the philosophical vocabulary for making this distinction between illocutionary and perlocutionary acts.

---

[13] Mullen quoted in James Henke, "Blessed Are the Peacemakers," *U2: The Rolling Stone Files*, p. 20.

## Exit

Speech act theory reminds us that the meaning of the words is just a first step in grasping the meaning of the total speech act. We want to understand the meaning of the word-string "Can you reach the salt?" only because we want to understand the speaker's point in uttering them. Iris Hewson and Michael Hutchence may have inspired "I Will Follow" and "Stuck in a Moment," but when Bono sings the songs, he invites us to ignore the fact that they are, for Bono, *about* those individuals. Bono invites us to make the songs relevant to our own situation, by treating them as about our own situations.

Popular breakthroughs of the kind that U2 enjoyed in 1987 and 2001 depend on constructing songs that many listeners can make relevant. The songs must involve emotions and themes that address the concerns of large numbers of people in the popular audience. What musicians and performers cannot control is what theme will simultaneously interest millions of people. *The Joshua Tree* has its preachy moments. Wisely, "Bullet the Blue Sky" was not the first single. Popular songs are also singable, offering melodies that permit the audience to take up the unspoken invitation to perform those words, literally making them their own by repeating them. With its sweeping melody and open-ended theme about love and vulnerability, "With or Without You" violated assumptions about how U2 should sound. With its borrowings from techno, so did the songs on *Pop*. Many members of U2's core audience may like *Pop*, but more casual listeners were not enticed into buying it.

One reason for its relative unpopularity is that *Pop's* first single was "Discotheque," and I suspect that many listeners heard it as Bono preaching at them. "You" is the most common word in "Discotheque" (it is repeated forty-three times), and the speaker is addressing someone listening to music ("be the song you hear"). So it is difficult to hear the song as anything but Bono's reflections on the emptiness of consumer culture. There are moments where the speaker includes himself in our collective predicament ("let's go, let's go"). Yet the dominant feel of the song is that of one person lecturing another. Songs like "Miami" and "The Playboy Mansion" are so thick with specific cultural references that they mainly come across as Bono's critique of the shallow enticements of consumerism. Bono sounds so intent on sharing his personal insights about contemporary culture that he suspends the invitation to the audience to make the songs relevant in original ways.

This analysis of the difference between *Pop* and *All that You Can't Leave Behind* assumes that audiences understand that performers have different intentions for different songs and performances. Yet an invitation to the audience to find ongoing relevance is not a blanket invitation to understand songs *however* one wishes. Performers have various perlocutionary intentions, things they hope to achieve by means of their performance. By performing at Live Aid in 1985, U2 hoped to raise awareness of starvation in Africa. Many songs are written and performed with perlocutionary aims that can only be reached by getting the audience to limit the range of interpretations placed on each song. For example, U2 does not want anyone to hear their songs as a call to answer violence with violence—on *Under a Blood Red Sky*, Bono calls attention to his thematic intentions for a song by saying, "This is not a rebel song. This song is 'Sunday Bloody Sunday.'" As speech acts, U2's performances betray both illocutionary and perlocutionary intentions. If the perlocutionary intentions become too obtrusive, much of the popular audience will no longer recognize an illocutionary act of inviting everyone to make the song relevant in a personal way.

So it's not a complete accident that *The Joshua Tree* and *All that You Can't Leave Behind* enlarged U2's audience, whereas *Pop* did not. The breakthrough singles from *The Joshua Tree* are less overtly Christian or political than the bulk of the songs on the first four albums. The same is true of much of *All that You Can't Leave Behind*, but through serendipity it also offered us "Stuck in a Moment" just as many of us got stuck in one. U2's music expands the group's audience when the songs successfully invite us to ignore Bono's life while accepting his unspoken invitation to use their songs to illuminate our own.

# 13

# "What You Don't Know, You Can Feel It Somehow": Knowledge, Feeling, and Revelation in U2

TIMOTHY CLEVELAND

We know many things. At least it is natural to say we do. We know that George Washington was the first President of the United States, that 2 + 2 = 4, that bachelors are unmarried. We know how to sing, how to play tennis, or how to ski. We know the Mona Lisa by sight, the sound of Bono and Bob Dylan as soon as we hear them sing, the smell of biscuits baking when we wake up in the morning. If we tried to list off the cuff all the things we would claim to know, we would soon give up. Feelings are equally ubiquitous. We feel anxious, depressed, angry, and elated. We feel love and hatred, *Angst* and *ennui*. We feel sorry for some people and attracted to others. We feel the wind in our hair and the sun on our face. We feel sleepy and feverish. We can feel certain our team will win or sure things are beyond repair. Feelings seem as common as consciousness.

Contrasting knowledge and feeling is cliché. It's easy to hear the songs of U2 as simply reiterating this commonplace. In "A Beautiful Day," the contrast is obvious: "What you don't know, you can feel it somehow." A similar distinction between thought and feeling is clear in "Vertigo," "Your head / can't rule your heart/ A feeling is so much stronger than / a thought," and the refrain connects this contrast to knowledge and feeling: "It's everything I wish I didn't know/ Except you give me something I can feel / Feel." The last capitalized and repeated "Feel" is sung as a command. U2 comes across as championing feeling but disparaging knowledge and thought. This message seems no better than the banal distinction between knowing and feeling. The substance of these U2 lyrics, however, may reflect more subtle insight into knowledge and feeling. The feeling that U2 champions may actually be akin to a kind of knowledge. U2's songs make frequent references to God and moral matters. Understanding how feeling is distinct from some kinds of knowledge may also be crucial to understanding the nature of revelation and moral motivation. A careful listen to U2's corpus raises the following questions: What is knowledge? How is knowledge distinct from feeling? What kinds of knowledge are there? How many ways can one feel? What is the relationship between knowledge and thought? Is feeling ever a kind of knowledge? When is feeling more important than knowing or thinking? One word the Greeks used for knowledge is *episteme*. Philosophers call the theory of knowledge *epistemology*. Behind Bono's lyrics and the music of U2 lurks a distinctive epistemology that may bring us "one step closer to knowing" the answers to some of these questions.

## The Varieties of Knowing

The verb "to know" is incredibly versatile. The direct objects of this verb can be many different things. We know *that U2 is a band, that Bono is the singer, that Edge is the lead guitarist, that Larry plays the drums, and that Adam plays the bass*. We can also say things such as, "I know *Bono whenever I hear his voice*" and his friends can say simply "I know *Bono*." Quite a different way to use the verb 'to know' is to say "I know *how to play U2 songs on the guitar*." If we are careful to distinguish these objects, then we see there are different ways to know, varieties of knowledge.

In the first examples above, the italicized direct objects of "know" are clauses beginning with the word *that*. We could say that what these clauses stand for are *facts*. That Bono is the singer is a fact. So in these examples what we know are facts. Here is another way to think of this use of the verb 'to know'. The sentence "Bono is the singer" says something that is either true or false. In this case it is true. The sentence "Bono is an Englishman" is false. Sentences that are true or false express propositions. The sentence "Bono is the singer" expresses the proposition *that Bono is the singer*. Knowledge *that* is called *propositional* knowledge. In ordinary talk we sometimes don't include the 'that' when we claim to know something. For example, the song "Beautiful Day" contains the line "I know I'm not a hopeless case." This line is an example of propositional knowledge even though it does not include the word 'that'. The first-person speaker is claiming to know a proposition—*that I am not a hopeless case.* Most of the examples of the propositional use of 'to know' in U2 songs are similar. In "Ultraviolet (Light My Way)," the verb 'to know' is used in the propositional sense without the word 'that': "you know I need you to be strong ..." *That I need you to be strong* is a proposition. In "I Still Haven't Found What I Am Looking For," there is the example "You know I believe it [in Kingdom Come]." *That I believe it* is a fact that is known. Propositional knowledge is knowledge of facts or truths expressed by true sentences. Often when we speak of knowledge we mean propositional knowledge.[1]

Contrast this propositional use of the verb 'to know' with the one in the second set of examples: I know *Bono whenever I hear his voice* and I know *Bono* (said by his friends). In these cases the object of the verb is not a proposition but a person, Bono. I don't know *that* something is the case. I know an object, in this case a person, Bono. The direct object of the verb 'to know' in this case is an object. Notice that this use of the word 'to know' is very close to the verbs 'to recognize' or 'to be acquainted with.' I recognize Bono simply by his voice. His friends are acquainted with him. Of course, they may know many facts about him (propositional knowledge) but they also know him directly. They have been in direct contact with him. This kind of knowledge is sometimes referred to as knowledge by *acquaintance.*

Propositions are expressed in sentences. So whatever propositional knowledge I have about Bono can be stated in true sentences about him—truths. Propositional knowledge is knowledge of truths. However it is possible that I know no truths about Bono but I can nonetheless recognize Bono by the sound of his voice or by seeing him. I could be directly aware of Bono without knowing any truths or facts about him. This kind of direct awareness is knowledge by *acquaintance.*

---

[1] Some philosophers argue that all knowledge is propositional knowledge. More on that to come.

The British philosopher Bertrand Russell (1872–1970) first noted the distinction between knowledge of truths and knowledge by acquaintance in his book *The Problems of Philosophy*: "We shall say we have *acquaintance* with anything of which we are directly aware, without the intermediary of any process of inference or any knowledge of truths," and "Knowledge of things, when it is of the kind we call knowledge by *acquaintance*, is essentially simpler than any knowledge of truths, and is logically independent of knowledge of truths . . ."[2] This kind of knowledge is closely tied to direct perception of things. I know Bono by the sound of his voice or how he appears to me. Such knowledge is common and crucial, though we often think of knowledge as knowledge of truths or facts. An example of this use of the verb 'to know' occurs in the song "Daddy's Gonna Pay for Your Crash Car": "You know everyone in the world, but you feel alone." The claim is hyperbole. No one can know everyone in the world. But the type of knowledge here is acquaintance. She is not said to know truths about everyone in the world but to be acquainted with everyone. Note also that in this song her knowledge is contrasted with a kind of feeling.

The last use of the verb 'to know' I mentioned was illustrated by "I know *how to play U2 songs on the guitar*." Here the object of the verb is neither a thing nor a proposition. It is a capacity or skill. This kind of knowledge is often referred to as knowing *how*. As in the case of knowledge by acquaintance, one may have knowledge *how* without any knowledge of truths. I may know how to play the guitar without knowing any truths about the techniques of guitar playing that allow me to play so well. This is a perfectly good and common use of the verb. Philosophers are prone to focus attention on propositional knowledge because it is closely connected with issues of truth and rationality. The epistemology implicit in U2's songs is a call to reconsider the importance of propositional knowledge. To appreciate this message we must first be careful to distinguish the ways one can be said to feel.

---

[2] Bertrand Russell, *The Problems of Philosophy* (Oxford University Press, 1912), p. 46. He adds in the passage above, "it would be rash to assume that human beings ever, in fact, have acquaintance with things without at the same time knowing some truth about them."

## Ways to Feel

The verb 'to feel' is even more flexible than the verb 'to know'. This flexibility is likewise found in the different direct objects that verb takes. These different uses of the verb are illustrated in many U2 songs. In "Where the Streets Have No Name," the lyric is "I want to feel sunlight on my face . . ." In "If God Will Send His Angels," Bono sings, "I want to feel my soul," and finally, "And I want to feel." Many times the verb is followed by a simile, "The sky falls / and you feel like it's a beautiful day," and in "Ultraviolet (Light My Way)": "Sometimes I feel like checking out." The line I already quoted from "Daddy's Gonna Pay for Your Crash Car" simply says, "You feel alone." The title of the song "Numb" is the feeling: "I feel numb." To lump all these different uses of the verb 'to feel' together into a simple category called 'feelings' is to court confusion. The common verb obscures important differences.

Consider the first example, "I want to feel sunlight on my face." Here we could say that there is some *thing* desired to be felt—the sunlight on my face. What the person wants to feel is a certain sensation that sunlight on one's face produces. In this case, 'feeling' is synonymous with 'sensation'. "I want to feel sunlight on my face" means "I want to sense sunlight on my face." Another example is found in Bono's song "The Wanderer": "I went out there / in search of experience/ To taste and to touch / and to feel . . ." Here feeling is a kind of experience or sensation like tasting or touching. We often think of feelings as sensations. We might call this *perceptual* feeling. Note that our sensations are things we are directly aware of. We know them by acquaintance. So perceptual feelings should be considered a kind of knowledge.

Feelings are frequently thought of as emotional states. The lines "you feel alone" and "I feel numb" do not refer to sensations. They refer to emotional conditions. Feeling alone is the condition of alienation. Though one can feel a sensation of numbness, say when a limb is anesthetized, in the song "Numb" it refers to a kind of emotional listlessness, *ennui*. U2 songs often mention the emotion love. "I feel love" is the use of 'feel' in the sense of an emotion. Call this use of the verb 'to feel' *emotional* feeling. Russell believed we have knowledge by acquaintance of our emotional feelings.

In the song "Acrobat," Bono sings "Don't believe what you hear / Don't believe what you see/ If you just close your eyes / You can feel the enemy." Here feeling is contrasted with perceptual states that make one aware of the world around them. The 'enemy' that one can feel is oneself. 'To feel' in this case refers to a kind of awareness one has of oneself independent of the sensations of the outside world. Feeling in this case could be called *introspection*. Like perceptual feeling it is a kind of direct awareness and so a kind of knowledge by acquaintance. Again feeling is a state of knowledge, not contrary to it.

Consider cases where 'feel' is followed by a simile. "Sometimes I feel like checking out" and "you feel like it's a beautiful day." The first example may seem to be a case of emotional feeling, expressing a state of depression. But I think this case actually illustrates another kind of feeling. 'Checking out' is a euphemism for committing suicide. That is why it is natural to think of this as emotional feeling. One usually has to be depressed to commit suicide. However, 'to feel' here is used very much like 'to believe': "I believe that I should commit suicide" or "I believe that suicide is a good idea." Now feeling like checking out is not the same as a belief but a kind of inclination to believe. Notice that the object of 'to believe' in this example is a proposition, *that I should commit suicide*. So feeling like checking out is having a positive attitude toward a proposition. The same is true of the example "You feel like / It's is a beautiful day." The feeling here is a positive attitude toward the proposition *that it's a beautiful day*.

'To feel' in these cases expresses a state of mind that is an inclination toward accepting a particular truth. If I feel like checking out, then I am inclined to accept as a truth the sentence "I should commit suicide." If you feel like it's a beautiful day, then you are inclined to accept as truth the sentence "It is a beautiful day." These examples illustrate what could be called *attitudinal* feeling. Attitudinal feeling is like propositional knowledge in that its object is a proposition. But usually we use the verb 'to feel' in this context to contrast this attitude with propositional knowledge. 'To feel' in these cases implies that one is not sure or does not have justification for one's inclination. This contrast is natural and obvious in the claims, "I don't know that I should kill myself, but I feel that I should" and "You aren't certain it's a beautiful day but you feel that it is." Attitudinal feeling is a state of mind that falls short of knowledge.

Sometimes the verb is intransitive—it lacks any object. For example, the lyric "I want to feel." This might mean "I want to be open to experiences and sensations" or it could mean "I don't want to be emotionally numb." Only the context can determine whether perceptual feeling or emotional feeling is intended. There are other uses of the verb 'to feel' besides perceptual, emotional, introspective, and attitudinal. These however should suffice to understand how feeling might provide an alternative to knowing.

## Knowledge and Thought

Philosophers usually think of knowledge as a kind of belief. In order to know that Bono was born in Dublin one must believe that he was. But people believe all kinds of false things. For belief to count as knowledge the belief must be true. If Bono was born in Dublin, then one cannot know he was born in Belfast. Yet one could just happen to believe that Bono was born in Dublin. Let's say one simply guesses so based on the fact that he is Irish. In that case, one has a true belief but one does not know that he was born in Dublin. One happens to have a true belief but one has no good *reasons* to believe he was born in Dublin. One cannot just happen to know something by having a true belief. One must have good reasons or justification for the belief. Philosophers debate what justification is and how much is needed for knowledge, but it is clear in this case that there is plenty of evidence available. One could confirm Bono was born in Dublin via hospital documents for instance. There is a long tradition in philosophy of defining knowledge as justified, true belief. Science is the paradigm of knowledge in this sense.

If knowledge is justified true belief, then it seems all knowledge will be propositional knowledge, knowledge of truths. Knowledge then will have to involve thought. To believe that the lead singer of U2 is Irish one must have that thought. And to think that thought one must understand the concepts of *being Irish, being a lead singer,* and *being a member of U2.* Concepts can apply to many different objects. For example, *being Irish* applies to many different objects, all the distinct individuals that are Irish. Put simply, thinking is the ability to relate objects with concepts. Relating the concepts of *being Irish, being a lead singer,* and *being a member of U2* in the appropriate way produces the thought that the lead singer of U2 is Irish, that is, a proposition. Belief occurs when one accepts the proposition as a fact, the way the world is. Knowledge occurs when the proposition is a fact and one has good reasons, evidence, or justification for accepting it. All such knowledge depends on thought, our ability to cut the world into categories with concepts.

This point can be put more clearly in terms of language and sentences instead of concepts and propositions. To believe that the lead singer of U2 is Irish is to believe the sentence "The lead singer of U2 is Irish" is true. To believe is to assent to the truth of a sentence. Sentences are made up of words related appropriately. The subject of the sentence is the description "The lead singer of U2" and the predicate is the phrase "is Irish." The thought is that the predicate applies to the object so described. The sentence is true if this is so, false if it is not. True sentences reflect the way the world is, false ones do not. A belief is true when the sentence one assents to is true. Propositional knowledge occurs when one has a justified true belief. One can think of knowledge in terms of propositions or in terms of sentences. Either way knowledge depends upon thought or language.

## Feeling as Knowledge: Revelation

When U2 songs favor feeling over knowledge, feeling seems to be contrasted with propositional knowledge, knowledge that depends on thought. But feeling can be thought of as perceptual, emotional, or introspective. All these kinds of feelings involve a different kind of knowledge however. They were all cases of knowledge by acquaintance. Knowledge by acquaintance is unlike propositional knowledge. Propositional knowledge of reality is mediated by thought or language. Knowledge by acquaintance is direct awareness of things. The feeling mentioned in the lyric "I want to feel sunlight on my face" is a direct awareness of the bodily sensation of sunlight unmediated by any concepts or language. It is pure feeling, we might say.

The song "Staring at the Sun" says, "Don't try too hard to think / Don't think at all." This seems to emphasize the importance of feeling over thinking in the same ways as the lines in "Vertigo":

"Your head / can't rule your heart / A feeling is so much stronger than / a thought." The importance of feeling here may be that, unlike propositional knowledge, it provides us with a direct access to reality, a reality that one will miss if one tries to think of it in terms of concepts or describe it in language. Feeling as knowledge by acquaintance is what has traditionally been described as 'intuition', and, in the religious case, 'revelation'. It is no wonder that U2, a band known for its religious sentiments and commitments, should plead the case for feeling as a way not only to have direct awareness of oneself and immediate connection to other people but as a way to relate directly to God. The song "When I Look at the World" seems to be sung in the voice of one who cannot experience such a feeling but recognizes the lack from seeing another who can: "So I try to be like you / Try to feel it like you do," but "I can't see what you see . . ."

The person longs to feel what the other person feels that allows him or her to see the world in a way that "bring[s] them [him/her] to their [his/her] knees." It is a religious revelation, a feeling that has transformed the person into someone with "an expression / So clear and so true / That it changes the atmosphere / When you [he/she] walk[s] into the room." The songs of U2 seem to champion feeling as the possibility of a kind of knowledge by acquaintance, a direct awareness, of God or divine reality. The feeling that the music of U2 is heavy with philosophical weight is not an illusion. They, in fact, find themselves in the company of a philosopher such as William James, who wrote in his classic *The Varieties of Religious Experience*:

> I do believe that feeling is the deeper source of religion, and that philosophic and theological formulas are secondary products, like translations of a text into another tongue. . . . When I call theological formulas secondary products, I mean that in a world in which no religious feeling had ever existed, I doubt whether any philosophic theology could ever have been framed. I doubt if dispassionate intellectual contemplation of the universe, apart from inner unhappiness and the need for deliverance on the one hand and mystical emotion on the other, would ever have resulted in religious philosophies such as we now possess.[3]

---

[3] William James, *The Varieties of Religious Experience* (London: Longmans, Green, 1905), p. 431.

U2 seems to express James's philosophical thesis in the emotions of their music—the agony of 'inner unhappiness,' the desire for 'deliverance,' and the ecstasy of religious revelation. Like James, the songs of U2 call for a kind of mysticism over a kind of religious understanding restricted by thought or concepts. Feeling is more important than knowledge when it comes to the matter of ultimate importance. That is, feeling as a kind of knowledge by acquaintance trumps propositional knowledge when it comes to what matters most.

This preference for feeling as knowledge by acquaintance over propositional knowledge also explains why Bono's Christianity seems controversial to more traditional believers. Traditionally, revelation has been thought of in propositional terms. Revelation is thought to occur when God communicates some truths to humans by extraordinary means. These truths are the propositions expressed by the sentences of the Scriptures. Faith, on this understanding of revelation, is believing this set of truths. Call this view *propositional* revelation. The view suggested in James and the songs of U2 is *mystical* revelation, revelation as an immediate experience or feeling. That this is how Bono understands the Scriptures is evident in an interview from his new book. He explains the importance of feeling in relating himself to God when he recounts this story about his father:

> He said: "You do seem to have a relationship with God." And I said: "Didn't you ever have one?" He said: "No." And I said: "But you have been a Catholic for most of your life."—"Yeah, lots of people are Catholic. It was a one-way conversation . . . You seem to hear something back from the silence!" I said: "That's true, I do." And he said: "How do you feel it?" I said: "I hear it in some sort of instinctive way, I feel a response to prayer, or I feel led in a direction. Or if I am studying the Scriptures, they become alive in an odd way, and they make sense to the moment I'm in, they're no longer a historical document." He was mind-blown by this.[4]

Mystical revelation is a direct relationship with God found in a momentary feeling. This knowledge of God does not result in a set of truths or propositional knowledge. In fact, this mystical

---

[4] Bono and Michka Assayas, *Bono in Conversation* (New York: Riverhead, 2005), p. 25.

revelation is *ineffable*—it cannot be expressed in truths of language. To try to articulate it is, as James says, "like translations of a text into another tongue."[5]

A serious philosophical problem arises for a defender of this kind of revelation as feeling, as knowledge by acquaintance. Simply put, one person's feeling is another person's pathology. James admits the epistemological limitations to this type of revelation: Religious feelings or experiences " . . . have the right to be absolutely authoritative over the individuals to whom they come . . . [but] no authority emanates from them which should make it a duty for those who stand outside of them to accept their revelations . . ." (*Varieties,* p. 422). There is no standard, beside the experiences themselves, for judging the veracity of these feelings or experiences. Do they come from direct relation with God or are they products of one's own mind? James calls this the problem of *origins.* He admits it has no answer. Does that refute the importance of feeling over thought and propositional knowledge? James thinks not. James articulated a view called *pragmatism.* The truth of an idea was determined solely by its results. This pragmatism also applies to religious passions. The test of a religious experience or feeling is its results. How does it affect the person's life? Don't try to confirm the origin of the feeling, but instead look to its consequences. Alluding to a Biblical passage, James writes, "By their fruits ye shall know them, not by their roots . . . The *roots* of a man's virtue are inaccessible to us. No appearances whatever are infallible proofs of grace. Our practice is the only sure evidence . . ." (*Varieties,* p. 20). The feeling Bono describes is only significant of a relationship with God if it is reflected in moral transformation.

Philosophers have long argued over whether feeling is necessary for moral motivation. Suppose one has propositional knowledge of what one should do. That is, one has a true moral

---

[5] James, *The Varieties of Religious Experience.* Neither James nor Bono think that propositional knowledge and reason are bogus or unimportant in religion. James says he does not wish "to defend feeling at the expense of reason" (p. 431) and "Conceptions and constructions are thus a necessary part of our religion" (p. 432). That Bono thinks that religious feeling and propositional knowledge and reason are compatible is evident in the song "Miracle Drug": "Of science and the human heart / There is no limit . . . Love makes nonsense of space / And time will disappear / Love and logic keep us clear / Reason is on our side, love." Both Bono and James think feeling has primacy over propositional knowledge.

belief based on impeccable reasons. Does that knowledge make
one act? The Scottish philosopher David Hume (1711–1776)
famously said that it could not. Reason without feeling never
leads to action. As he put it, "Reason is, and ought only to be
the slave of the passions, and can never pretend to any other
office than to serve and obey them."[6] The importance of revelation as feeling manifests itself as the impetus of moral transformation. The feeling that most inspires the Christian vision
expressed in the songs of U2 is love. Bono says, "Well, I think I
know what God is. God is love, and as much as I respond [*sighs*]
in allowing myself to be transformed by that love and acting in
that love, that's my religion" (*Bono in Conversation*, p. 200). The
relationship with God that he finds in feeling manifest itself in
his concern for social justice and equality for the poor and the
oppressed. One can always remain skeptical of feeling as a kind
of knowledge or revelation. But if feeling can transform the
world, then one may want to reconsider the importance of feeling over knowledge and wish to embrace U2's message: "What
you don't know, you can feel it somehow."

---

[6] David Hume, *A Treatise of Human Nature* (Oxford: Oxford University Press, 1951
[1736]), p. 415.

# 14

# The Ancient Quarrel between Philosophy and Poetry: U2 and Trash

CHRIS TOLLEFSEN

U2, sadly, suffer on occasion from Misplaced Artistic Pretension, despite having the potential to be one of the great trash bands of all times. And this is in consequence of their willing and adept embrace of high imagery.

Why do I, a long-time follower of U2, now think this? Before we can understand the success and failure of U2, we need to have a look at Plato.

## Philosophy versus Poetry

In Plato's *Republic*, Socrates famously remarks that there is an ancient quarrel between poetry and philosophy, a quarrel which he believes is well-founded, and in which he joins on the side of philosophy. Central to his attack on poetry is the role of mimesis, or imitation, in poetry, and the relation between imitation and our "inferior part"—the part of our soul governed by the emotions. Plato's radical thesis was that imitations corrupted the soul by way of their appeal to this part.

What could such a quarrel possibly have to do with the the rock band U2? Quite a bit. For the overwhelming success of U2 as the world's greatest rock 'n' roll group, is in large part a consequence of their mastery of images—imitations—and their exploitation of the connection between imitations and emotions. To argue this thesis, I shall do three things.

First, I shall lay out a series of claims about the relation between imitations and emotions, and suggest why the connection should be worrisome. Second, I shall show how these claims relate to Plato's description of the origins of the ancient quarrel. Finally, I shall attempt to indicate some of the ways in which U2 are eminently skilled in the production of certain types of images and the corresponding emotions. The images in question are not trivial; one reason U2 is so successful is that their imitations—in their lyrics, their music, and their staging— are imitations of realities that transcend the personal, especially love, religion, and community. The grip of such imitations on our emotions is correspondingly strengthened.

## Imitative Emotions

Some types of imitations work, and appeal to us, in part because of their ability to stimulate in us further imitations—imitations of the emotions that we typically feel, or think we should feel, in the presence of the reality which is the object of the original imitations. These emotions are not themselves the emotions we feel in the presence of the reality. Compare our emotions in the presence of the death of a loved one, with our emotions at the death of a beloved character in a play, novel, or movie. Typically, the former emotions are in themselves more complex psychological states, often they are more disabling, and they are more linked to a wide set of other cognitive and psychological states than are what I am calling the imitative emotions. Finally, a point Plato makes much of, we enjoy those emotions I am calling imitative in a way that typically we do not enjoy genuine emotions.

To say that the emotions are more complex in the presence of the reality is to draw attention, for example, to certain temporal features of those emotions: we feel these emotions more and less pressingly at different times; sometimes we can go for a considerable period of time in which we do not "feel" the emotions actively. But we can reasonably say that we feel sorrow for a very long time after the death of a loved one. Sorrow at a death is not simply a matter of a fleeting state. Nor is it even always isolable as a particular feeling with a particular phenomenology—the sorrow of a death is often mixed up with guilt, sometimes with relief, with worry, with fear, and so on. Is there one emotion or many here? It seems difficult to say.

By contrast, imitative emotions are often quite pure: we feel distinctly and keenly the loss of the beloved character without a mingling of other emotions, and we feel it for a more or less distinct period of time. No one can be said to sorrow over Hamlet's death for much beyond his stay in the theatre, nor does anyone really feel guilty about his death or fearful of its consequences.

Nor has sorrow over Hamlet, or, to take an example from the Harry Potter series, Sirius Black, often disabled mature agents for very long; to allow oneself to become undone by such emotions is more an indulgence than anything else. The temporal limitedness of imitative emotions plays a role here, obviously, since part of the reason we are not disabled is that the emotion so quickly disappears. But even apart from that, I suspect that few people had any difficulty leaving the theaters after *Schindler's List*, nor did many people vomit up their popcorn; were we magically, and horribly, transported to an actual gassing of Jews on the other hand, it would be immensely hard to recover.

Finally, as the complexity and mingling of emotions would indicate, emotions in response to real events are typically integrated into a very wide set of cognitive and psychological states—memory, for example, intentions to act or not act in certain ways in consequence of the event, and a host of attendant emotions, desires, wishes, and beliefs, such as religious beliefs. Imitative emotions play a much weaker role in the cognitive and psychological economy of an individual. In general they are much less closely tied to subsequent intentions—the personal experience of crushing poverty typically leads to greater lifestyle changes than the quasi-experience of poverty in film, or novels, or paintings.

However, in their own way, and for reasons related to the differences, imitative emotions can appear to be much more powerful than some genuine emotions. While many of the most significant aspects of our lives are marked by equally significant events, still, many such aspects are experienced also in routine everyday settings: marriage, religion, community, country, love, death and mourning—all have moments and periods of intense emotion, but all equally have emotional down time, and some of the most important elements of these parts of our lives are more cognitive, or willed, than felt. The commitment that underwrites a marriage, for example, or the belief that the sacraments of one's religion are truly sacramental, putting one in touch with God, while occasionally, and sometimes intensely, felt, are not always felt, or felt intensely. Yet they require a more or less constant upkeep of the commitments they involve, and of the beliefs implicated by those commitments.

By contrast, the imitative emotions associated with such transcendent aspects of our lives as love, God, and community—all of which, I shall show, are fundamental to the imagery of U2—are by their nature intensely felt within a discernable period of time. Moreover, and this is a crucial difference, they are experienced with relatively little effort compared to the effort needed to sustain a marriage, or religious devotion, or community or country. Dealing with the realities in question, in each case, requires genuine and sustained work—one reason, I suspect, for the come-and-go quality of their attendant emotions. Focus is on the work, and the object of the work, and emotion can go unnoticed, or disappear altogether in the labor.

In consequence, for many agents, on many occasions, the imitative emotions offer a welcome substitute for the strenuous, and sometimes tedious labors of love or religion and so on. Surely much political rhetoric, many forms of advertising, and the dubious use of stirring music at important moments, all take advantage of this fact, encouraging participants to feel the moment in a way that actually discourages the thought that more needs to be done to achieve or appreciate the reality in question.

I'm suggesting that our response to imitations is often itself imitative—that is, it involves emotions that are themselves imitations of the emotions we experience in the presence of the realities which artistic imitations imitate. There is, in fact, a frequently added level of imitation in these parts: the arts can imitate the objects of our emotions: a dying man, a beautiful woman, the crucifixion. Or, the arts can imitate the emotions we feel in the presence of such objects. Music in a minor key seems arguably like this, as do some poems, paintings, and so on. Given our tendency to take on the emotions of those around us, these imitations of emotions typically have the same effect that imitations of their objects have. Finally, I have suggested that allowing ourselves to experience the imitative emotions can be corruptive, because we may be encouraged to think that we have experienced, and are fully engaged in, the reality imitated.

## Plato and the "Ancient Quarrel"

My account thus far overlaps substantially, though not entirely, with the explanation, and justification, Plato gives for the "ancient quarrel between poetry and philosophy." Plato's attack on imitation in Book X of the *Republic* operates on two fronts. The first concerns the epistemic status of imitative poetry. Is it the case, asks Plato, that Homer, for example, has knowledge of the things he imitates, and are his imitations accurate, knowledge producing, or veridical?

I can't here go into detail over Plato's answers to these questions, or defend them. Roughly, Plato argues that it is implausible to think that Homer does have knowledge of the realities he imitates. Plato addresses Homer, asking "What city gives you credit for being a good lawgiver who benefited it . . . is there any war in Homer's time remembered that was won by his generalship and advice?" and ". . . as befits a wise man, are many inventions and useful devices in the crafts or sciences attributed to Homer . . .?" (*Republic*, 599e–600a).

More radically, Plato argues that by their nature, artistic imitations are unsuitable for conveying truth. In Book X, Plato famously compares the bed itself, or the form of the bed, to the bed made by the craftsman in imitation of the form. The artistic imitation of the craftsman's bed is thus an imitation of an imitation and therefore "three removes from the truth." But, most importantly, Plato argues that the artistic imitation is not even an imitation of the craftsman's bed itself, but only of the appearance of that bed—from the side, or the front, or what have you. Thus, "imitation is far removed from the truth, for it touches only a small part of each thing and a part that is itself only an image. And that, it seems, is why it can produce everything."[1]

This combined attack on the knowledge of artists, and the ability of works of art to convey truth is the first front of Plato's quarrel. The second has to do with the relationship between imitations and the emotions. :"[O]n which of a person's parts does [imitation] exert its power?" Plato answers that it is on the emotional part of the soul—reason and spirit are overcome, and indeed often willingly give way, for they think it nobler to weep

---

[1] For a defense of Plato's claims on the epistemic status of works of art see Olaf Tollefsen, "Realism, Art, and *Republic X*" in *Foundationalism Defended* (Bethesda: Cambridge Press, 1995), pp. 181–193.

at another's sorrows than at one's own. But by playing to the emotions, Plato thinks "imitation really consorts with a part of us that is far from reason, and the result . . . is neither sound nor true."

It is here that my analysis differs slightly from Plato's. Plato arguably takes one of the strictest lines on the emotions in the history of philosophy. While certain desires might be acceptable in order to enable us to meet basic demands of life—desires for food and sex, for example, when tightly controlled by reason—Plato seems not to recognize a wider role for the emotions in the moral life. Whereas Aristotle, and Aquinas following, would suggest that a rather wider variety of emotions could be educated by reason, and that the virtuous agent was one whose emotions were in harmony with, rather than suppressed by, reason, Plato appears to advocate suppression of emotions. So imitations are problematic for Plato because they make us weep at all, not because, as on my account, of the nature of the emotions that accompany weeping at works of art.

On my view, there is very likely good reason to weep at real death, to rejoice in spiritual goods, to find one's marriage or faith uplifting, to be angry at injustice and so on.[2] My quarrel is not, thus, with these emotions as such, but with their imitations, a quarrel intimately related to, but slightly different from, Plato's.

## High and Low Imagery and Emotion

I would argue that most popular music is characterized by two qualities. First, to the extent that it is imitative, and produces imitative emotions, they are typically what I shall call "low" emotions. Much popular music is about infatuation and sex, not love. The low emotions are produced by low imagery—the imagery of sexual conquest, of being with one's posse, of chillin' with a beer or some alternate substance. By contrast, what I would call the high emotions are those associated with realities that transcend, or claim to transcend, the immediately personal: love, religion, country, and community, to name four of considerable importance.

---

[2] A slightly different sort of case, for Plato, since he believes anger to be part of the "spirited part" of the soul.

Second, popular music is simple. This is a great part of the reason for its success: it makes few cognitive demands, and can be followed by those with a relatively limited attention span. Popular music is typically highly rhythmic, and enjoyable for that reason; in provoking listeners to dance, it provides a context for the enjoyment of the good of play more than, I would argue, it does the good of beauty. Popular music, I would argue, is typically not beautiful, and thus only minimally instantiates the primary good of art: aesthetic enjoyment of the beautiful. The enjoyment taken in a work of popular art, especially popular music, typically involves a combination of low-level aesthetic pleasure, and the pleasure of play, especially physical play.

The following, then, can be called Tollefsen's Taxonomy of Popular Music. On my view, pop music, like many other forms of popular entertainment such as movies, can move in four directions. First, some pop entertainment becomes art. But it does this, I would argue, *not* because of a move from low emotion and imagery to high, but because of a move to greater complexity. It is the complexity of the interplay of parts that, when arranged in a pleasing whole, provides the depth to genuine art that we can call beauty. And the development of such depth out of the play of the popular is certainly possible, whether by individual artists who take a form of popular entertainment and revolutionize it, or by cultures through time, whose popular forms of entertainment become increasingly layered and complex.

Tollefsen's Principle of Misplaced Artistic Pretension, however, holds that on occasion popular entertainers mistakenly come to think that it is the other typical feature of popular entertainment that makes the difference between entertainment and art: the focus on low imagery and emotion. Thus, attempted moves to the status of art are accomplished by replacement of the low imagery with high, and the production of high, rather than low emotion in listeners, viewers, readers, etc. But the pretension truly is misplaced: the complexity of a work of beauty may be achieved in the structuring of the low as well as the high—*The Miller's Tale* deserves a place on a list of great works of literature just as the *Divine Comedy* does.

Trash is what good popular entertainment should be. Essentially a form of rhythmic play, whether in music, movies, fiction or the visual arts, trash does not seek to instruct, but simply to entertain. This does not mean it is unskilled: far from it.

Good trash takes work, often considerable technical skills, and an awareness of what one is doing. Entertainment is, it seems to me, also what the beautiful enables, so we must see something of a continuum between the popular arts and the high arts (a different high low distinction than that between the low and the high emotions). As Pauline Kael writes in her essay "Trash, Art, and the Movies," to which the concept of trash in this essay owes much, "Movie art is not the opposite of what we have always enjoyed in movies, it is not to be found in a return to that official high culture, it is what we have always found good in movies only more so."[3]

Cynical trash, by contrast, which is the fourth spot on my taxonomy, attempts to do the work of trash, while taking advantage of people's manifest need and desire for entertainment, and their willingness to settle for what is poorly made, pandering and cheap. Hollywood's sequel mentality is largely a consequence of a commitment of cynical trash rather than good trash. One familiar quasi-technical term to designate this branch of the taxonomy is "crap."

To put the taxonomy to work, let me suggest the following. *Jaws*, the Spielberg movie, is trash. *AI*, the Spielberg movie, is trash pretending to be art. *Schindler's List*, the Spielberg movie, is art, or at least reasonably close to it. And *Hook*, the Spielberg movie, is cynical trash, or, if you will, crap.

## The U2 Formula

U2, sadly, suffer on occasion from Misplaced Artistic Pretension, despite having the potential to be one of the great trash bands of all times. And this is in consequence of their willing and adept embrace of high imagery.

The case for this must be made in the first case by reference to the imagery itself. I believe that much of the imagery of U2, lyrically, but also in other ways, works according to the following fourfold sequence. First, the songs begin with a kind of idealized love, possibly, but not necessarily romantic; they are typically not about sex, but about a common idea of love as transcendent, as able to raise people out of and above them-

---

[3] Pauline Kael, "Trash, Art and the Movies," in *Going Steady* (New York: Marion Boyars, 1994), p. 106.

selves. Second, to solidify this image of the transcendent, these songs of love are frequently rife with religious imagery—the love of a woman, and the love of God, are sometimes difficult to disentangle. To this point, we are essentially working within the realm of the lyrics or the songs. The third aspect concerns the music. The ringing and chiming guitars for which the Edge is famous seem the right counterpart to Bono's soaring lyrics and voice; moreover, U2 songs often begin slow and rise in pitch, or have a quiet moment in the middle after which the music again crashes in. It is Big Moment music, or, as it was called in the 1980s, when bands such as the Waterboys, the Alarm and Big Country worked in U2's shadow, the Big Music.[4]

The fourth stage is essentially tied to U2's performances, and involve the extension of the "you" addressed in the songs to the crowd of fans to whom Bono is singing. The "you" might be the beloved offering salvation, or the beloved to whom salvation and transcendence is offered; but the great achievement of a U2 concert is to create the appearance that the group and the fans are all a community together, all bound up in the transcending love the raises people up and out of themselves. This is part of the group's self-understanding; at a concert at the University of Notre Dame in 2000, Bono exhorted the crowd "Take it to church; that's right, you're in church."[5]

An example of this may be seen in the "Elevation" tour performance of "I Will Follow." A song from U2's first album, it is an amazingly simple but also surprisingly affecting, and hence effective piece.[6] This song might be about the love of Bono's mother, or it might be about romantic love (the fact that it is ambiguous is important to U2's success, as we shall see below). But the voice of the song is "looking at myself...blind, I could not see." Here we have both the self-enclosedness to which transcendent love is the antidote, and also the intertwining of reli-

---

[4] From a song by Mike Scott on the Waterboys' first EP.

[5] Bono, quoted in Steve Braden, "U2's Hi-Tech Tent Revival," *America* 186 (7th January, 2002), p. 20. There is, of course, another form of imagery used by the group—the video imagery and the costumery, utilized massively on the Zooropa and Popmart tours. I am less concerned with this use of images, since in part its function was to deliberately call attention to itself *as* a use of images. In consequence, it was, I think, less powerful and seductive than the band's more straightforward approach on the Elevation tour.

[6] U2 lyrics may be found at http://lyrics.interference.com/u2/lyrics/index.html.

gious imagery, in the allusion, one of several, to "Amazing Grace." Arguably, the way out of the blindness, the alienation indicated both by being "outside" and by being "inside," is to follow the beloved; again, the phrase "I will follow" has clearly religious overtones, hearkening to Christ's injunction to follow him.

The use of harmonics in the middle eight calls to mind bells, possible church bells, a reference Bono makes explicit in the Elevation tour—"Make those bells ring, Edge, ring those bells," he urges before singing "Boston lift me up on your shoulders, let's get to a place where we'll never get older." The audience has now been incorporated into the U2 community, and invited to be the bridge to a transcendent space to which Bono aspires. As he sings "Your eyes make a circle, I see you when I go in there," Bono might still be addressing the audience, or some other beloved; in any event, the audience has been by this point sufficiently encouraged to think of themselves as pursuing with Bono whatever transcendent love he is following. The four stages of a U2 song have been achieved.

There can be no doubt that U2's audience do take themselves to form a community with the group, and that they take this to be healing, and even ennobling. This has been especially apparent since September 11th, 2001. Since that time, the ambiguity of reference in U2's lyrics, and the band's offer of love as a way above the solipsism of the self has been understood by fans as specifically an offer of relief for the solipsism of the *grieving* self.

The Elevation tour video is interesting in this regard. It was recorded several months before September 11th, but it would be almost impossible for someone watching it and not knowing the temporal location not to think it was addressed to an audience scarred by that day's events. Beginning with "Elevation" ("Love / lift me up out of these blues / Won't you tell me something true / I believe in you") and including, within the first ten songs, "Beautiful Day" ("Touch me, take me to that other place / Teach me, I know I'm not a hopeless case"), "Stuck in a Moment You Can't Get Out Of," (reportedly about Michael Hutchence's suicide, but including the promise that "if your way should falter / Along the stony pass / It's just a moment / This time will pass") "New York," "I Will Follow," and "In A Little While ("In a little while . . . I'll be there / In a little while / This hurt will hurt no more / I'll be home love.")

Analysis of this nature could continue indefinitely. And as someone who attended several U2 shows in younger and perhaps happier days, I can attest to the way in which a U2 show leaves one with the sense of having participated in a "culture," to use Bono's words, a huge community in which all are one. But the community is an image only, an appearance, generated by the powerful imagery of U2, but not, for that reason, more real. And the Platonic worry that all this raises, is whether in the end this is really a good thing. Is there genuine healing or redemption at a U2 show, genuine transcendence of the evils of the day, evils as horrible as those of 9/11, or are audience members allowing a lesser part of themselves—the part seduced by imitative emotions, to convince them that they have received in two hours what it can take a lifetime to fail to achieve?[7]

---

[7] Thanks to Pete, Tom, Heather, Heidi, Rick, Art, Debbie, Mike, Cheryl and Laurie: U2 concert companions, 1985–1989.

# 15

# Aristotle, U2, and the Abolition of Man: "A Feeling Is So Much Stronger than a Thought"

DAVID WERTHER

U2's *How to Dismantle an Atomic Bomb* begins with "Vertigo," a song that contrasts thoughts and feelings.

> Lights go down. It's dark
> The jungle is your head
> Can't rule your heart
> A feeling is so much stronger than
> A thought

"Vertigo" is followed by "Miracle Drug," a song Steve Stockman tells us is based on "the life and disability of Christopher Nolan, a school colleague of the band."[1]

> After a difficult birth, the motor center of his brain was so damaged that he could not coordinate his limbs. His voice was so distorted it was unintelligible. When he was eleven, he was given a new miracle drug called Lioresal, which relaxed his muscles so that he could move his neck ever so slightly. He was given a unicorn stick that was strapped to his forehead and allowed him to type . . . the tiniest movement of his neck revealed a genius who had been captive in a dysfunctional body for years . . . Nolan arrived at Mount Temple around the end of U2's time there. That he became a great Irish writer who won the Whitbread Book of the Year in 1987 also endeared him to Bono. (*Walk On*, pp. 219–220)

---

[1] Steve Stockman, *Walk On: The Spiritual Journey of U2* (Orlando: Relevant Books, 2005), p. 219.

In "Miracle Drug" the feelings of confusion and disorientation in "Vertigo" are replaced by a very different emotion, compassion. Bono underscores the importance of this emotion by drawing upon Jesus's story of justice and judgment: the parable of the sheep and the goats. There, Jesus identifies the people of his kingdom as those who cared for him by looking after the neediest.

> Then the king will say to those on his right hand, 'Come you that are blessed by my Father, inherit the kingdom prepared for you from the foundation of the world; for I was hungry and you gave me food, I was thirsty and you gave me something to drink *I was a stranger and you welcomed me*, I was naked and you gave me clothing, I was in prison and you visited me.' Then the righteous will answer him, 'Lord, when was it that we saw you hungry and gave you food, or thirsty and gave you something to drink? And when was it that we saw you as a stranger and welcomed you in, or naked and gave you clothing? And when was it that we saw you sick or in prison and visited you?' And the king will answer them, 'Truly I tell you, just as you did it to the least of these who are members of my family, you did it to me.' (Matthew 25: 34–40, emphasis added)

Toward the end of "Miracle Drug" Bono's lyrics borrow from the gospel.

> Beneath the noise
> Below the din
> I hear a voice
> It's whispering
> In science and in medicine
> *'I was a stranger*
> *You took me in'* [emphasis added]

## "The Jungle Is Your Head, Can't Rule Your Heart"

Compassion means "to suffer along with." Listening to "Miracle Drug" provides one with the opportunity not only to sense something of Bono's compassion but also to share it. The philosopher Aristotle (384/3–322/1 B.C.) tells us that "goodness consists in feeling delight where one should, and loving and hating aright."[2] Further, such feelings can arise in response to music and result in "a change of the soul" (*Politics*, 1340a 17, p. 344). If Aristotle is right about this then responding appropriately to "Miracle Drug" can make us better people.[3] And, I think that the same goes for other U2 songs. "Pride (In the Name of Love)" and "Crumbs from Your Table" come immediately to mind.

Some people will respond with incredulity to my suggestion that experiencing U2's music may result in moral growth. However, with some reflection on an Aristotelian line of reasoning and some of U2's songs, I hope to show that such skepticism is unjustified.

In the following passage Aristotle makes a connection between music and morality.

> Since music belongs to the category of pleasures, and since goodness consists in *feeling delight* where one should, and loving and hating aright, we may clearly draw some conclusions. First there is no lesson which we are so much concerned to learn, and no habit which we are so much concerned to acquire, as that of forming the right judgments on, and feeling delight in, fine characters and good actions. Next, musical times and tunes provide us with images of character-images of fortitude [courage] and temperance [self-control], and of all the forms of their opposites; images of the other states-which come closer to their actual nature than anything else can do. This is a fact which is clear from our own experience; to listen to these images is to undergo real change of soul. Now to acquire a habit of feeling pain or taking delight in an image is something closely allied to feeling pain or taking delight in the actual reality. (*Politics*, 1340a 17, p. 344)[4]

---

[2] Aristotle, *The Politics of Aristotle* (Oxford: Oxford University Press, 1875), 1340a17, p. 343.

[3] My claim here is not that Aristotle would have so regarded the song "Miracle Drug." Rather, I am merely committing myself to the broadly Aristotelian claim that our responses to music can sometimes have a positive impact on our souls, and as I see it, "Miracle Drug" is a case in point.

[4] I came to see the significance of this passage, and a good deal more about moral development, from M.F. Burnyeat, "Aristotle on Learning to be Good" in *Essays on Aristotle's Ethics*, ed. Amelie Oksenberg Rorty (Berkeley: University of California Press, 1980).

Now consider an argument inspired by Aristotle's thought and applied to the music of U2.

**PREMISE 1:** Forming right judgments regarding character and action, and feeling delight in fine characters and good actions is an important lesson.

**PREMISE 2:** U2's music can provide us with images of fine characters and good actions, and move us to feel delight in them.

**PREMISE 3:** If we are exposed repeatedly to U2's images of fine character and good action and moved to delight in them, we may come habitually to delight in these things.

**CONCLUSION:** Repeated exposure to U2's musical images of fine characters and good actions can result in habitual delight in them.

This argument is valid that is, if its premises are true, then its conclusion must be true. Are its premises true? The truth of Premise 1 seems uncontroversial. If you think otherwise ask yourself the following question: "Would my view of Bono change dramatically if I were to learn that instead of channeling millions to the poor, he has been embezzling millions from charities?" Unless you can answer "no" you affirm the truth of the first premise.

Skipping over Premise 2 for the moment, note that an affirmation of Premise 3 does not commit one to the implausible view that listening to any U2 music inevitably leads to a habitual delight in good persons and right actions. The claim is only that by listening to the music of U2 *that does portray* right actions and virtuous persons we *can* come habitually to delight in that which is morally positive. Note also that this premise does not assert the strong claim that repeated exposure to certain sorts of music *must* result in certain sorts of habits, but the weaker claim that repeated exposure *may* result in certain sorts of habits. And, since habits are the products of repeated actions, or in this case passions (being moved), Premise 3 seems to be acceptable.

## Until the End of the World

Matters become more complicated and controversial when we consider Premise 2: U2's music can provide us with images of fine characters and good actions, and move us to feel delight in them.

Some might argue that Bono would find Premise 2 to be problematic as he seems to have conceived of music as catharsis or release.[5]

> **SPIN:** Is music purifying?
>
> **BONO:** For me, yes. I don't think that I could do anything else. I don't think that I am capable of doing anything else. Rock 'n' roll has always been a release for me. That's what it should be. It's a purging thing.[6]

Talk of release, purging, and purification brings us back to Aristotle, as he also recognized music's cathartic role.

Students of Aristotle offer two interpretations of catharsis.[7] On both views catharsis concerns the emotions of fear and pity. On one of the views, catharsis plays a role of purification, such that the soul is cleansed through pity and fear. This is the so-called religious reading of catharsis. On the other view, catharsis plays a role of purgation, such that the soul is freed from, as it were, excess pity and fear. This is the so-called medical reading of catharsis. Whichever view one ultimately takes, a case can be made for the cathartic significance of U2's music.

Consider two powerful songs, "Exit" and "Until the End of the World." "Exit" evokes feelings of fear, fear of losing control, giving into one's dark side, perhaps even taking one's life. "You know he got the cure . . . but then he went astray, / He used to stay awake / To drive the dreams he had away / He wanted to believe / In the hands of love . . ."

---

[5] See Chris Tollefsen's comments on U2 and catharsis at the end of Chapter 14 in this volume.

[6] "U2," Interview by Jeff Spurrier in *Spin* (May 1985), p. 23.

[7] For my discussion of Aristotle's aesthetics I am indebted to the very clear summaries by Frederick Copleston and Sir David Ross. Frederick Copleston, S.J., *A History of Philosophy: Greece and Rome Volume I Part II* (Garden City, New York: Image Books, 1962), pp. 100–112. Sir David Ross, *Aristotle* (London: Methuen, 1964), pp. 276–290.

In his commentary on "Exit," Niall Stokes describes the song as one of "purgation."

> That was the point of "Exit" to convey the state of mind of some-one driven, by whatever powerful urges, to the very brink of des-peration. . . . *it was a method of purging* the band's own demons, their own anger and fury at the vicissitudes fate had thrust upon them. It was a way of coming to terms with death and grief. It was an exorcism."[8]

Here, then, is an instance of the medical role of catharsis.

In contrast to "Exit," where there is an experience of purga-tion, in "Until the End of the World" there is a possibility of purification. In this song the betrayal of Jesus is told from Judas's perspective. In listening to the song one can identify with Judas and imagine oneself "drowning in sorrows" and experiencing "waves of regret." The song does not offer us relief from fear, purgation. Rather, it produces what, given the subject of the song, might be appropriately called a "holy fear," providing a possibility of purification and self-examination for those who, in the words of the betrayed, "have ears to hear."

It seems that however one understands Aristotle's notion of catharsis, some of U2's songs play primarily that role. Some but not all. In affirming premise 2 of the original argument, "U2's music can provide us with images of fine characters and good actions, and move us to feel delight in them," I am not thereby denying a cathartic role for U2's work. I am merely refusing to restrict U2's music to that role.

## Pride in the Name of Love

In keeping with Premise 2, U2 expresses a number of moral ideals, including courage and justice. The courageous person, Aristotle tells us, neither shuns danger, as do the cowardly, nor feigns fearlessness, as do the reckless.[9] Rather, this person endures even that which is most dreadful, death, but does so only if "it is noble to do so or base to refuse" (*Nicomachean Ethics*, 1116a 12, p. 71). One way in which we can begin to cultivate

---

[8] Niall Stokes, *U2 Into the Heart* (New York: Thunder's Mouth, 2001), p. 76. Emphasis added.

[9] Aristotle, *Nicomachean Ethics* (Indianapolis: Bobbs-Merrill, 1985), 1115b 24–1116a9, p. 71.

courage is to be moved by the sacrifices of those who have fallen before us. U2 relates one such sacrifice that of Dr. Martin Luther King Jr. in "Pride (In the Name of Love)."

Rock critic Kurt Loder was not much moved by the song. He refers to it rather dismissively as "well-intentioned" and adds that it "gets over only on the strength of its resounding beat (a U2 trademark) and big, droning bass line, not on the nobility of its lyrics, which are unremarkable."[10] It has also been noted that Bono did not get his facts straight: "Early morning, April four / Shot rings out in the Memphis sky / Free at last, they took your life / They could not take your pride." King's assassination took place in the evening not the morning.

In terms of the song's power to move listeners, the time of King's assassination is irrelevant. Certainly no one who agrees with the judgment expressed in "Top 100 Singles of the Last 25 Years", that "Pride in the Name of Love" is "one of the most inspirational songs of this decade"[11] will be much worried about the fact that Bono botched the time of day. Many will concur with the Edge's perspective, "As you get to know it better, it draws you in and becomes something personal to you" (*U2*, p. 132).

A case can be made that Adam Clayton was drawn in. The following story told by Bono underscores the inspirational force of "Pride (In the Name of Love)."

> 1987. Somewhere in the south. We'd been campaigning for Dr. King, for his birthday to become a national holiday. In Arizona, they are saying no. We're campaigning very hard for Dr. King. Some people don't like it. Some people get very annoyed. Some people want to kill us. Some people are taken very seriously by the FBI. They tell the singer that he shouldn't play the gig because tonight his life is at risk, and he must not go on stage. And the singer laughs. Of course we're playing the gig. Of course we go onstage, and I'm singing "Pride (In the Name of Love)"—the third verse—and I close my eyes. And you know, I'm excited about meeting my maker, but maybe not tonight. I don't really want to meet my maker tonight. I close my eyes and when I look up I see Adam Clayton standing in front of me, holding his bass as only

---

[10] Kurt Loder, "*The Unforgettable Fire* Album Review" in *U2: The Ultimate Compendium of Interviews, Articles, Facts, and Opinions from the Files of Rolling Stone* (San Francisco: Hyperion, 1994), p. 21.

[11] "Top 100 Singles of the Last 25 Years" in *U2: The Ultimate Compendium*, p. 132.

Adam Clayton can hold his bass. There are people in this room who'd tell you they'd take a bullet for you, but Adam Clayton would have taken a bullet for me.[12]

## Crumbs from Your Table

U2's treatment of courage in "Pride (In the Name of Love)" is positive. In contrast, U2's treatment of the virtue of justice in "Crumbs from your Table" is negative. The band provides us with a picture of injustice which calls forth feelings of anger, indignation, and shame. As the title suggests we listen to the cry of an impoverished person who desires only our leftovers. It's hard not to feel ashamed of our affluence and pious platitudes when hearing the chorus: "You speak of signs and wonders / I need something other / I would believe if I was able / But I'm waiting for the crumbs from your table." And, it is hard not to feel guilty knowing that "where you live should not determine whether you live or whether you die" and realizing that in sharing only crumbs we have had a hand in determining needless deaths.

In "Crumbs from Your Table" and "Pride (In the Name of Love)" U2 succeeds in the Aristotelian task of providing moral images in music and producing appropriate feelings in some of its listeners. At the risk of seeming to disparage these excellent songs, I think that it's fair to say that neither song demands much of the listener. It's pretty hard to miss the point.

## Wake Up Dead Man

Sometimes the band's message is expressed less directly and some listeners just don't get it. For example, some fans did not realize that when Bono took on the guise of McPhisto ( = Mephistophiles = the devil) he was attempting to mock the devil.[13] Presumably most of these fans were just turned off. But, it is possible that some fans completely misconstrued the message. Thus, someone unfamiliar with psalms of lament might consider "Wake up Dead Man" to be impious.[14]

---

[12] "Transcript: U2's Rock and Roll Hall of Fame Induction Speeches", http://www.atu2.com/events/05/rockhall.

[13] For some helpful commentary see *Walk On*, pp. 105–06.

[14] For an insightful discussion see Brian J. Walsh "Wake Up Dead Man: Singing the Psalms of Lament" in Raewynne J. Whitelely and Beth Maynard, eds., *Get Up Off Your Knees Preaching the U2 Catalog* (Cambridge, Massachusetts: Cowley, 2003), pp. 37–42.

Jesus, Jesus help me
I'm alone in this world
And a fucked up world it is too
Tell me, tell me the story
The one about eternity
And the way it's all gonna be
WAKE UP WAKE UP DEAD MAN
WAKE UP WAKE UP DEAD MAN
Jesus, I'm waiting here boss
I know you're looking out for us
But maybe your hands aren't free . . .

Instead, this song is an instance of what Bono calls "Honesty, even to the point of anger":

> He [the psalmist David] was forced into exile and ended up in a cave in some no-name border town facing the collapse of his ego and abandonment by God. But this is where the soap opera got interesting, this is where David is said to have composed his first psalm—a blues. That's what a lot of psalms feel like to me, the blues. Man shouting at God . . .
>
> I hear echoes of this holy row when un-holy bluesman Robert Johnson howls "There's a hellhound on my trail" or when Van Morrison sings "Sometimes I feel like a motherless child." . . .
>
> Abandonment, displacement, is the stuff of my favorite psalms. The Psalter may be a font of gospel music, but for me it's in his despair that the psalmist really reveals the nature of his special relationship with God. Honesty, even to the point of anger. "How long, Lord? Wilt thou hide thy face forever?" (Psalm 89) or "Answer me when I call" (Psalm 5).[15]

My case then for the positive moral significance of U2's images of fine characters and good actions is a modest one. I grant that some songs have no such role and some have primarily a cathartic effect. And I grant that the band sometimes fails to get its message across. But that does not negate the fact that the band sometimes succeeds and does so spectacularly.

If, as I have argued, all three of the premises in our argument are true, we arrive at an interesting and surprising conclusion:

---

[15] Bono, "Introduction," in *Selections from the Book of Psalms* (New York: Grove Press, 1999), pp. vii–viii.

Repeated exposure to U2's musical images of fine characters and good actions can result in habitual delight in them. And, this conclusion is consistent with Bono's words to his father early in the band's career.

> I hope our lives will be a testament to the people who follow us, and to the music business where never before have so many lost and sorrowful people gathered in one place pretending they're having a good time. It is our ambition to make more than good music. (*Walk On*, p. xiv)

Some might be tempted to downplay the significance of my argument for the positive moral significance of U2's music, pointing out that properly trained emotions alone are not sufficient for moral maturity. True enough. But from the fact that delight in good character is insufficient for moral maturity it does not follow that it is insignificant. In *The Abolition of Man*, C.S. Lewis tells us:

> It still remains true that no justification of virtue will enable a man to be virtuous. Without the aid of trained emotions the intellect is powerless against the animal organism. I had sooner play cards against a man who was quite sceptical about ethics, but bred to believe that "a gentleman does not cheat," than against an irreproachable moral philosopher who had been brought up among sharpers. In the battle it is not syllogisms that will keep the reluctant nerves and muscles to their post in the third hour of the bombardment.[16]

If Lewis were alive today he might have written, "I had sooner ask for a contribution to Amnesty International from someone who was skeptical about ethics but brought up listening to U2 than an irreproachable moral philosopher who finds no delight in goodness."

## "I'm at a Place Called Vertigo"

Ideally each of us would be virtuous. Most of us are not there yet. Aristotle argues that getting there requires appropriate feel-

---

[16] C.S. Lewis, *The Abolition of Man* (New York: Macmillan, 1975), pp. 33–34.

ings, feelings of delight in virtuous character and right action. We may develop these feelings listening to the music of U2. In the current state of cultural vertigo ("It's everything I wish I didn't know") U2 gives us something we *should feel*, and that is no morally insignificant matter.[17]

> The jungle is your head
> Can't rule your heart
> A feeling is so much stronger than
> A thought.

[17] I am grateful to Jamie Henke, William Irwin, Mark Linville, Tim Paustian, Susan Werther, and Mark Wrathall for comments and corrections. Thanks too to Jessica for talking with me about "the legendary Bono."

# U2 Albums

| Album | Peak Billboard Position [1] |
|---|---|
| *How to Dismantle an Atomic Bomb* (2004) | #1 |
| *All That You Can't Leave Behind* (2000) | #3 |
| *Pop* (1997) | #1 |
| *Zooropa* (1993) | #1 |
| *Achtung Baby* (1991) | #1 |
| *The Unforgettable Fire* (1990) | #12 |
| *Rattle and Hum* (1988) | #1 |
| *The Joshua Tree* (1987) | #1 |
| *Under a Blood Red Sky* (1983) | #28 |
| *War* (1983) | #70 |
| *October* (1981) | #107 |
| *Boy* (1980) | #107 |

---

[1] Information comes from www.billboard.com.

# U2 Grammy Awards

## *2005*

General Album of the Year: *How to Dismantle an Atomic Bomb*
General Song of the Year: "Sometimes You Can't Make It on Your Own"
Best Rock Performance by a Duo or Group with Vocal: "Sometimes You Can't Make It on Your Own
Best Rock Song: "City of Blinding Lights"
Best Rock Album: *How to Dismantle an Atomic Bomb*

## *2004*

Best Rock Performance by a Duo or Group with Vocal: "Vertigo"
Best Rock Song: "Vertigo"
Music Video—Best Short-form Music Video: "Vertigo"

## *2001*

General Record of the Year: "Walk On"
Best Pop Performance by a Duo or Group with Vocal: "Stuck in a Moment You Can't Get Out Of"
Best Rock Performance by a Duo or Group with Vocal: "Elevation"
Best Rock Album: "All that You Can't Leave Behind"

## *2000*

General Record of the Year: "Beautiful Day"
General Song of the Year: "Beautiful Day"
Best Rock Performance by a Duo or Group with Vocal: "Beautiful Day"
Best Music Video—Long Form: *Zoo TV—Live From Sydney*

## *1993*

Best Alternative Music Album: *Zooropa*

### 1992

Best Rock Performance by a Duo or Group with Vocal:
  *Achtung Baby*

### 1988

Best Rock Performance by a Duo or Group with Vocal: "Desire"
Best Performance Music Video: "Where the Streets Have No Name"

### 1987

General Album of the Year: *The Joshua Tree*
Best Rock Performance By A Duo Or Group With Vocal: *The Joshua Tree*

# U2 Internet Resources

The official website of U2 can be found at **u2.com**. It contains news, information on tours, song lyrics, an online store offering clothing and tour merchandise, exclusive content (including interviews, video and photo footage, and stories on the band's activities), and discussion boards. Membership (for a fee) is required for access to some portions of the site.

**www.atu2.com** contains news stories on the band from many sources, with a search engine to search the archives back to 1978. It also houses blogs written by the @U2 staff, free podcast downloads, pictures of the band organized by band member and tour, information and help for U2 paraphernalia collectors, a monthly cartoon, and links to many fan sites and resources. Other excellent weblogs devoted to U2 include **www.u2log.com** and **u2sermons.blogspot.net**. The latter contains extensive resources for under- standing the religious relevance of U2's music and activities.

Other good sources for U2 news, images, and discussion are **www.interference.com** and **www.u2station.com.** The latter site also contains an extensive instrumental tablature of U2 songs.

Very specific infomation about U2 tour news and rumors, as well as summaries of particular U2 concerts can be found at **www.u2tours.com.**

**Www.u2source.com** contains an archive of U2 interviews, a "chatcast" or podcast of discussions about U2, and links news from other fan sites. In addition to the usual links and news, **Www.u2exit.com** contains images and descriptions of U2-related sites in Dublin. For answers to a wide array of U2-related questions, see **www.u2faqs.com**.

# Author Profiles

**STAN BENFELL** is Associate Professor in Comparative Literature and Chair of the Department of Humanities, Classics, and Comparative Literature at Brigham Young University. His research and writing primarily concern literature and thought in the Middle Ages and Renaissance, but he also has an interest in modern continental philosophy. He became a fan of U2 back in 1984, when his younger brother played the lp "War" for him, and he was hooked.

**TIMOTHY CLEVELAND** is Professor of Philosophy and Head of the Philosophy Department at New Mexico State University. He is the author of *Trying Without Willing: An Essay in the Philosophy of Mind* (1997) as well as articles on the philosophy of action, philosophy of logic, and metaphysics. In 1992, he took a transatlantic flight and stayed up over thirty-six hours to catch U2's great performance at Globen in Stockholm. He likes to ask: "Am I buggin' you? Don't mean to bug ya."

**CRAIG DELANCEY** is an Assistant Professor of Philosophy at the State University of New York at Oswego. He writes about rationality, the philosophy of mind, and environmental ethics. Everybody here is having a good time, except him: he keeps talking about the end of the world.

**HUBERT L. DREYFUS** is Professor of Philosophy in the Graduate School at the University of California at Berkeley. His publications include *What Computers (Still) Can't Do* (third edition, 1993), *Being-in-the-World: A Commentary on Division I of Heidegger's Being and Time* (1991), *Mind over Machine: The Power of Human Intuition and Expertise in the Era of the Computer* (with Stuart Dreyfus, 1987), and *On the Internet* (2001). Professor Dreyfus is dangerous, because he is honest.

**THEODORE GRACYK** teaches philosophy in Minnesota. He is the author of two books about popular music, *Rhythm and Noise: An Aesthetics of Rock* and the award-winning *I Wanna Be Me: Rock Music and the Politics of Identity*. Philosophically, he agrees that some days are better than others, but doubts that you can leave by the back door and throw away the key. His formative years were dominated by Catholic elementary school and Irish nuns, so he wonders why anyone thinks that the members of U2 speak with accents.

A former pupil from the Ecole Normale Supérieure in Paris, **BÉATRICE HAN-PILE** is a Reader in Philosophy at the University of Essex, England. She is the author of *Foucault's Critical Project: Between the Transcendental and the Historical* (2002) and of many articles on Schopenhauer, Nietzsche, and Heidegger. She is currently working on a book entitled *Transcendence Without Religion*.

**JEFF MALPAS** is Professor of Philosophy at the University of Tasmania where he is also the Director of the Centre for Applied Philosophy and Ethics. He completed his Ph.D. at the Australian National University, and is the author of *Place and Experience* (1999) and *Heidegger's Topology* (2006) as well as other works.

**JENNIFER MCCLINTON-TEMPLE** is Assistant Professor of English at King's College in Pennsylvania. She has published articles on post-colonial fiction and composition theory and is a co-editor of *The Encyclopedia of Native American Literature* (forthcoming). Thanks to an accommodating projectionist friend, she was, without question, the first person in Conway, Arkansas, to see *Rattle and Hum*.

**MARINA MCCOY** is an assistant professor of philosophy at Boston College and teaches courses in Plato, the history of philosophy, and feminism. As the mother of two children (Katie and James), she is versatile in both Plato and Playdough. She moves in mysterious ways.

**TRENTON MERRICKS** is Professor of Philosophy at the University of Virginia. He is the author of *Objects and Persons* (2001), *Truth and Ontology* (forthcoming), and about thirty journal articles. He contributed to this volume mainly because he really, really wants to meet Bono, and thought this might somehow help.

**ABIGAIL MYERS** has worked as an editor in educational and technical publishing, and served as an editorial assistant for several books in the Popular Culture and Philosophy series while studying with Bill Irwin and the rest of the gang at King's College in Wilkes-Barre,

Pennsylvania. She has begun her studies for a master's degree in education while teaching high school English through the New York City Teaching Fellows program. She spent nine hours sitting outside Madison Square Garden in the pouring rain on 8th October, 2005, when she was rewarded with a front-row spot *inside the ellipse*, right at Adam Clayton's feet. She figures this must have been like sitting in the Garden with Epicurus. Or something.

**KERRY SOPER** received his Ph.D. in American Studies from Emory University, learning there to stand up straight and carry his own weight. He studies the history of popular culture, satire, and comedy, trying to educate his mind—explain all these controls. He is currently an assistant professor at Brigham Young University where he teaches in the Humanities and American Studies programs; in classes, he enjoys hearing the sound of his own voice, though he admits to being a bit of an intellectual tortoise.

**IAIN THOMSON** is Associate Professor of Philosophy at the University of New Mexico. He is the author of *Heidegger on Ontotheology: Technology and the Politics of Education* (2005) and has published more than a dozen articles on Heidegger and other leading figures in existentialism, phenomenology, and postmodernism. His work has been frequently reprinted and translated into French, Polish, and Japanese. He is currently writing a book on Heidegger's phenomenology of death and its impact on contemporary continental philosophy, called *Thinking Death After Heidegger.* He has the right shoes to get him through the night.

**CHRIS TOLLEFSEN** is Associate Professor of Philosophy at the University of South Carolina. He has published scholarly articles in meta-ethics, normative theory, and applied ethics, and is especially interested in the difference between appearance and reality in the moral life. He has taught philosophy in Ghana, and studied percussion in Guinea, West Africa; so if Larry Mullen needs a break . . .

**DAVID WERTHER** is a member of Geneva Campus Church, and a faculty associate in Philosophy in the Department of Liberal Studies and the Arts, University of Wisconsin-Madison. In addition, he teaches theology in the extension program of Trinity Evangelical Divinity School. He has published a number of papers in philosophical theology in *Ars Disputandi, Philosophia Christi, Religious Studies,* and *Sophia.* David and his daughter Jessica have a special fondness for the *U2 Go Home-Live from Slane Castle* DVD, especially "Walk On." David would love to see U2 again in the Aragon Ballroom.

**MARK WRATHALL** teaches philosophy, and there's a lot of things if he could he'd rearrange. He is the Humanities Professor of Philosophy at Brigham Young University, the author of *How to Read Heidegger* (2006), and the editor of numerous books including *A Companion to Heidegger* (2005) and *A Companion to Phenomenology and Existentialism* (2006).

# Index

Made in the USA
San Bernardino, CA
08 October 2015